Survival

GLOBAL POLITICS AND STRATEGY
Volume 51 Number 2 | April–May 2009

The International Institute for Strategic Studies
Arundel House | 13–15 Arundel Street | Temple Place | London | WC2R 3DX | UK
Tel +44 (0)20 7379 7676 Fax +44 (0)20 7836 3108 E-mail survival@iiss.org Web www.iiss.org

Survival Online www.informaworld.com/survival

I0867087

Aims and Scope *Survival* is one of the world's leading forums for analysis and debate of international and strategic affairs. Shaped by its editors to be both timely and forward thinking, the journal encourages writers to challenge conventional wisdom and bring fresh, often controversial, perspectives to bear on the strategic issues of the moment. With a diverse range of authors, *Survival* aims to be scholarly in depth while vivid, well written and policy relevant in approach. Through commentary, analytical articles, case studies, forums, review essays, reviews and letters to the editor, the journal promotes lively, critical debate on issues of international politics and strategy.

First published 2009 by Routledge

2 Park Square, Milton Park, Abingdon, Oxfordshire OX14 4RN
52 Vanderbilt Avenue, New York, NY 10017

Routledge is an imprint of the Taylor & Francis Group, an informa business

First issued in paperback 2019

ISBN 13: 978-1-138-45888-8 (hbk)
ISBN 13: 978-0-415-49839-5 (pbk)

50 YEARS

Survival
GLOBAL POLITICS AND STRATEGY
Volume 51 Number 2 | April–May 2009

Contents

Cover: MICHAEL KAPPELER/AFP/Getty Images

On the cover
German Chancellor Angela Merkel and Russian Prime Minister Vladimir Putin review an honour guard during an official welcoming ceremony in Berlin, 16 January 2009.

New on the web
Visit http://www.iiss.org/publications/survival, our new look website: Interviews with authors, related articles and more.

IISS Voices
A new blog from the editors of *Survival* and other IISS staff. Http://www.iiss.org/whats-new/iiss-voices.

Plus

Review Essays

Closing Argument

About the IISS The IISS, a registered charity with offices in London, Washington and Singapore, is the world's leading authority on political–military conflict. It is the primary independent source of accurate, objective information on international strategic issues. Publications include *The Military Balance*, an annual reference work on each nation's defence capabilities; *Strategic Survey*, an annual review of world affairs; *Survival*, a bi-monthly journal on international affairs; *Strategic Comments*, a monthly analysis of topical issues in international affairs; and the *Adelphi* series of books on issues of international security.

SUBMISSIONS

To submit an article, authors are advised to follow these guidelines:

- *Survival* articles are around 4,000–10,000 words long including endnotes. A word count should be included with a draft. Length is a consideration in the review process and shorter articles have an advantage.
- All text, including endnotes, should be double-spaced with wide margins.
- Any tables or artwork should be supplied in separate files, ideally not embedded in the document or linked to text around it.
- All *Survival* articles are expected to include endnote references. These should be complete and include first and last names of authors, titles of articles (even from newspapers), place of publication, publisher, exact publication dates, volume and issue number (if from a journal) and page numbers. Web sources should include complete URLs and DOIs if available.
- A summary of up to 150 words should be included with the article. The summary should state the main argument clearly and concisely, not simply say what the article is about.
- A short author's biography of one or two lines should also be included. This information will appear at the foot of the first page of the article.

Submissions should be made by email, in Microsoft Word format, to the Managing Editor, Jeffrey Mazo, survival@iiss.org. Alternatively, hard copies may be sent to *Survival*, IISS, Arundel House, 13–15 Arundel Street, Temple Place, London WC2R 3DX, UK. Please direct any queries to Jeffrey Mazo.

The editorial review process can take up to three months. *Survival*'s acceptance rate for unsolicited manuscripts is less than 20%. *Survival* does not normally provide referees' comments in the event of rejection. Authors are permitted to submit simultaneously elsewhere so long as this is consistent with the policy of the other publication and the Editors of *Survival* are informed of the dual submission.

Readers are encouraged to comment on articles from the previous issue. Letters should be concise, no longer than 750 words and relate directly to the argument or points made in the original article. A response from the author of the article will normally be solicited.

Back issues: Taylor & Francis retains a three-year back issue stock of journals.

The issue date is April–May 2009.

NATO and the UN

Michael F. Harsch and Johannes Varwick

When the secretaries-general of NATO and the United Nations, Jaap de Hoop Scheffer and Ban Ki Moon, signed a joint declaration in September 2008, it came as a surprise to many observers. After almost 60 years of wary coexistence, the two organisations established, for the first time, a formal relationship between the headquarters and a framework for expanded consultation and cooperation. The organisations already cooperate to safeguard Kosovo's fragile stability and to manage a deteriorating situation in Afghanistan, and NATO has until recently protected UN food-aid shipments to Somalia against the growing threat of pirate attacks. The UN is involved in virtually all ongoing NATO operations in one way or another, but relations have always been troubled.[1] The Alliance is still seen by many UN members and parts of the UN bureaucracy as a Cold War military machine and US 'tool box'. Given the tensions between the two, even UN staff wonder why Ban decided to sign the declaration. Put into a broader strategic perspective, however, the joint declaration fits within the trend towards a stronger role for regional actors in global security.

The agreement offers the opportunity for substantial strategic dialogue, which could make fragmented UN–NATO efforts to stabilise and rebuild war-torn countries such as Afghanistan more coherent. Given the difficult history of relations between the two, however, closer UN–NATO cooperation is likely to face continuing challenges.

Michael F. Harsch is a Visiting Fellow at Johns Hopkins University's School of Advanced International Studies (SAIS) in Washington DC and a PhD candidate in Political Science at the Freie Universität Berlin. **Johannes Varwick** is Professor of Political Science at the University of Kiel and an independent consultant in Berlin.

Survival | vol. 51 no. 2 | April–May 2009 | pp. 5–12 DOI 10.1080/00396330902860744

Regional organisations and security

When the UN founders met in San Francisco in 1945, they expected that 'regional arrangements' would play a significant part in a new system of collective security. Chapter VIII of the UN Charter encourages the settlement of local disputes by regional organisations, and the UN Security Council can use regional organisations for enforcement action under its authority. With the beginning of the Cold War, however, the role of regional organisations could not develop as anticipated.

De jure, the Security Council is the only body with the authority to legitimise the use of force in international relations. The only exception is provided by Article 51 of the UN Charter, which sets out the right of individual or collective self-defence. In reality, the UN's lack of resources and military capabilities impede its ability to enforce its decisions, and its authority is frequently ignored. NATO's very creation in April 1949 as an alliance for collective defence demonstrated that Western Europe had serious doubts about the UN's ability to fulfil its promise of collective security. The North Atlantic Treaty does not mention Chapter VIII of the UN Charter. As a Chapter VIII organisation, NATO would have been constrained to take military action only after Security Council authorisation. This would have given permanent Security Council members Russia and China the power to veto an Alliance decision. The drafters of the Treaty chose to rely instead on Article 51, which obliges the Alliance simply to report to the Security Council after collective self-defence measures have been taken.

NATO and the Warsaw Pact quickly earned reputations as vehicles for superpower interests, marginalising the UN. Other regional organisations were seen as ineffective debating chambers, lacking the necessary capacities for resolving crises.[2] As a result, Security Council resolutions made no reference to regional organisations throughout the Cold War.[3]

A new beginning

Since 1991, the UN has made ever more frequent references to regional organisations. While critics warn that such organisations pursue the particular interests of their member states and lack the neutrality and impartiality necessary to resolve conflicts, supporters argue that regional organisations enjoy comparative advantages in crisis management, such as geographical proximity and understanding of the actors and issues involved.

UN Secretary-General Boutros Boutros-Ghali expressed a central rationale for the trend toward regional management of conflicts in 1995: 'It is increasingly apparent that the United Nations cannot address every potential and actual conflict troubling the world.'[4] UN peacekeeping has evolved from the Cold War practice of deploying unarmed or lightly armed forces to supervise ceasefires in permissive environments to the current large-scale, multidimensional peace-building missions under challenging conditions. One way to relieve the increased pressure is to delegate tasks to regional actors. The European Union (EU), for instance, has led several UN-mandated crisis-management missions, and is the most important financial contributor to UN peacekeeping.

Regional organisations have various motives for cooperating with the UN. For the EU, the UN is the cornerstone of a multilateral world order, and a viable option for tackling conflicts in places where EU members would prefer not to send their troops. NATO is interested in UN mandates for its missions, which provide legitimacy for the use of force and increase domestic and international support for operations.

NATO in Bosnia was the first regional organisation authorised by the Security Council to use force

In 1992, in Bosnia, NATO became the first regional organisation authorised by the Security Council to use force, but the overall record of UN–NATO cooperation has been mixed. NATO has complained of UN ineffectiveness, and the UN has been angered by NATO's willingness to initiate military action without authorisation. Cooperation in Bosnia and Kosovo has functioned well, although both sides face persistent problems with information- and intelligence-sharing. Institutional collaboration has been limited to a single military liaison officer (with no civilian staff) and ad hoc desk-to-desk contacts. The EU, by comparison, has two fully staffed delegations in New York, one representing the Council of the European Union and the other the EU Commission.

Since 2004, however, there have been growing signs that the UN is ready to take relations with regional organisations to a new level. Both the UN Secretary-General's High-level Panel on Threats, Challenges and Change and Kofi Annan's March 2005 report 'In Larger Freedom' advocated closer links with regional bodies.[5] The September 2005 UN World Summit called for expanded 'consultation and cooperation between the United Nations and regional ... organizations through formalized agreements between the respective secretariats'.[6]

The long road to a joint declaration

It was at the 2005 summit that NATO first proposed a draft joint declaration. The UN secretary-general's authority to sign joint declarations without further consultation of the member states made it possible to avoid a vote in the UN General Assembly, where NATO critics dominate. Nevertheless, the project encountered severe obstacles.

NATO faces enduring negative perceptions in the UN, where it is often linked to US global military ambition and viewed as being at odds with the UN mission of maintaining international peace. For many in the UN, it was therefore symbolically important that an agreement with NATO take place only after accords with other regional organisations such as the EU, the African Union (AU) and the Association of Southeast Asian Nations (ASEAN).

Most importantly, many UN members and staff are afraid that a stronger reliance on NATO assets could reduce UN decision-making autonomy and operational independence. The main troop-contributing countries such as Pakistan, Bangladesh, India and Nigeria are especially concerned about possible NATO influence on UN command-and-control structures. The UN's humanitarian bodies and agencies have also been critical of the declaration, fearing that closer cooperation with NATO could jeopardise their neutrality and impartiality in conflict areas and put their staff at risk.

When Ban Ki Moon came into office in January 2007, he continued his predecessor's policy of forging stronger links to regional organisations, but was not keen to tackle the sensitive issue of NATO–UN relations, giving priority to other partnerships instead. In November 2006, outgoing

Secretary-General Annan had signed a declaration for enhancing cooperation with the AU, which was followed by a joint communiqué of the UN Security Council and the AU Peace and Security Council in June 2007. That same year, a joint statement on UN–EU cooperation in crisis management and a memorandum of understanding with ASEAN were signed.

An updated NATO declaration was ready to sign by early 2008, but the UN again put it off, first arguing that it wanted to wait for a report on UN personnel safety, then that it was preoccupied with the humanitarian crisis in Burma. Another failure seemed likely, as tensions between the UN and NATO rose during the summer over UN criticism of the international forces in Afghanistan for causing too many civilian casualties and over the Georgia crisis.

NATO members, which are also important UN members, continued to push the issue of the declaration, pressuring the UN secretary-general. The UN secretariat had to weigh the risks and benefits of its decision. On the one hand, the UN's main troop contributors were against the declaration, and important members such as Russia, China, Brazil, Indonesia and South Africa had voiced concerns. On the other, NATO's potential to provide desperately needed strategic-airlift and naval capabilities in Africa seemed to outweigh the risks. On 23 September 2008, Ban and de Hoop Scheffer finally signed the declaration in the offices of the UN Secretary General.

The signature has left the UN uneasy. In an effort not to upset the non-Western Security Council members further, the UN secretariat urged NATO not to publish the accord, and ordered its staff to keep the issue as low-key as possible. The 'quiet signing' nevertheless caused a public outcry in Russia. Foreign Minister Sergey Lavrov accused Ban Ki Moon of 'secretly' concluding an agreement without properly consulting Security Council members. Russia's ambassador to NATO, Dmitry Rogozin, even called the declaration 'illegal'. The NATO and UN secretariats argue, however, that they held sufficient briefings and that a joint declaration of the secretaries-general does not require approval from UN members.[7]

Considering that it took three years to agree on a text, the result is not very remarkable. The two-page document acknowledges the organisations' past operational cooperation, and the secretaries-general declare their intention to establish a framework for consultation and cooperation, including regular exchanges at senior and working levels. It then lists areas of common interest in which cooperation should be further developed: communication and information-sharing, including issues pertaining to the protection of civilians; capacity-building, training and exercises; lessons learned; planning and support for contingencies; and operational coordination and support.

Although NATO Spokesman James Appathurai was quick to emphasise that there were 'no politics attached to this', the main value of the agreement, which lacks any technical details, is political.[8] NATO hopes that it will now be easier to improve its relations with non-governmental and other regional organisations, such as the AU and the League of Arab States.[9] Most importantly, the document sends a clear message from the top to the organisations' bureaucracies that cooperation and coordination are desirable and necessary – something that has not always been clear in the past.

A stronger role for regional organisations?

Despite its remarkable transformation since the end of the Cold War, NATO has essentially remained a military organisation. In peace-building operations, such as the one in Afghanistan, success depends on the capacities and expertise of the UN and its special agencies in such areas as institution-building, rule of law, humanitarian assistance and development. If progress lacks in these fields, the Alliance will not be able to achieve its goals. The UN, in turn, has a growing need for the Alliance's capabilities for peacekeeping operations. It faces increasingly complex missions in sometimes hostile environments, as in the Democratic Republic of the Congo, Sudan and Afghanistan, which require robust forces, air and sea transport, and aerial-reconnaissance capabilities.

Given the complexity of the current operational environment, the world's security architecture is under stress. A complete remodelling of the system is, however, unlikely to occur in the foreseeable future, and international organisations will have to find ways to create synergy and intensify coordination. The signature of a joint declaration between NATO and the UN has the potential to improve institutional relations, but operational cooperation is likely to remain limited. NATO members are hardly able or willing to provide capabilities for UN peacekeeping in regions which they perceive to be of minor strategic interest. The UN, for its part, potentially possesses the authority and legitimacy to become the actor that coordinates efforts in stabilisation operations. Afghanistan is in particularly desperate need of coordinated political, security and reconstruction activities, and NATO is not suited to fulfil this task. If NATO members accepted a stronger UN coordination role, this would end a situation in which all actors call for coordination, but nobody wants to be coordinated.

Closer ties between the organisations could also result in common planning for responses to humanitarian crises and natural disasters like the devastating earthquake in Pakistan in 2005, where both sides worked together to provide relief. Making progress in these fields will be difficult, as each body will have to give up some of its operational and decision-making autonomy. In the long run, however, scarce resources, pressing security challenges, and determined political leadership could lead to more effective cooperation in some of the most troubled regions of the world.

Acknowledgements

The authors would like to thank Lindsay P. Cohn for her valuable comments.

Notes

1 Janka Oertel and Johannes Varwick, 'NATO und Vereinte Nationen: Eine ambivalente Beziehung mit Entwicklungspotenzial', *Vereinte Nationen*, vol. 56, no. 4, pp. 160–66; David S. Yost, *NATO and International Organizations* (Rome: NATO Defense College, 2007), pp. 31–71.

2 Louise Fawcett, 'Regional Governance Architecture and Security Policy', *FES Briefing Paper*, February 2006, p. 2, http://library.fes.de/pdf-files/iez/global/50187.pdf.

3 Ban Ki Moon, 'Report of the Secretary-General on the Relationship between the United Nations and Regional Organizations, in particular the African Union, in the Maintenance of International Peace and Security', UN Doc. S/2008/186, 7 April 2008, para. 4.

4 Boutros Boutros-Ghali, 'Report of the Secretary General: Improving Preparedness for Conflict Prevention and Peacekeeping in Africa', UN Doc. A/50/711–S/1995/911, 1 November 1995, para. 4.

5 'A More Secure World: Our Shared Responsibility, Report of the High-level Panel on Threats, Challenges and Change', UN Doc. A/59/565, 2 December 2004, para. 273; Kofi Annan, 'In Larger Freedom: Towards

Development, Security and Human Rights for all', UN Doc. A/59/2005, 21 March 2005, para. 213.

6 UN General Assembly, '2005 World Summit Outcome', UN Doc. A/RES/60/1, 24 October 2008, para.170 (a).

7 Associated Press, 'Russia Official Blasts "Secretive" UN–NATO Deal', *International Herald Tribune*, 9 October 2008, http://www.iht.com/articles/ap/2008/10/09/europe/EU-Russia-NATO-UN.php.

8 Weekly press briefing by NATO Spokesman James Appathurai, Brussels, 1 October 2008, http://www.nato.int/docu/speech/2008/s081001a.html; interviews with NATO and UN officials in Brussels, Pristina and New York, 2008.

9 Jaap de Hoop Scheffer, 'Keynote Address at the 54th Annual Session of the NATO Parliamentary Assembly', Valencia, 18 November 2008, http://www.nato.int/docu/speech/2008/s081118a.html.

Rebooting NATO–Russia Relations

Oksana Antonenko and Bastian Giegerich

Twenty years after the fall of the Berlin Wall and five years after the establishment of the NATO–Russia Council, the August 2008 war between Russia and Georgia sparked a crisis in NATO–Russia relations. NATO suspended normal cooperation through the council and Moscow responded by freezing military exchanges. The crisis exposed how dysfunctional cooperation had become. But rather than lament the failure of cooperation, NATO leaders should use the opportunity to fundamentally reassess the goals of and strategy for engagement with Russia and develop a new, pragmatic approach that stresses mutually beneficial problem-solving. The war between Russia and Georgia has reset NATO–Russia relations; it is high time to think about how to reboot them.

A troubled history

The history of NATO–Russia relations is one of problems, mistrust and misperceptions; the relationship could hardly be characterised as a true partnership even before August 2008. Moreover, the fabric of cooperation, including the NATO–Russia Council, has not produced meaningful strategic rapprochement in terms of overcoming the legacy of Cold War perceptions or developing a common assessment of threats and capabilities to deal with them. From Moscow's perspective, relations during the 1990s and early 2000s involved a string of humiliating experiences in which NATO

Oksana Antonenko is IISS Senior Fellow (Russia and Eurasia). **Bastian Giegerich** is IISS Research Fellow for European Security.

 DOI 10.1080/00396330902860751

or significant member states exploited temporary Russian weakness: NATO enlargement in 1999 and again in 2004, the war in Kosovo, the non-ratification of the Conventional Forces in Europe Treaty, US withdrawal from the Anti-Ballistic Missile Treaty, Western support for the 'colour revolutions' in Georgia and Ukraine, US plans for deploying missile defences in Europe. While Russian interpretations of some of these may be somewhat peculiar, others do support the claim that the West does not hesitate to ignore Russian positions when doing so carries little cost.

The Russia–Georgia war caught NATO completely unprepared. It was the EU, benefitting from the activism of the French presidency, which helped negotiate the ceasefire and deployed a civilian observer mission to monitor it, with the side effect that Russia has discovered the EU as a potential security actor. Together with the time-honoured Russian preference for bilateralism over engagement with multilateral institutions, currently reflected in an attempt to develop a new security dialogue with the new American administration, this has, for Moscow, put relations with NATO on the back burner. Russian leaders have accused NATO of breaking off relations and say it is now up to NATO to restore them. Moreover, senior Russian policymakers repeatedly assert, with thinly veiled reference to NATO operations in Afghanistan, that NATO needs Russia more than Russia needs NATO. But the argument over who needs whom more is pointless; nobody gains from not talking.

The problem of Russia–NATO relations involves Cold War legacies, differences in strategic culture, and a preoccupation with process over substance. Cold War legacies still shape mutual perceptions. Russians still view NATO as an anti-Russia organisation which remains a threat to their security, despite NATO's clear statement that the Alliance is defensive and not directed against anyone. Russian policymakers also view NATO as an instrument of US policy in both Europe and Eurasia. Finally, they believe that NATO enlargement is a zero-sum attempt to provide security for NATO states at Russia's expense.

NATO Allies are divided in their perceptions of Russia. Many Western European states do not view Russia as a threat, as the president of France reiterated at the Munich Security Conference in February, and want to build a partnership with Moscow to manage regional and out-of-area problems, including Afghanistan. But a number of member states, including some of Russia's neighbours, still view Russia as a potential threat, due to a large extent to historical grievances and Moscow's increasingly assertive posture. A number of these states sought membership primarily for the Article 5 commitment to deter potential aggression from Russia. The 2007 cyber-attacks on Estonia and the cut-off of natural-gas supplies from Russia in 2009 as a result of a dispute between Moscow and Kiev only confirmed that threats still exist and are becoming more complex. The new pressure to reaffirm the Article 5 guarantees through explicit contingency planning to reassure Russia's neighbours could reinforce Russia's concerns over NATO endorsement of US missile-defence plans and its continued open-door policy with regard to future enlargement. NATO argues that it will not, and should not, relinquish its decision-making autonomy, but an awareness of the deep-rooted historical suspicions on both sides would certainly help to avoid misunderstandings.

Russia still views security in terms of geography and realpolitik

Major differences in strategic culture shape threat perceptions and responses to security threats. Russia still views security in terms of geography and realpolitik. Its leaders remain worried about the influence of external actors in what they consider to be Russia's security space and continue to see such matters as a zero-sum game. Russian security-policy elites feel that vulnerability comes from regions adjacent to Russia's borders, which it sought to dominate for centuries. As one expert observed, Russia has gone from a Cold War to a pre-Cold War security mindset.[1]

Moscow remains reluctant to cooperate with other players to address potential sources of insecurity in Eurasia, viewing the presence of other major powers in the region as an important vulnerability and challenge in itself. Moreover, given their zero-sum view of security, most Russian leaders believe the most effective strategy for managing relations with other players in the South Caucasus or Central Asia is through competition. Hence President Dmitry Medvedev's proposal to NATO and the West in general to recognise the post-Soviet space as a zone of Russian 'privileged interests'.[2]

NATO security culture is different, and not just because it is much less concerned with geography since the end of the Cold War. NATO and its member governments stress the deterritorialised nature of many contemporary security threats and are much more preoccupied with out-of-area missions such as Afghanistan. Unlike Russia, NATO is a multilateral organisation where different strategic cultures coexist. Moscow finds the resulting diversity confusing and tends to mistrust NATO pleas to abandon geopolitics in favour of functional cooperation on a common agenda, or agreement to disagree when cooperation cannot be achieved. It is telling that Russia and NATO have been engaged separately in security cooperation with different Central Asian states for over a decade, but have never really cooperated in addressing regional security challenges.

Finally, the strategic bargain behind the Russia–NATO partnership is built on unrealistic and asymmetric expectations. These were exposed as a result of the war between Russia and Georgia. For NATO members the expectation has been that the more they talk to the Russians, through the NATO–Russia Council or associated meetings and working groups, the more understanding can be developed. NATO sought to envelop Russia in a tight network of dialogues, meetings and exchanges in the hope that it would transform or influence Russia's behaviour and its perceptions of NATO and its own security interests. The institutionalisation of the relationship, however, seems to have done little to change underlying assumptions. The development of common threat perceptions, common capabilities to address them and the trust to employ them when a crisis occurs have all been found wanting.

On the Russian side the assumptions were different but equally unrealistic. During a 2008 meeting with the Valdai Discussion Club, a group of international experts invited each year by RIA Novosti to meet with top Russian officials, Prime Minister Vladimir Putin complained that he had been misled by NATO on the NATO–Russia Council. He argued that NATO had promised to make the council into a 27-member decision-making and discussion forum, while in practice Russia was always confronted with a united NATO position, a 26+1 format. This suggests Putin thought the council could offer Russia a sort of back-door membership in which it could be embraced as an equal partner without being forced to embrace and respect NATO's institutional culture, membership criteria and obligations. The misunderstanding and frustration fostered by this unrealistic expectation pushed cooperation down the list of priorities for both NATO and Russia at a time both were redefining their identities and developing new instruments to address security challenges.

With hindsight, it is surprising that neither Russia nor NATO saw a need for more meaningful engagement. NATO, and in particular the United States, did not initially seek Russian cooperation in Afghanistan, believing that Moscow had little to contribute (including lessons from the Soviet experience), preferring to engage with Central Asian states directly on matters such as basing or border security. Moscow did not see NATO as a natural partner for promoting Eurasian security, including stabilising Afghanistan, and resolving or preventing regional conflicts. Instead, NATO-bashing was used as a tool to mobilise domestic public opinion against an external enemy, reinforcing the popularity and legitimacy of the ruling elite.

This short-sighted complacency over meaningful cooperation meant there were neither sufficient institutional mechanisms nor political will to deal effectively with the August 2008 crisis in Georgia. The ensuing formula of 'no business as usual' was convenient at the time, insofar as neither side had important vested interests in the way the usual business had been conducted. Coming up with a formula for a business 'better than usual' will not be easy. The starting point should be to abandon reassuring but virtual institutions and unrealistic expectations, and to take as many immediate, functional and mutually beneficial measures as realistically possible.

Building blocks

Afghanistan is one important area of common interest. Russia signed an agreement with Germany allowing for the transit of German cargo for the NATO-led force (ISAF) by rail through Russian territory, underlining a readiness to cooperate with NATO members bilaterally. At the NATO Bucharest Summit in 2008 Russia and NATO agreed on the transit through Russia of non-lethal cargo to support ISAF. Recent Russian involvement in Kyrgyzstan's moves to end US access to the Manas air base seems to contradict this trend. Nonetheless, it would be important to discuss transit agreements in an official NATO–Russia framework to avoid bilateralism in an area of concern to the Alliance as a whole.

Consultations on Afghanistan could also take place between NATO and the Shanghai Cooperation Organisation, which has already set up a contact group on Afghanistan, and between NATO and the Collective Security Treaty Organisation, which has been engaged in training Afghan army units. Russia has emphasised that a premature withdrawal of NATO troops from Afghanistan could undermine stability in Central Asia. Moscow has a clear interest, for example, in stopping drug trafficking from Afghanistan. If cooperation in this area can be developed, Russia and other Central Asian states will likely be more sympathetic to NATO use of military facilities in the region.

The high point of NATO–Russian cooperation was on the ground in Bosnia

NATO and Russia should also seek to re-establish military-to-military cooperation in general. While this would help generate stronger capacity and interoperability to address shared challenges, its main purpose would be confidence building. The high point of NATO–Russian cooperation in the last two decades has been working together on the ground in the NATO-led Stabilisation Force in Bosnia.

In the longer term it is important to find opportunities for real operational engagement, such as anti-piracy operations or confidence-building measures between navies in the Arctic, and for developing joint capabilities for peace-support operations which might one day be implemented jointly under a UN mandate. Although it might seem far-fetched, joint units could be established between Russia and some NATO member states, modelled perhaps on the Polish–Ukrainian Peace Force Battalion or the Franco-German Brigade, to develop interoperability and trust. This could be achieved in the context of Russian defence reform, which has the declared objectives of restructuring and professionalising Russian forces and developing specialised peacekeeping forces. If such an experiment were successful joint units could eventually be used for peace-support operations, possibly even in sensitive areas like Nagorno-Karabakh, provided a political settlement is agreed by parties.

With a new US administration unlikely to push for NATO enlargement and with both Ukraine and Georgia preoccupied with domestic problems, NATO and Russia have a window of opportunity to develop a strategic dialogue on Eurasian security. NATO should define its various partnership policies more precisely and disentangle them from enlargement. On the one hand, NATO will need to clarify that its Article 5 collective-defence clause applies to members only and that there cannot be implicit guarantees with regard to candidate countries, with or without Membership Action Plans. On the other hand, other ways should be found to reassure countries, such as Ukraine and Georgia, that feel vulnerable. Such reassurances should come both through closer ties between NATO and its partners and from a more open and strategic dialogue between NATO and Russia on Eurasian security. Russia and NATO should move away from the zero-sum dynamic and accept each other as legitimate players – even partners – in promoting security in the common neighbourhood.

One region where NATO–Russia cooperation should be explored further is the Black Sea. Following the August war tensions arose between the United States and Russia over US naval deployments to deliver humanitarian aid to Georgia and between Russia and Ukraine over the involvement of the Russian Black Sea Fleet in the conflict. Reviving and even expanding confidence-building measures in the Black Sea, such as information exchanges and joint exercises like those proposed in 2008 during a friendly call on the Russian Black Sea port of Novorossiisk of warships from Germany, Greece, and Turkey, would be a step in this direction.

Missile defence will be an important factor shaping both US–Russia and NATO–Russian relations. The new US administration has put deployment plans on hold but has not overturned agreements with Poland and the Czech Republic . Russia has responded by delaying deployment of *Iskander* missiles in Kaliningrad, always intended as a bargaining chip. But it is not enough to simply pause. NATO–Russia cooperation on theatre missile defence, where the two parties have common interests and could both make contributions in terms of technology and doctrine, should be revived and accelerated.

Avoiding errors

It is important that NATO develop a collective strategy on how to engage partners in the East, particularly Georgia and Ukraine. The George W. Bush administration's decision to conclude, in its final weeks, a special bilateral pact – the US–Georgia Charter on Strategic Partnership – with a significant security and defence component could undermine NATO unity, provoke Russia and weaken the credibility of such NATO policies as the NATO–Georgia Commission. The new US administration should adhere to the multilateral approach and seek to get other allies on board in its efforts to develop a comprehensive security strategy for Europe and Eurasia.

Finally, the recent determination, first declared at NATO's Riga Summit, on the part of some NATO members to develop a strong role for the Alliance in the field of energy security urgently needs clarification, not least because it could provoke a new crisis in relations with Russia. Energy security is an important concern for many NATO members, but it should be dealt with primarily through economic and political means, with military or police limited to dealing with the physical security of energy infrastructure and possibly maritime situational awareness, as is the current, yet not clearly communicated, consensus within NATO. The EU and the private sector should play a crucial role in Eurasian energy security by promoting diversification of supplies and energy efficiency.

* * *

One way to build a new NATO–Russia cooperation agenda will be through discussion of the new European Security Treaty proposed by Medvedev. Although there is disagreement as to the substance and forum for such discussions, it will be important for NATO to develop ideas, identify red lines and outline its own proposals. At the very least NATO should seek to clarify what the Russian president has in mind. Even if such discussions take place through the Organisation for Security and Cooperation in Europe, it would be useful for the distinct NATO–Russia dimension to be reflected.

An important dimension of such discussions should involve arms control, but this is also an area where past mistakes are most likely to repeat themselves. The Conventional Forces in Europe Treaty seems to be dead, and there is a danger that arms control more generally has been discredited. It is up to NATO to get the ball rolling on reviving the treaty or negotiating new confidence-building and transparency mechanisms to replace it.

The war between Russia and Georgia brought NATO–Russia cooperation, which in any case had failed to deliver tangible benefits to either side, to a screeching halt. Cooperation is not an end in itself, but should serve both strategic interests and pragmatic problem-solving. Trust can only be rebuilt over time; pragmatic, real-world cooperation offers better chances of creating it than the institutional shell of the past.

Acknowledgements

This commentary draws on an IISS expert workshop on NATO–Russia relations, which was organised with the support of NATO's Public Diplomacy Division.

Notes

1 James Sherr, 'Russia and the West: A Reassessment', The Shrivenham Papers no. 6, Defence Academy of the United Kingdom, January 2008, http://www.russiaprofile.org/page.php?pageid=CDI+Russia+Profile+List&articleid=a1200420940.

2 Dmitry Medvedev, interview with leading Russian TV channels, 31 August 2008, http://www.kremlin.ru/eng/speeches/2008/08/31/1850_type82912type82916_206003.shtml.

Noteworthy

No pressure, though

'We have only four years left for Obama to set an example to the rest of the world.'

NASA scientist Jim Hansen warns that only urgent action will save the world from the devastating effects of climate change.[1]

'If Obama does not manage to extricate the nation from the crisis in two or three years, the [Republicans] will unveil their real candidate, and Obama's presidency will finish earlier than expected.'

Pravda online offer their interpretation of the challenges faced by the Obama administration.[2]

'I really hope you put America back together. No pressure though.'

Sheenie Shannon Yip, age 13, from her letter to President Obama published in Thanks and Have Fun Running the Country: Kids Letters to President Obama *(McSweeney's Books).*[3]

$167.5 million

Estimated budget shortfall faced in 2009 by the US Defense Department's Security Development Plan for the Pakistan–Afghanistan border region[5]

$1.75 trillion

Deficit projected by US President Obama's 2010 budget proposal for the current fiscal year[6]

Threatening Tsvangirai

'He will not last. I swear to you. We just want to buy time.'

A ZANU-PF official, speaking on condition of anonymity, gives reason to doubt that President Robert Mugabe of Zimbabwe will long cooperate with new Prime Minister Morgan Tsvangirai.[19]

Starting out

'And for those who seek to advance their aims by inducing terror and slaughtering innocents, we say to you now that our spirit is stronger and cannot be broken. You cannot outlast us, and we will defeat you.'

US President Barack Obama speaks at his inauguration on 20 January 2009.[7]

No more nukes?

'I suppose that every foreign-policy speech by any foreign minister anywhere in the world at the moment says the Obama administration creates an opportunity, but in this case it's true.'

UK Foreign Secretary David Miliband speaks at the IISS on the prospects for strengthening nuclear non-proliferation regimes and even achieving the abolition of nuclear weapons, London, 3 February 2009.[8]

'I do not share for one moment the ambition for a nuclear-free world. I am delighted that nuclear weapons were invented, I thank God they were invented when they were, and I thank God they were invented by the Americans and not the Germans or … the Japanese.'

John Gilbert, former UK defence minister, voices his opposition to British government efforts to explore prospects for nuclear abolition.[9]

DOI 10.1080/00396330902860991

Financial fiascos

'We will rebuild, we will recover, and the United States of America will emerge stronger than before.'

President Obama speaks to a joint session of the US Congress, 24 February 2009.[10]

'We are seeing a kind of lemming-like approach, trying to get to the precipice first without any idea of what that money is going to buy.'

South Africa's Finance Minister, Trevor Manuel, expresses doubts about the bailout strategies adopted by several countries to counter the global financial crisis.[11]

'Wall Street and bankers are still not getting it. They are acting like Marie Antoinette and redecorating their offices.'

Ariana Huffington speaks at the World Economic Forum, 28 January 2009.[12]

'Headache … low blood pressure – and depression.'

A doctor at the on-site infirmary in the Davos Congress Center identifies the ailments for which a higher number of people than usual sought treatment during the 2009 World Economic Forum.[13]

Special delivery

'We are very polite at UNRWA – we don't open other people's mail.'

Christopher Gunness of the United Nations Relief and Works Agency in Gaza City says he doesn't know the contents of a letter left at the UNRWA compound for US President Obama. The letter is believed to have come from Hamas.[14]

'Basically it is a Palestinian decision – whether they want to send flowers or rockets.'

Maj. Peter Lerner, spokesman for the Israeli Defense Ministry, reflects on the possibility of permitting Gaza to resume exports after a single shipment of Gazan carnations was allowed to depart for Europe in time for Valentine's Day.[15]

6.2%

Annual rate at which US GDP shrank in the fourth quarter of 2008[17]

1,200%

Percentage increase in sales of J.K. Galbraith's 1954 classic *The Great Crash, 1929*[18]

Defining torture

'His treatment met the legal definition of torture.'

Susan J. Crawford, convening authority of military commissions at Guantanamo Bay detention facility, explains why she did not refer detainee Mohammed al-Qahtani's case for prosecution.[4]

No regrets

'I will always be proud about what I did for Pakistan.'

A.Q. Khan emerges from five years of house arrest for selling nuclear secrets to Iran, North Korea and Libya.[16]

Sources: 1 Robin McKie, 'President "Has Four Years to Save Earth"', *Observer*, 18 January 2009; **2** 'Barack Obama Takes Office as Republicans' Scapegoat', *Pravda*, 20 January 2009; **3** Greg Toppo, 'Kids Shower Obama with "Running the Country" Advice', *USA Today*, 3 February 2009; **4** William Glaberson, 'Detainee Was Tortured, a Bush Official Confirms', *New York Times*, 14 January 2009. **5** US Government Accountability Office, 'Securing, Stabilizing and Developing Pakistan's Border Area with Afghanistan', February 2009, p. 23; **6** Jackie Calmes, 'Obama Plans Major Shifts in Spending', 26 February 2009, *New York Times*; **7** Barack Obama, Inaugural Address, 20 January 2009, http://www.whitehouse.gov/blog/inaugural-address/; **8** David Miliband, 'Lifting the Nuclear Shadow', http://www.iiss.org/recent-key-addresses/david-miliband-address/; **9** John Gilbert, IISS, London, 4 February 2009, http://www.iiss.org/recent-key-addresses/david-miliband-address/; **10** Barack Obama, Address to Joint Session of Congress, 24 February 2009, http://www.whitehouse.gov/the_press_office/remarks-of-president-barack-obama-address-to-joint-session-of-congress/; **11** Carter Dougherty, 'A Sense of Despair, But Clashing Views on How to Respond', *International Herald Tribune*, 28 January 2009; **12** 'Gauging the Pain Around the World', *New York Times*, 28 January 2009; **13** 'For the Depressed, a Sweet Solution', *New York Times*, 1 February 2009; **14** 'US Received Hamas Letter for Obama: State Dept', AFP, 20 February 2009; **15** Isabel Kershner, 'Israel Opens the Gaza Border for 25,000 Carnations, Bound for Europe', *New York Times*, 12 February 2009; **16** Saeed Shah, 'Pakistan Releases "Father" of Nuclear Bomb from House Arrest', *Guardian*, 6 February 2009; **17** Timothy R. Homan, 'U.S. Economy: GDP Shrinks 6.2%, More Than Estimated', Bloomberg.com, 27 February 2009, http://bloomberg.com/apps/news?pid=20601087&sid=aKMkV532Xkq0&refer=home; **18** Dan Sabbagh, 'Crash of 1929 Gives Unlikely Support to Pearson Profit', *Times* (London), 3 March 2009; **19** Celia W. Dugger, 'Mugabe Swears In His Rival as Prime Minister of Zimbabwe', *New York Times*, 11 February 2009.

China's Democratised Foreign Policy

Denny Roy

The rise of China generates excitement in some quarters but anxiety in others. A possible mitigating factor against the worst-case scenario of a belligerent, outlaw superpower is the prospect of democratisation in China. For many liberal theorists, China's apparently permanent commitment to free-market economics raises the expectation that a loosening of the Chinese political system cannot be far behind. It has become a truism that an authoritarian state is likely to undergo political liberalisation when its average per capita gross domestic product reaches between $5,000 and $6,000.[1] A Chinese economist at a government-affiliated think tank recently projected that, based on current trends, China's per capita GDP will reach $3,000 by 2010 and $6,000 by 2020.[2] There are of course many uncertainties lying ahead. Especially in light of the global financial and economic crisis, China could see an economic downturn and a political retrenchment before realising its anticipated potential. China might also prove to be an exception to the $5,000 rule. Nevertheless, an optimist could hope that about the time Chinese power and influence begin to rival those of the United States, China will have some form of democratic political system.

The potential impact of democratisation on Chinese foreign policy is enormous if one accepts the assertions of what is commonly called 'democratic peace theory'. Unfortunately, democratisation of China's political system will probably not bring about a dramatic pacification of Chinese foreign policy, as important aspects of Chinese foreign policy are already

Denny Roy is a Senior Fellow at the East–West Center, Honolulu.

 DOI 10.1080/00396330902860769

'democratic' in the sense that most of the Chinese people support, if not demand, them.

Democratic peace theory

Immanuel Kant argued in his essay 'Perpetual Peace' that democracies are disinclined to go to war because they give the general public, which is inherently peace-loving, veto power over a country's foreign policy through the ballot box.[3] Wars have been frequent in history, Kant argued, because the ruling class made the decision to fight while the mass public bore the costs of the fighting. But if the common man actually had a voice in foreign-policymaking, war would become infrequent. In a democracy, a decision for war must account for public opinion. National leaders who contemplate subjecting their people to an unpopular war risk being voted out of office.

Recent scholarship has suggested additional reasons why democracies might be disinclined to fight wars against one another. One argument is that democracies tend to develop rich networks of institutional and cooperative linkages, which act as restraints and disincentives against violent conflict. Another rationale is that the political culture of negotiation, compromise and peaceful resolution of differences that develops within democratic systems carries over into bilateral relations between democracies. Finally, democracies might see one another as sharing similar values, engendering a mutual respect that steers them toward managing their disputes peacefully.[4]

Observers of recent US foreign policy will recognise the influence of democractic peace theory. President Bill Clinton proclaimed in 1994 that 'the best strategy to ensure our security and to build a durable peace is to support the advance of democracy elsewhere. Democracies don't attack each other. They make better trading partners and partners in diplomacy.'[5] President George W. Bush opened his second term with the statement:

> The survival of liberty in our land increasingly depends on the success of liberty in other lands. The best hope for peace in our world is the expansion of freedom in all the world ... It is the policy of the United States to seek and support the growth of democratic movements and institutions in every nation and culture, with the ultimate goal of ending tyranny in our world.

Bush sounded even more Kantian later that year: 'The reason why I'm so strong on democracy is democracies don't go to war with each other. And the reason why is the people of most societies don't like war, and they understand what war means.'[6]

Public opinion and Chinese policymaking

Chinese President Hu Jintao often speaks of his desire to develop 'socialist democracy' in China, citing goals such as greater public participation in decision-making and greater transparency in government. Neither Hu nor other top leaders, however, appear interested in a multiparty system in which voters choose their national leaders from a slate of parties with substantial programmatic and philosophical differences. Furthermore, Beijing still sees the broad civil liberties that Westerners identify with democracy as destructive of the highly valued objective of social and political stability.

China today is a one-party system under the Chinese Communist Party (CCP), and CCP leaders have no intention of giving up their monopoly on power. The system does not allow for groups outside the ruling party to compete for control of the government. Nor does it ensure a separation of powers or checks and balances among the key government organs. The role of the Chinese press is not to evaluate or criticise government policies, but rather to purvey the positions dictated by the leadership. Still, a modest degree of political ferment is visible today in China. The government has introduced local-level elections, though most of the candidates are CCP members, and in any case the state requires the winning office-holders to hew to the policies passed down by the central government. The Chinese press is now much freer than in the recent past to pursue certain kinds of potentially sensitive stories, such as corruption among officials. Chinese citizens now challenge their government in court and sometimes win, also unheard of until recently. The leadership appears interested in pursuing democratisation *within* the CCP, which could yield a system in which different factions function somewhat like competing parties. In sum, the pace with which China is changing raises the possibility of a dramatically transformed system emerging within two or three decades, with liberalisation representing one of the directions in which China might move.

To understand how democratisation might affect Chinese foreign policy, we must understand the role of public opinion in Chinese policymaking today. The relationship between public opinion and the national leadership has been interactive. The CCP has shaped public expectations through decades of discourse reinforcing particular points intended to bolster the party's legitimacy. From its early years the CCP has styled itself as a patriotic party that has defended China's sovereignty in contrast to past regimes that permitted losses of Chinese territory, rights and dignity. In the 1990s the central government emphasised the victimisation of China during the 'century of shame' (1842–1949), particularly the Japanese invasion during the Pacific War, as a means of mobilising public support for economic development to strengthen China so it would never again be vulnerable to foreign exploitation. In recent years the Chinese media have continuously promoted the view that China's accomplishments have entitled the country to international recognition and respect.

Beijing now has the burden of living up to the people's demands

Having fostered nationalist fervour and pride among the public, Beijing now carries the burden of living up to the people's demands. In general, the Chinese people expect their government to obtain the resources and economic opportunities necessary to maintain a continued increase in China's wealth and living standards. They expect Beijing to protect China's 'sovereignty', commonly understood as land, sea and airspace owned or claimed by China. And the Chinese expect their leaders to insist that the international community accord China due respect and prestige. As China scholar Peter Hays Gries put it, 'aware that popular nationalists now command a large following, the [Chinese Ministry of Foreign Affairs] is actively seeking to appease them … The Party must gain face for China before international society to earn the support of nationalist audiences at home.'[7] According to China expert Minxin Pei, 'the Communist Party is very eager to demonstrate to the Chinese people that their government has international respect and legitimacy. That's why the Chinese government … spent so much political capital to try to get practically all the foreign leaders to attend the [Beijing Olympics] opening ceremony.'[8]

Obtaining greater supplies of resources, protecting against perceived threats to sovereignty, and upholding national honour are all areas that are prone to spark conflict: a forceful Chinese initiative or reaction could quickly raise tensions with one or more foreign governments. Yet anything less than a forceful move on China's part would carry a strong risk of the leadership failing to meet the people's demands and thus losing a measure of legitimacy. Jiang Zemin frequently came under widespread public criticism for his perceived failure to stand up resolutely to the United States over issues such as the 1999 accidental bombing of the Chinese Embassy in Belgrade and the negotiations over China's accession to the World Trade Organisation.[9] More recently, during the Tibetan protests in spring 2008, many Chinese judged Hu Jintao's government to be 'weak and cowardly' in its response to the unrest.[10] Authoritarian governments are not immune to adverse public opinion. In some circumstances China's leadership faces pressures comparable to those on democratic national leaders who seek re-election.

But wouldn't democratisation in China change this? It might be argued that public support of Chinese foreign policy today reflects the lack of a 'marketplace of ideas' due to the CCP's dominance over the Chinese media and education systems. Authoritarian governments are notorious for exploiting their monopoly over political discussion and the ignorance of their people to mobilise support for government policies, including policies such as war that require heavy sacrifices by the populace. Liberalisation of Chinese domestic politics, some believe, would allow for free discussion of alternative foreign policies by the media and create space for competing political parties to offer different perspectives on China's foreign relations. Given more of an opportunity than they now enjoy to learn all the options and evaluate the rationale for each, Chinese citizens might favour engaging their Asia-Pacific neighbours in more peaceful and conciliatory ways.

This argument, however, has little relevance to China. Chinese are not ignorant of alternative viewpoints. China has more Internet and mobile-phone users than any other country in the world. Nearly 41 million Chinese travelled abroad in 2007, and the number is rising rapidly as China's middle class grows.[11] Neither does the simple model of the one-party state dictating opinion to the masses explain public support for Chinese foreign policy. The Chinese people have learned not to accept their government's pronouncements uncritically. Despite government spin, Chinese observers do not always agree that their leaders are doing what is best for China's national interests. The Chinese public bases its evaluations of foreign affairs on a worldview formed by deeply held assumptions about China's role in world history and its treatment by other countries. On some foreign-affairs issues, particularly Chinese relations with Japan and the United States, the Chinese public is often more belligerent than Beijing.[12] In a newly and formally democratised China, political parties vying for votes would have to satisfy widespread Chinese nationalist sensibilities to have a chance of capturing control of the government. Thus, it is easy to imagine China fitting into the theoretical argument that young democracies are especially war-prone.[13] In China's case, democracy would eliminate the bulwark that has stood between nationalism-fuelled public opinion and foreign-policy decision-making.

China and East Asia

On two specific issues the Chinese public supports strong foreign-policy positions that keep East Asia in a perpetual state of near-crisis. Firstly, the Chinese public is unwilling to accept post-war Japan as a fully rehabilitated country until the Japanese satisfy Chinese indignation over issues related to the Pacific War. Secondly, the people of mainland China insist that Taiwan eventually unite politically with the mainland, even if it must be through war.

China and Japan

During most of the Cold War, Chinese hard feelings over Japan's Pacific War aggression and atrocities were not a major issue in Sino-Japanese relations. The Chinese government chose not to stoke anger and resentment against Japan. Beijing took a relatively conciliatory position, hoping to encourage socialist revolution among the Japanese and to develop bilateral economic relations. Mao's government also chose to soft-pedal the suffering China's people endured at Japanese hands during the war in the belief that this theme was defeatist and discouraging.[14] Beijing did not ask for reparation payments as part of the agreement to normalise Japan–China relations in 1972, settling for a tacit understanding that Tokyo would subsequently supply China with generous economic assistance.

In the 1980s, however, the Chinese government sought a new approach to energise a people disillusioned by the Cultural Revolution and other failings of communist ideology. Press reports of whitewashed Japanese history textbooks prompted strong Chinese condemnation. The CCP began changing China's education system to emphasise Chinese victimisation, with demonisation of the Japanese an unavoidable corollary.[15] This programme reached a crescendo in the 1990s. The authorities allowed Chinese researchers to delve into and publicise Japanese wartime atrocities, and museums and memorials commemorating Chinese sacrifices in the 'War of Resistance Against Japan' sprang up throughout the country. Discussions of foreign (especially Japanese) outrages against the Chinese people, often presented in ghastly detail, became the vehicle for encouraging nationalism and spurring greater efforts toward lifting China into the ranks of the major powers.

By turning the attention of the Chinese public and media to the previously suppressed topic of Japanese war crimes, Chinese leaders unleashed a societal tide that they proved unable to control. Grassroots movements pushed the Chinese government to reluctantly take steps it initially did not support, such as publicly backing attempts by Chinese citizens to sue for compensation in Japanese courts. True, Chinese authorities have occasionally tried to prevent or limit anti-Japanese protests that threatened to damage bilateral ties beyond a level Beijing thought prudent. In 2002 and 2003, some Chinese strategists proposed 'new thinking' toward Japan: leaving aside historical grievances and forging a relationship with Japan that accords with China's current strategic interests. Chinese leaders reportedly saw merit in the idea, but negative public reaction preventing them from pursuing it.[16]

In Japan, meanwhile, Prime Minister Junichiro Koizumi's insistence on openly attending the Yasukuni Shrine was representative of Japanese guilt fatigue. Koizumi held that the Japanese no less than any other people have the right to honour their war dead, and that this practice should not be subject to veto by foreigners. Koizumi was three years old when the Pacific

War ended. His and succeeding generations of Japanese who have known only post-war Japan are far less likely to accept the idea that Japan must accommodate permanent regional demands for Japanese compensation and self-restrictions based on Japan's Pacific War aggressions.

Chinese society has moved in the opposite direction. Influenced by the heavy anti-Japan content in Chinese education and media in the 1980s and 1990s, younger Chinese who did not personally experience the war are at least as anti-Japanese as the wartime generation.[17] Since President Jiang Zemin's visit to Japan in 1998, when he irritated his hosts by lecturing them on the war-crimes issue, Beijing seems to have realised the danger of overplaying the history card. The Chinese public, however, was just getting started at the time of Jiang's visit. Japan's inability or unwillingness to satisfy Chinese indignation over the war deeply rankled them. A series of Chinese demonstrations, protest campaigns and riots (participants in which were mostly young people rather than the wartime generation) erupted spontaneously in reaction to a variety of triggers: in 2001, a famous Chinese actress offended her compatriots by appearing on a magazine cover wearing a dress that displayed a stylised Japanese rising-sun flag; Chinese observers thought two Toyota advertisements in a Chinese auto magazine in 2003 intentionally implied Japanese superiority over China; the Chinese press reported that Japanese businessmen visiting Zhuhai had hired a large number of Chinese prostitutes during the 2003 anniversary of the Mukden Incident, which led to Japan's takeover of Manchuria in 1931; Japanese students at a university in Xian performed a skit that Chinese onlookers considered obscene; China hosted the 2004 Asian Cup soccer tournament and saw its national team beaten by the visiting Japanese; and in 2005, a United Nations report suggested that Japan should have a permanent seat on the UN Security Council, while the Japanese Ministry of Education again approved textbooks that the Chinese believed under-reported Japan's Pacific War misdeeds. Chinese authorities attempted to manage these anti-Japanese outbursts, which were clearly not part of Beijing's preferred programme for pursuing its objectives

Younger Chinese are at least as anti-Japanese as the wartime generation

vis-à-vis Japan. A pattern emerged: anti-Japanese sentiment in China spontaneously flared up, public opinion forced Beijing to take a tough position with Tokyo, Chinese authorities let their people blow off steam, but tried to contain the protests and then quickly restore order, reminding the populace that a working relationship with Japan is in China's interest.

President Hu's visit to Japan in May 2008, the first by a Chinese president since Jiang's counterproductive trip in 1998, marked a resuscitation of the bilateral relationship that had reached a nadir in 2005. The meeting was at best only a moderate success in terms of substance, but the fact that a meeting between Hu and Japanese Prime Minister Yasuo Fukuda took place at all, particularly with Hu striking a moderate tone, signalled that both governments were eager to re-stabilise the relationship. Yet this hardly assuages concerns that Sino-Japanese relations remain vulnerable to another society-driven downturn.

China and Taiwan

Since gaining control of mainland China, the CCP has insisted that Taiwan remain politically a part of China and eventually return to its previous status as a domain of the central government in Beijing (although the CCP has never ruled Taiwan).

The Chinese public has internalised the decades-old CCP refrain that Taiwan belongs to China and that preventing 'separatists' from declaring Taiwan's formal independence is a core national interest. In their view, Taiwan belongs to the 1.3 billion Chinese on the mainland as much as to the 23m who live on Taiwan. Mainlanders are too quick to dismiss Taiwanese nationalism as the product of brainwashing by Japan, which governed Taiwan for 50 years, or rabble-rousing by Taiwanese politicians. Ultimately, however, for mainlanders the possibility that residents of the island might desire a different destiny is irrelevant: the Taiwanese do not have the right to decide Taiwan's fate independent of the wishes of Chinese on the mainland.

Much of the Chinese public now embraces the belief that China cannot become a great power without reclaiming its most valuable piece of 'lost' territory. As China scholar Tang Shiping put it, 'a China without Taiwan would no longer be China'.[18] Even if Chinese leaders would prefer to reach a modus vivendi with Taipei that would permanently reduce cross-Strait tensions, public opinion will not allow any deal that Taiwan's leaders would be likely to accept, even under new President Ma Ying-jeou, who must disprove his opponents' warnings that he will sell out Taiwan to China. Mainland Chinese are not only prepared to bear the costs of a war to prevent Taiwan's independence, they would not forgive a government that shrank from such a fight. The Chinese public's perception that Taiwan is a national-security issue makes Taiwan a regime-security issue for the CCP. The top leaders in Beijing could survive in power even if they lost a war over Taiwan if the consensus perception was that they demonstrated Chinese resolve but were unable to overcome the technological superiority of the enemy forces. On the other hand, the highest level of officials could not remain in power if they allowed Taiwan to move permanently to formal independence without Beijing employing the last resort of military force.

As with China–Japan relations, the CCP's discourse on Taiwan over many years has contributed to public attitudes that now constrain Beijing's Taiwan policy.[19] This is particularly unfortunate in view of the fact that the attitude of mainland-Chinese leaders toward Taiwan has varied throughout history. During part of the Qing Dynasty, the central government was ambivalent about claiming Taiwan as part of China.[20] Before he conquered the mainland, Mao Tse-tung said Taiwan (then a Japanese colony) should be independent.[21] The post-1949 CCP might have chosen another way to formulate the relationship. Beijing might have argued, for example, that since most of Taiwan's inhabitants are ethnically and culturally Chinese it does not matter if they do not have formal political ties to the mainland. Taking this position today, however, would be politically impossible, and will remain so for perhaps another generation.

The Taiwan Strait conundrum well illustrates the possibility of war-proneness between two peoples who are parties to a dispute that is not easily settled through compromise and who might value their nationalist aspirations even higher than peace. And this despite the robust and growing economic ties across the Taiwan Strait that create a strong disincentive for conflict.

Democratic authoritarians

Contrary to the Kantian caricature, although China is an authoritarian state, some of its assertive and conflict-accepting foreign-policy positions have the support of the Chinese mass public. Similarly, it would be dangerously erroneous to assume, as Kant might lead us to do, that Chinese national leaders are not sensitive to public opinion because they are not popularly elected. Discounting the impact of domestic opinion on Chinese foreign policy might lead to miscalculation. Outsiders might judge that a certain policy would not serve China's long-term national interests and assume that Chinese leaders would reach the same conclusion. These observers might then rule out the possibility of China pursuing such a policy. But as policymakers in all states realise, the public often sees issues differently than government officials. The masses tend to be more emotional, strategically short-sighted and concerned with moral principles than office-holders. A mobilised Chinese public could force Beijing to act against the government's own cold-blooded calculations, putting a seemingly 'irrational' course of action back on the table, perhaps unbeknownst to foreign analysts attempting to anticipate contingent Chinese behaviour.

> *Most Chinese do not cheer criticism of their government*

Western human-rights pressure on China seems premised on a belief in an adversarial relationship between the Chinese government and Chinese society, a situation that requires outsiders to speak on behalf of a suppressed Chinese populace that wishes for greater civil liberties. Most Chinese, however, do not cheer this criticism of their government. Rather, they rally to the CCP's positions that China has made historically unprecedented progress in socioeconomic human rights by raising the living standards of tens of millions of its people, that immediate introduction of Western-style civil and political liberties would create chaos that could threaten China's recent gains, and that this pressure for political liberalisation from the West is largely driven by groups that want to embarrass rather than help China.[22]

The anti-China protests attracted by the Chinese Olympic torch as it toured the globe prior to the 2008 Beijing Olympic Games further illustrated, if not deepened, the bond between the Chinese people and their government when it comes to China's foreign relations. Although the protestors professed humanitarian concerns such as fair treatment of Tibetans and asylum for North Korean refugees, Chinese generally saw these protests as mean-spirited attempts to deny China its duly earned international prestige. Chinese communities abroad responded to the call for pro-China counter-demonstrations with enthusiasm – in the case of Seoul, excessive enthusiasm. Similarly, the general reaction of the Chinese public to discussions of possible boycotts of the Olympic opening ceremony by foreign leaders was not one of gratitude, but rather resentment. Because the Chinese people embraced the Beijing Olympics as a source of national unity and pride, it made a poor venue for pressing the Chinese government on unrelated grievances.

Foreign governments working with Chinese officials should understand that Chinese officials have a need for political 'cover' comparable to elected leaders in multiparty democracies. Most outsiders are not aware of the price Jiang paid in the form of criticism from the general public and from nationalist and conservative groups within the political and military elite for his emphasis on accommodating the United States. His successor Hu Jintao likewise avoids directly challenging the United States but appears more focused on strengthening China's relationship with the rest of Asia than with the United States, an approach more in line with public sentiment.

* * *

The conclusion that the democratisation of China would not substantially reduce tensions with China's democratic neighbours calls into question democratic peace theory. As realist scholar John Mearsheimer notes, democracies are just as concerned as non-democracies about survival in a competitive and uncertainty-filled international environment.[23] Democratic countries can be involved in disputes that are not resolvable through peaceful negotiation or compromise. Circumstances – and not just governments – can drive democratic polities to choose to go to war with one another. Over the long term, the freer exchange of ideas that accompanies democratisation might engender more cosmopolitan thinking among the Chinese public, including a reassessment of topics such as national sovereignty, nationalism, globalisation, and the goals and costs of conflict. Perhaps a later generation of Chinese will re-think the Taiwan issue and lay aside the history issue with a Japan that has become a completely different country during the post-war period than it was during the Pacific War. In the short term, however, democratisation would not by itself extinguish Chinese nationalism; rather, it would provide nationalist urges with more direct influence over policy. Adding China to the international pool of democracies would not necessarily make military conflict between China and any of its democratic Asia-Pacific neighbours obsolete. Chinese tensions with the United States, Japan and Taiwan could be expected to continue.

China's emergence as a regional and global great power represents a massive shift in the political, economic and strategic geology of the international system. The challenge for the United States and the other major powers is to employ their limited influence wisely toward the objective of channelling China toward conformity with global norms and practices accepted as lawful and constructive. China's huge population longs not only for security and prosperity, but also for the international prestige they believe China deserves. Statesmen and strategists must account for the pressure that domestic opinion places on Chinese policymakers on issues that evoke strong nationalistic sentiment. This does not mean the international community must accommodate China on every issue over which the Chinese public becomes agitated, regardless of the justice or merits of the Chinese position. Rather, governments bargaining with China must understand that on some issues foreign pressure may be a less compelling force on Chinese leaders than countervailing domestic pressure. Chinese leaders may prefer to follow the course urged by the international community but conclude that they cannot because of expectations at home. In such circumstances, a better understanding of the constraints under which Chinese leaders operate might facilitate the realisation of a face-saving solution rather than leaving both sides frustrated and empty-handed.

Chinese society harbours an outlook shaped by intense nationalism, a belief in China's inherent greatness, and a deep sense of outrage over foreign mistreatment of China throughout the modern era. This outlook, its power to agitate the mass public, and the influence of an energised populace upon the making of foreign policy are durable phenomena that will persist through any democratic transition in the medium term. Although there are good reasons to hope for democracy in China, the anticipated rescue from China's most serious bilateral disputes should not be among them.

Notes

1 Henry S. Rowen, 'Elections in China', *The National Interest*, no. 45, Fall 1996, pp. 68–9; Fareed Zakaria, *The Future of Freedom: Illiberal Democracy at Home and Abroad* (New York: W.W. Norton, 2003), p. 79.

2 'Expert: China's Per Capita GDP to Hit $3,000 by 2010', Xinhua News Service, 4 January 2008, http://news.xinhuanet.com/english/2008-01/04/content_7364497.htm.

3 Immanuel Kant, 'Perpetual Peace', in Hans Reiss (ed.), *Kant: Political Writings* (Cambridge: Cambridge University Press, 1991).

4 A few representative works on this much-studied topic are Bruce Russett, *Grasping The Democratic Peace: Principles For A Post-Cold War World* (Princeton, NJ: Princeton University Press, 2001); Stewart Weart, *Never At War: Why Democracies Will Not Fight One Another* (New Haven, CT: Yale University Press, 1998); and Karen Rasler and William R. Thompson, *Puzzles of the Democratic Peace: Theory, Geopolitics and the Transformation of World Politics* (New York: Palgrave Macmillan, 2005).

5 Bill Clinton, '1994 State of the Union Address', *Washington Post*, 25 January 1994, http://www.washingtonpost.com/wp-srv/politics/special/states/docs/sou94.htm.

6 'Bush: "No Justice without Freedom"', CNN, 20 January 2005, http://www.cnn.com/2005/ALLPOLITICS/01/20/bush.transcript/index.html; 'Bush and Blair Discuss the Mideast', *New York Times*, 12 November 2004, http://www.nytimes.com/2004/11/12/international/middleeast/12text-bush.html.

7 Peter Hays Gries, 'Nationalism and Chinese Foreign Policy', in Yong Deng and Fei-ling Wang (eds), *China Rising: Power and Motivation in Chinese Foreign Policy* (Lanham, MD: Rowman & Littlefield, 2005), pp. 111, 112.

8 Quoted in Larisa Epatko, 'Olympics Mark China's "Coming of Age"', Online Newshour, 16 May 2008, PBS, http://www.pbs.org/newshour/indepth_coverage/asia/china/2008/olympics.html.

9 Joseph Fewsmith, 'China and the WTO: The Politics Behind the Agreement', in National Bureau of Asian Research, *NBR Analysis*, vol. 10, no. 5, December 1999, p. 23.

10 Jim Yardley, 'Chinese Nationalism Fuels Tibet Crackdown', *New York Times*, 31 March 2008, http://www.nytimes.com/2008/03/31/world/asia/31china.html.

11 '21.6 mln Chinese to Travel Abroad in First Half 2008', Xinhua News Service, 8 February 2008, http://news.xinhuanet.com/english/2008-02/08/content_7582359.htm.

12 In 2003, for example, chemical weapons buried by the Japanese in Qiqihar, northeastern China, during the Pacific War were accidentally unearthed, killing one Chinese and harmed 40 others. A petition demanding an apology and compensation from Japan garnered over one million Chinese signatures within a month. The Chinese government bowed to this manifestation of public opinion, allowing activists to deliver a letter of protest to the Japanese Embassy in Beijing. But this was clearly a reluctant concession, as the Chinese media did not cover it and Chinese diplomats in Japan denied knowing about it. Tim Luard, 'Anti-Japan Protests Worry China', BBC News, 18 September 2003, http://news.bbc.co.uk/2/hi/asia-pacific/3118850.stm. In 2007, as Beijing was attempting to repair relations with Japan, the Chinese government imposed restrictions on media outlets against publishing inflammatory memorials of the 70th anniversary of the Japanese invasion of China. Li Datong, '"Public Opinion" and China's Japan Policy', openDemocracy, 17 April 2007, http://www.opendemocracy.net/democracy/china_japan_4537.jsp. Beijing has also tried to restrain anti-Japan activism by Chinese citizens in connection with the Senkaku/Diaoyu Islands dispute. Yang Jian, 'China's Security Strategy Towards Japan: Perceptions, Policies, and Prospects', Centre for Strategic Studies Working Paper No. 17/01, Victoria University of Wellington, pp. 11–12.

13 Edward D. Mansfield and Jack Snyder, *Electing to Fight: Why Emerging Democracies Go to War* (Cambridge, MA: MIT Press, 2005).

14 Yinan He, 'History, Chinese Nationalism and the Emerging Sino-Japanese Conflict', *Journal of Contemporary China*, vol. 16, no. 50, February 2007, p. 7.

15 Peter Hays Gries, *China's New Nationalism: Pride, Politics, and Diplomacy* (Berkeley, CA: University of California Press, 2004), pp. 69–86.

16 National Institute for Defense Studies, *East Asian Strategic Review 2004* (Tokyo: Japan Times Press, 2004), pp. 107, 108.

17 Many observers have confirmed this trend, citing various reasons for it: younger people have grown up in a period during which the authorities permitted, if not cultivated, the practice of blaming Chinese problems on foreign governments; younger Chinese are emboldened by China's growing international prominence to demand rectification of old injustices; and inflammatory anti-Japan sentiment is easily spread through the Internet (heavily used by younger people) and is much less likely to invoke government censorship than discussions of such topics as democratisation or the shortcomings of high-ranking Chinese Communist Party officials. See Justin McCurry and Jonathan Watts, 'China's Angry Young Focus Their Hatred on Old Enemy', *Guardian*, 30 December 2004, http://www.guardian.co.uk/

world/2004/dec/30/china.japan; Joshua Kurlantzick, 'China's Next-generation Nationalists', *Los Angeles Times*, 6 May 2008, http://articles.latimes.com/2008/may/06/opinion/oe-kurlantzik6; Aaron Kyle Dennis, 'Today Anti-Japan, Tomorrow Anti-Beijing?', *Asia Times*, 27 April 2005, http://www.atimes.com/atimes/China/GD27Ad01.html; Fujiwara Hidehito, 'Beijing Can't Keep Love–Hate Relations', *International Herald Tribune/Asahi Shimbun*, 12 April 2005, http://www.japanfocus.org/_Asahi_Shimbun-_Nationalism_and_the_China_Japan_Conflict.

18 Tang Shiping, 'Lixiang Anquan Huanjing yu Xinshiji Zhongguo Dazhanlue', *Zhanlue yu Guanli*, no. 6, 2000, p. 43. Most China-watchers would agree with the observation of a *New York Times* journalist who concluded that 'the idea that Taiwan will inevitably reunite with the mainland is probably the most emotional, deeply held belief of ordinary Chinese, from college students to retired factory workers'. Elisabeth Rosenthal, 'Decision in Taiwan: the Mainland', *New York Times*, 20 March 2000. In a 2000 survey of mainland Chinese, over 95% supported the use of force to prevent Taiwan independence. Sangwon Suh, 'Anxious Countdown', *Asiaweek*, 19 May 2000, http://cgi.cnn.com/ASIANOW/asiaweek/magazine/2000/0519/nat.security.html.

19 Thus, Beijing may not be deterrable in a Taiwan scenario, in no small measure because of public opinion.

20 Denny Roy, *Taiwan: A Political History* (Ithaca, NY: Cornell University Press, 2003). p. 19.

21 Edgar Snow, *Red Star Over China* (New York: Modern Books, 1944), p. 96.

22 Muhammad Cohen, 'Why China Loves the Olympics', *Guardian*, 11 August 2008, http://www.guardian.co.uk/commentisfree/2008/aug/11/olympics2008.usa; 'China Digital Times Interview Series: Chinese Journalists Talk About the Olympics, Tibet, and Cross-Cultural Understanding', *China Digital Times*, 7 July 2008, http://chinadigitaltimes.net/2008/07/interview-with-a-chinese-journalist/; Ming Zhang, 'The Shifting Chinese Public Image of the United States', Strategic Forum No. 89, November 1996, Institute for National Strategic Studies, National Defense University, Washington DC, http://www.ndu.edu/inss/strforum/SF_89/forum89.html.

23 John J. Mearsheimer, *The Tragedy of Great Power Politics* (New York: W.W. Norton, 2001), p. 4.

The Euro and the Financial Crisis

Erik Jones

The global financial crisis is the first major challenge for the euro as a multinational currency. Many wonder whether it will also be the last. Although early indications suggest that the eurozone countries are weathering the storm, this has not stopped prominent economists such as Martin Feldstein from cautioning that 'the current financial crisis may provide a severe test of the euro's ability to survive'.[1]

This is not the first time that Feldstein has issued such a warning. He published an even stronger statement in the pages of *Foreign Affairs* shortly before the euro was formed. Then he speculated that conflicts between participating countries, or between those inside and outside the euro, could even escalate to war.[2] Few took the prospect seriously, either during the launch of the single currency or in the years that followed. As the current crisis continues to deepen and popular protests begin to mount, however, many fear Feldstein's nightmare scenarios are no longer so absurd.[3] War is not on the cards, but a deep and divisive conflict over the functioning of the single currency cannot be ruled out. Such a conflict would not only set European countries against one another, but could also undermine the solidarity of the European Union as a whole.

In an effort to determine whether the survival of the eurozone is threatened, commentators have naturally turned to the economic data. What they find is troubling. Real unit labour costs relative to major trading partners

Erik Jones is Professor of European Studies at the SAIS Bologna Center of the Johns Hopkins University and a Contributing Editor to *Survival*. He is the author of *Economic Adjustment and Political Transformation in Small States* (Oxford University Press, 2008).

 DOI 10.1080/00396330902860785

(a rough measure of national competitiveness) are moving against some of the poorer southern countries of the eurozone, Italy in particular. The same is also true for some countries outside the eurozone, such as the United Kingdom. The difference is that these countries at least retain the ability to restore national competitiveness by devaluing their national currencies.

A further problem is that the poorer and more highly indebted countries of the eurozone are witnessing an increase in the relative cost of long-term sovereign borrowing. The difference in the yields on ten-year benchmark government bonds between Greece and Germany, for example, has increased by a multiple greater than five. Again, borrowing costs are rising for some countries outside the eurozone as well, but they have control over their own monetary policy and so – at least in extremis – are able to print their own money and inflate away the difference. Countries that have adopted the euro do not have this pressure-release value. Hence the threat is not so much that countries will leave the eurozone but that they may default. The only hope defaulters can have for salvation lies in the possibility that the richer countries such as Germany will find the economic resources and political will to bail them out.[4]

The closer one looks at the problem, the worse it becomes, particularly if the economic data are to be believed. Nevertheless, there is good reason to believe that the situation is much better than most commentators are willing to admit. The trick is to dissect the economic analysis, much of which not only exaggerates the significance of recent trends but also underestimates or ignores the costs and benefits of the most likely alternatives.

The simple conclusion is that Europe's economic and monetary union is not only much stronger than many fear, it is also much better than the system of fixed but adjustable exchange rates that it replaced. Far from engendering conflicts, the single currency has diffused them. Along the way, it has also insulated politicians from being forced to make inevitably unpopular and difficult choices. Thus, the eurozone is more likely to get larger than it is to get smaller.

Competitiveness lost and found

The Italian case clearly illustrates the cost of giving up the exchange rate as a policy instrument. Even before the global financial crisis, economists noticed that Italian real unit labour costs were losing ground relative to near competitors, Germany in particular. These same economists pointed out that the old Italian policy response would have been to devalue the lira against the German mark. This devaluation would have lowered the relative cost of Italian exports abroad even as the real cost of Italian labour domestically continued to rise. Italian consumers and non-traded industries would have suffered from the rising cost of imports but Italian manufacturing profits would have stabilised or increased. Now that Italy is trapped within the single currency, however, Italian manufacturing can expect to receive no such reprieve. This means that Italy either has to leave the eurozone and bring back the lira at a lower value, or witness the demise of its manufacturing industry as it goes through the long and painful process of bringing its real unit labour costs back into line. If these are the alternatives, it is small wonder that some have already started questioning whether the eurozone will crack.[5]

The data are striking. The European Commission publishes a series that reflects the real unit labour costs for the total economy in national currency relative to the 15 pre-2004-enlargement member states of the European Union. If relative labour costs are set to equal 100 in the year 2000, which is how they are published on the European Commission's website, then by 2008 Germany was at 94.2 while Italy was at 106.9. Britain, by contrast, remained relatively unchanged at 99.7. The interpretation of this data seems straightforward. Within the single currency, Germany has gained in competitive terms and Italy has lost. Outside the euro, British competitiveness is much the same.

The German economy was struggling in 2000

The problem with this easy interpretation is that it depends on the base year for the index: 2000 = 100. There is a seductive logic to the arbitrary choice made by the Commission. Not only is the year 2000 a round number and a millennial date change, it is close to the start of the single currency. Choosing it implies that national performance that year was somehow normal and therefore that it is an appropriate basis for comparison. Yet there is good reason to believe that it was not. The German economy was struggling in 2000 and the situation

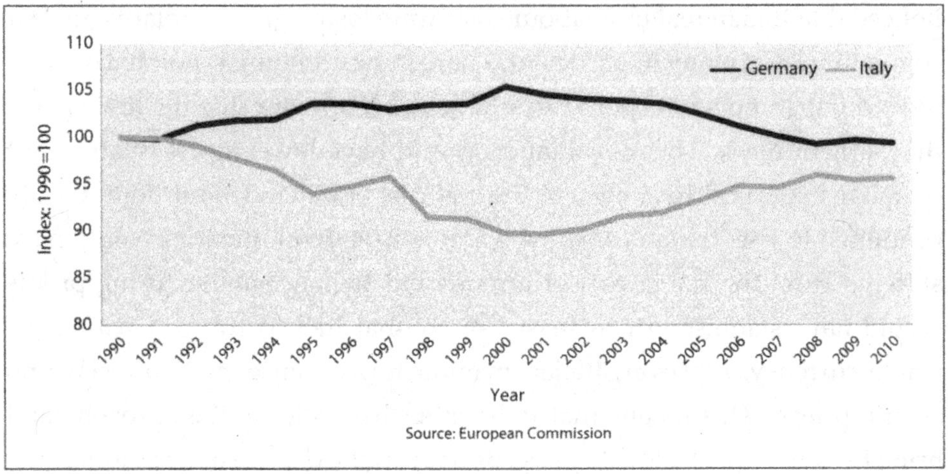

Figure 1. Competitiveness in Germany and Italy

would get worse before it got better. Meanwhile, the Italian economy was just emerging from reforms made to join the single currency in the first place, measures that included both a healthy dose of fiscal austerity and strong efforts to bring relative unit labour costs under control. The importance of these conditions can be seen if we shift the baseline for the index back by a decade (1990 = 100). This has the added advantage of revealing the implications of the German unification shock. The evolution of German and Italian labour costs using this new index can be seen in Figure 1, which also includes the European Commission's estimates for 2009 and 2010.

Figure 1 clearly shows the impact of the German unification shock on German labour-cost competitiveness. It also reveals the scale of the effort made by Italy to prepare for entry into the European single currency after 1996. Both of these effects reached their peak intensity in the year 2000, which was anything but a normal year for either country – it was also when the difference between the two was at its greatest. Both economies have since begun to move back toward the centre. In terms of relative labour-cost competitiveness, however, Italy is still ahead of Germany. The European Commission's latest projections suggest that this positive difference in Italy's favour is likely to remain in effect for at least the next two years. While this does not mean that the Italian economy is necessarily stronger than Germany's, it is hard to see why Italy would leave the eurozone.

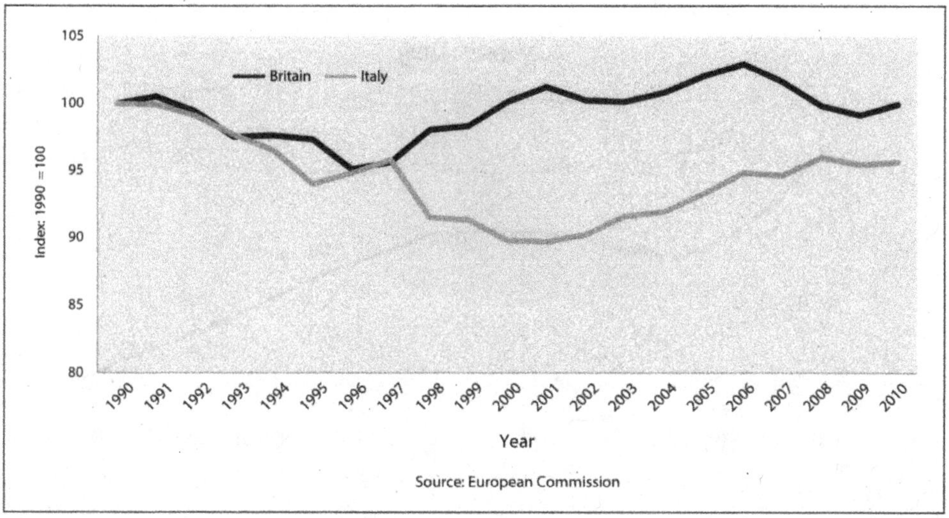

Figure 2. Competitiveness in Britain and Italy

In any case, the more telling comparison is not between two countries within the eurozone, but between a country that is in and another that is out. This is where the British case becomes interesting. If we look at the data series based in the year 2000, it is possible to claim that the United Kingdom did better for not having joined because its relative competitive position remains unchanged. If we base the data in 1990, however, the picture looks very different. Where Italy made great efforts to join the single currency, Britain did not. UK labour-cost competitiveness in manufacturing suffered as a result. This can be seen in Figure 2, which repeats the data for Italy but replaces Germany with Great Britain. The striking feature is how much British relative real unit labour costs deteriorate after 1997, only recovering after 2006.

How do we know which story gives the more accurate description of changes in relative economic competitiveness? Again, the point to emphasise is that these stories emerge from an analysis of an index that is itself dependent on the choice of base year. If we are going to choose between different versions of the same index, we should do so with reference to a different line of data.

In this case, it is useful to look at the data for manufacturing employment. Because manufacturing is exposed to international competition,

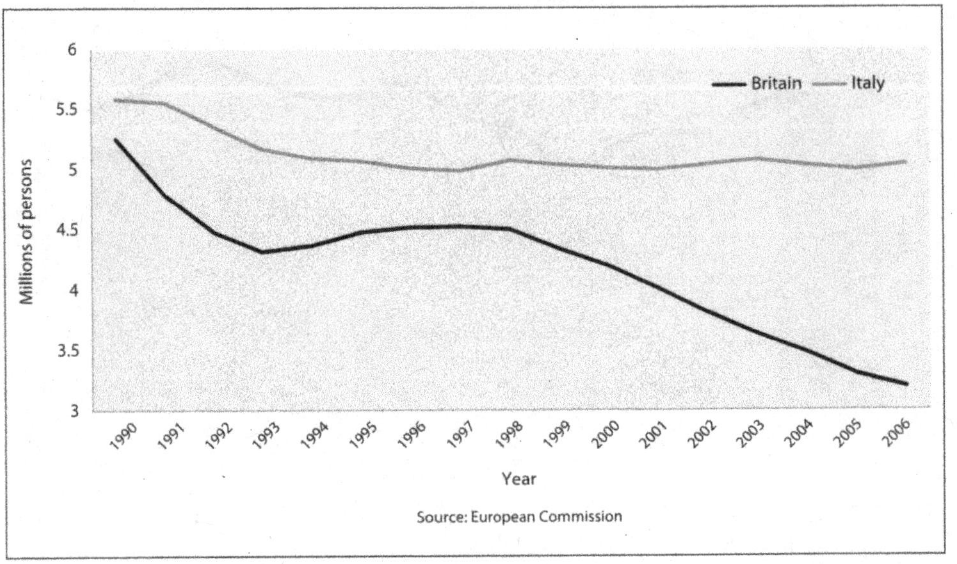

Figure 3. Manufacturing employment

manufacturing employment should go up or down depending on the relative level of international competitiveness (among other factors). If the story based on 2000 as a normal year is accurate, then all things being equal Italy should do worse than the United Kingdom in terms of holding on to manufacturing jobs. If the story based in 1990 is more accurate, then the trends in manufacturing employment should go the other way around. These data are presented in Figure 3. What they reveal is the secular decline in British manufacturing employment from 1997 to 2006 (the latest year for which figures are available from the European Commission). By contrast, Italian manufacturing employment remains roughly constant. The argument here is not that British manufacturing employment declined because of the deterioration in relative real unit labour costs, although that loss in competitiveness surely did not help. Rather, the data suggest that the relative merits of staying outside the euro rather than joining are not obvious on the competitiveness front. If the British experience is representative, Italy is better off staying inside.

Relative unit labour costs tell only part of the story. A fuller account would have to take into consideration both the cost of capital and the cost of doing business. Once again, it is hard to make the case for abandoning the euro. One of the major benefits of joining the eurozone is that it has offered members both greater liquidity and a lower cost of capital. For highly indebted countries such as Italy, Greece or Belgium, this meant that they could borrow larger amounts at longer maturities and lower prices in 'domestic' currency. During the months leading up to the start of the single currency, interest rates on long-term sovereign-debt obligations across the eurozone converged to within one-half of one percent. As refinancing recycled increasing volumes of public debt into longer maturities with lower yields, public finances in highly indebted countries benefitted to the tune of several percent of domestic GDP in foregone debt-servicing requirements. Corporate borrowers also benefitted as bond holders adapted expectations to a lower-risk, lower-inflation environment. Finally, manufacturers across the eurozone no longer have to deal as frequently with multiple currencies. The savings that this foregone cost of changing currencies implies may not be great, but are not negligible either.

> *Bond holders adapted expectations to a lower-risk environment*

Show me the money

The worry is that at least some of the principal benefits of joining the eurozone are coming undone. Where Greek debt used to trade at yields within one-half of a percentage point of Germany's, they now yield an additional 2.5% or more. This widening of the yield differential during the current financial crisis implies a significant increase in the relative cost of Greek government debt-financing at a time when fiscal accounts are already being stretched by automatic stabilisers in the form of lower taxes (on lower incomes) and higher benefits payouts because of higher unemployment. Worse still, Greece, like many highly indebted countries, still has much to do in preparation for the costs of an ageing population and the burden on government finances that this will entail. If the Greeks are highly indebted now, this is nothing to what they face in the future. As the relative cost of debt financing rises, or so the argument runs, the risk that the Greek government will default on its commitments begins to creep up as well. On

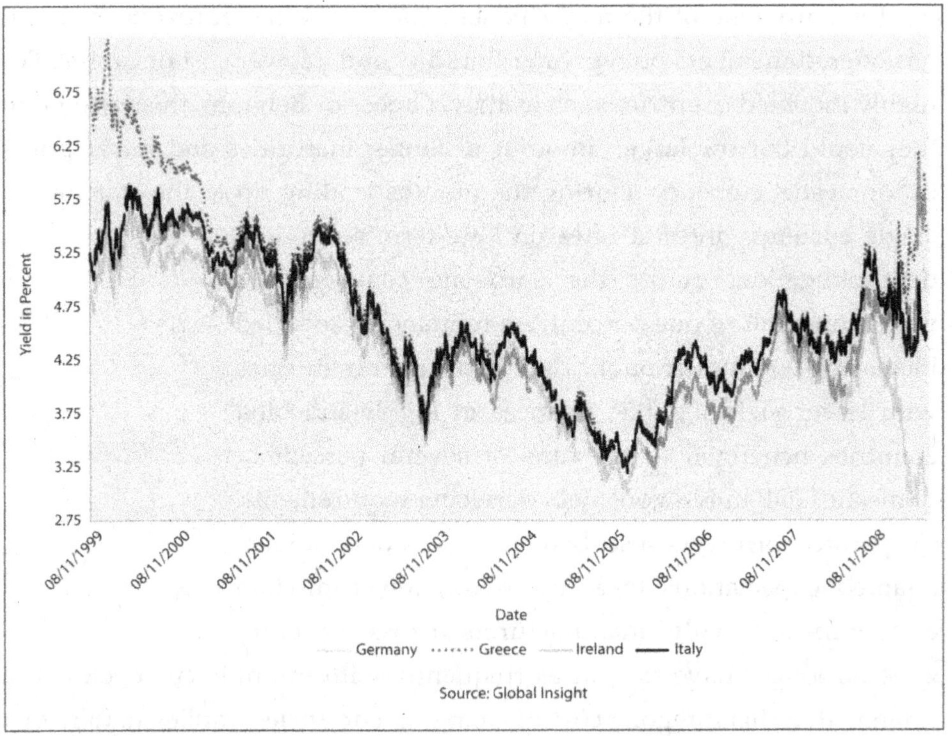

Figure 4. Long-term bond yields in the eurozone

14 January 2009, Standard & Poor's downgraded the Greek government's creditworthiness from A to A⁻ for long-term borrowing and A-1 to A-2 for short-term.[6]

The Greek government's default risk is increasing, but the point to note is that it would surely be higher outside the single currency than it is now. Although the yield differential with Germany has increased, this is largely due to the fact that while Greek sovereign-debt yields have been relatively stable, German sovereign-debt yields have gone down. As a result, Greece is still paying a lower interest rate on its long-term debt than it was just before it joined the single currency in 2000. The relative cost has increased but the absolute cost has not. This can be seen in Figure 4, which shows the yield on 10-year sovereign-debt obligations for four countries in the eurozone: Germany, Greece, Ireland and Italy. Germany is the benchmark; the other three are subject to varying degrees of concern about their creditworthiness.

Toward the middle of February 2009, the situation began to look more worrying. Both Ireland and Greece witnessed a sudden spike in their long-term yield rates, taking them to record highs since they entered the eurozone. Nevertheless, it is still worth noting that neither country has experienced a general run on its government securities, and what went up has started to come back down. Much of this new-found confidence in the market is due to suggestions made by German Finance Minister Peer Steinbrück that no eurozone member would be allowed to default.[7] Regardless, the threat of default is a long way off.

In real terms – that is, when relative inflation rates are taken into account – the long-run interest rates in Greece and Germany are much closer than the nominal yield spreads would suggest. According to data from Eurostat, prices rose by 2.4% more per annum on average in Greece than in Germany for 2008 (similar data for Ireland are still unavailable). If we subtract this inflation differential from the yield differential, the real rate of interest paid by the Greek government is not that much higher than that paid by Germany. This 'real' equivalence is not important to the large institutional investors that trade in sovereign bonds because most such institutions have Europe-wide interests and so perceive only a single real interest rate for the eurozone as a whole. This explains why the yield differentials were so tight across the eurozone before the current crisis. What has changed is the sudden increase in demand for safe-haven investments. Even including the most recent spike, German bond yields have gone down at least as much as Greek yields have gone up.

The threat of default is a long way off

The real interest-rate differential is important to national governments, however. National tax receipts tend to move in line with the national rate of price inflation and so the relatively higher rate of Greek inflation means that the Greek government's ability to manage its debt is not yet much affected by the increase in yields relative to Germany. Of course, the difference in inflation rates is diminishing under the weight of the current crisis and Greece still has to prepare for its ageing population. Nevertheless, the situation could be much worse.

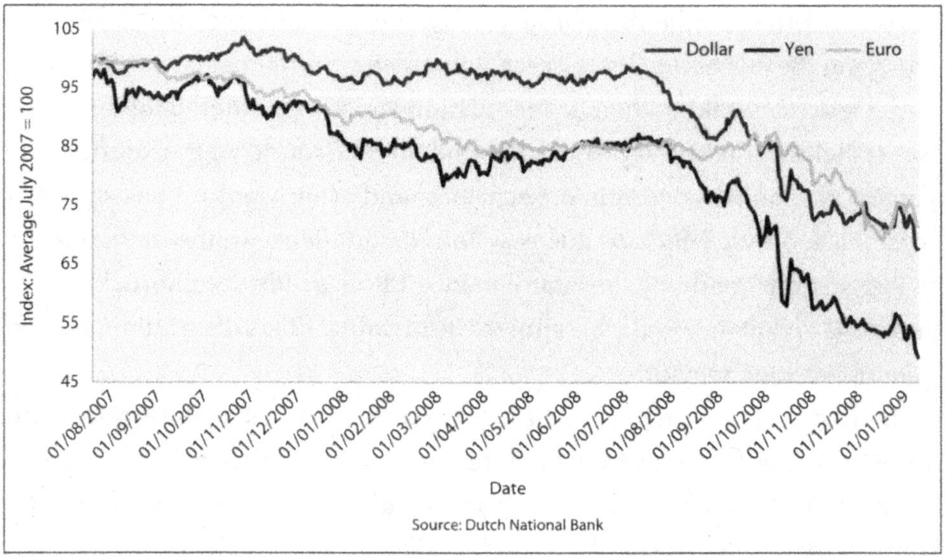

Figure 5. Exchange rates against the pound

Indeed, if Greece were outside the eurozone it probably would be. At the moment, Greek sovereign bonds benefit from the liquidity of deep eurozone markets. Were Greek bonds traded in drachmas rather than euros, much of that liquidity would evaporate. The same is true for Italy, Ireland, Spain and Portugal. The rule would apply to banks in those countries as well, with the implication that any run on the national currency would effectively become a run on the banks, and any run on the banks could trigger a run on the currency. Hence Greece would not only face a higher cost of borrowing, but it would also have to deal with the cost of exchange-rate volatility.

The British case shows just how quickly and erratically exchange rates can move. Since the start of the global financial crisis in August 2007, the United Kingdom has experienced an unprecedented increase in the volatility of exchange rates relative to the pound. As a result, not only has the pound lost value relative to other major world currencies, but its position in the triangular relationship between foreign currencies has gyrated as well. The effects can be seen in Figure 5. In turn, this increase in exchange-rate volatility has greatly complicated the process of manufacturing for export, because so much of what Britain exports to foreign markets is first imported from abroad.

Sophie's choice

Most governments in Europe are envious of the liquidity that is available in the eurozone and cannot tolerate the high degree of exchange-rate volatility that has been experienced by countries outside the zone, such as Great Britain. Hence their alternative to participation in the euro is to open their capital markets and peg their exchange rates. Denmark is a good example, but the same thing loosely applies to Norway, Sweden and Iceland, not to mention many of the countries of Central and Eastern Europe.

There is nothing new in this formula. It is roughly the same as what the eurozone countries did within the European Monetary System before they formed the single currency. The difference is that the eurozone countries have made an important structural choice. In exchange for capital-market liberalisation and irrevocably fixed exchange rates, they have agreed to maintain a common monetary policy. Those countries outside the eurozone have left themselves a bit more discretion. They can choose to maintain open capital markets and fixed exchange rates at the cost of an autonomous monetary policy, or not to fix the exchange rate and seek greater monetary policy autonomy instead, or to close their capital markets altogether.

What the countries outside the eurozone cannot choose is when they will have to exercise their discretion and at what cost. The obvious example is Iceland, which had to close its capital markets when a run on the currency threatened to bring down the country's entire economy. The timing of that decision was not in the hands of Iceland's politicians. Instead, it was determined by the weight of market forces that were driving the Icelandic krona into the ground. Now, as the Icelandic authorities look to reopen their capital markets to the outside world, they must also consider whether they would have more autonomy within the eurozone than without.

The Danish example sits at the other extreme. The exchange rate between the Danish krone and the euro fluctuates in a very tight band around 7.45 krone to the euro. Danish monetary authorities maintain this tight link by anticipating the policy decisions made at the European Central Bank (ECB). By October 2008, however, this strategy began to break down, confronting Danish monetary authorities with a choice. They could either cut interest rates and see the krone devalue against the euro, or raise them even as the ECB was cutting its own. In the end, the Danish authorities opted to fix the exchange rate by raising their discount rate to 4.5% on 8 October even as the ECB prepared to cut the rate on its main refinancing operations to 3.75% a week later. The gap between Danish and ECB policy rates widened further in early December. Only by mid January 2009 did the difference in policy rates begin to come back down.

The Swedish case shows a middle alternative. Throughout much of the financial crisis Sweden has sought to stabilise the fluctuation of its krona against the euro within a wider band than Denmark. To do so meant raising the Swedish central bank's policy rate by 50 basis points above that in the eurozone. As Denmark began to raise its rates in October, Sweden decided to follow the ECB down. This meant giving up some control over the value of the krona, which has continued to depreciate against the euro as Swedish interest rates have fallen.

None of these Nordic countries can be happy with its situation

None of these three Nordic countries can be happy with its situation. Each is rumored to be re-evaluating its official position with respect to participation in the eurozone. In contrast to the rumours circulating about Italy and Greece, these reports are plausible. Although reasonable people might disagree, it is possible to see how the Nordic countries could benefit from membership. It is much harder to make a realistic case that the existing member states could benefit from getting out.

Still in the woods

The euro as a multinational currency is not as vulnerable as it may first appear. Indeed, it provides a bulwark against the forces currently wreaking havoc in the global economy. It has eliminated exchange-rate volatility between participating countries, insulated them from having to make unpopular choices, lowered the relative cost of borrowing for the highly indebted, and created an incentive for countries like Italy to gain control over their relative unit labour costs along the way. This has not prevented Europe from staggering under the weight of the global financial crisis, but it has blunted at least some of the blow. Despite its advantages, however, the euro and the eurozone suffer from two obvious problems.

The first is that macroeconomic-policy coordination has not gotten any easier just because many European countries now use the same currency. This is evident as Europe struggles to come up with an effective macroeconomic stimulus package. (It was also evident when Europe struggled to engineer a lasting consolidation on fiscal accounts.) Like it or not, European fiscal politics has a very parochial focus, and even when there appears to be a Europe-wide pattern of coordination, chances are the 'pattern' is more coincidence than anything else.[8] This is not fatal for the single currency, nor is it a reason to believe that macroeconomic coordination would be better without one. All it means is that when called upon for a coordinated response to the global financial crisis, the countries of the eurozone are going to find it just as difficult to make concessions as anyone else.

The second problem is that the euro does not encompass the whole of the European Union, so whatever advantages it offers are, from an EU-wide perspective, at best only partial. Of course, one could argue that those countries that chose to remain outside the eurozone – either deliberately or through inaction – have only themselves to blame. Perhaps there is merit in this position for the United Kingdom, Denmark or Sweden: these countries not only understood the risks but also have the resources to withstand the consequences. The countries of Central and Eastern Europe are a different matter. Whether they chose to delay entry (Czech Republic, Hungary, Poland) or strove to enter and failed (the Baltic States, particularly Lithuania), these countries are even more ill-equipped to be outside the eurozone in such a turbulent global environment than they are to enter. The problem is not just that they cannot bear the costs of market volatility, but that they cannot contain them within their borders either. From inside the eurozone looking out, refusing to allow the Central and East European countries a firm commitment to enter into the single currency is unwise if not exactly unfair.[9]

The problem of macroeconomic-policy coordination within the eurozone is unlikely to be solved. Fiscal politics is politics after all, and all politics is local. The problem of the euro hold-outs is more easily handled. The eurozone will survive the current crisis. The question is how soon and how quickly it will start getting larger.

Acknowledgements

This article has benefitted greatly from the comments and advice of a number of colleagues, including Dana Allin, John Heilbrunn, Wolfgang Munchau, Michael Plummer and Francisco Torres. Laura Beke and Saskia van Genugten provided excellent research and writing support. The usual disclaimer applies.

Notes

1 Martin Feldstein, 'Will the Euro Survive the Current Crisis?', Project Syndicate, November 2008, http://www.project-syndicate.org/commentary/feldstein5.

2 Martin Feldstein, 'EMU and International Conflict', *Foreign Affairs*, vol. 76, no. 6, November–December 1997, pp. 61–2.

3 David Marsh, 'France, Germany and Fissures in the Eurozone', *Financial Times*, 12 January 2009, p. 9.

4 Wolfgang Münchau, '"What If" Becomes the Default Question', *Financial Times*, 20 January 2009, p. 9.

5 Simon Tilford, *Will the Eurozone Crack?* (London: Centre for European Reform, September 2006).

6 David Oakley and Karin Hope, 'S&P Cuts Greece's Credit Rating', *Financial Times*, 15 January 2009.

7 Rainer Buergin and Holger Elfes, 'Steinfrueck Say Euro States May Bail Out Members (update 2)', bloomberg.com, 14 February 2009, http://www.bloomberg.com/apps/news?pid=20601068&sid=aGwRmgq6Tz7w&refer=home.

8 Mark Hallerberg, *Domestic Budgets in a United Europe: Fiscal Governance from the End of Bretton Woods to EMU* (Ithaca, NY: Cornell University Press, 2004).

9 Wolfgang Münchau, 'Eastern Crisis That Could Wreck the Eurozone', *Financial Times*, 23 February 2009, p. 9.

NATO at 60

Mats Berdal and David Ucko

In October 2006 the International Security Assistance Force (ISAF) in Afghanistan, under NATO command since August 2003, assumed operational control of the whole of the country. With nearly 40,000 troops drawn from more than 35 countries, the Alliance was now charged with providing security and bringing stability to a deeply fractured country outside its treaty-defined area of operations. The range of tasks given to NATO forces in Afghanistan is broad and complex, from combat operations at one end to the rebuilding of roads, bridges and schools at the other. On the face of it, the assumption of such extensive responsibilities is testimony to an extraordinary transformation on the part of the Alliance, evidence of just how far it has come from its early and initially timid forays into peacekeeping on the European continent in the early 1990s.

And yet, NATO's first operation outside the Euro-Atlantic area has proved a far greater challenge than initial planning assumptions, many of them simplistically lifted from its experiences in the Balkans, appeared to suggest. By early 2009, the progress made by NATO forces in their efforts to extend the authority of the Afghan government outside Kabul remained patchy at best. NATO military operations have manifestly failed to reverse the steady resurgence since 2002 of Taliban influence, which now extends beyond the movement's traditional strongholds in the southern provinces

Mats Berdal is Professor of Security and Development in the Department of War Studies, King's College London. He was formerly Director of Studies at the International Institute for Strategic Studies. **David Ucko** is a Transatlantic Fellow at the RAND Corporation. He is the author of *The New Counterinsurgency Era: Transforming the U.S. Military for Modern Wars* (Washington DC: Georgetown University Press, 2009).

 DOI 10.1080/00396330902860793

of Helmand, Uruzgan and Kandahar.[1] Holding on to territory recaptured from Taliban forces continues to be hampered by NATO's limited troop strength, the use of 'national caveats' by Allied governments and, not least, by the slow pace at which Afghan security forces are being turned out.[2] The resulting insecurity has stifled reconstruction and development activities and has added to the already difficult job of raising troops for the mission. Continued instability has also complicated efforts aimed at enhancing cooperation with key civilian players on the ground, including not only the Afghan authorities but also the myriad outside agencies and international and non-governmental organisations based in the country. This in turn has exacerbated differences among NATO Allies about the balance of strategic priorities for Western engagement in Afghanistan and, by extension, about the relationship between the political aspirations of the Alliance and its military missions and capabilities.

The view that NATO's involvement in Afghanistan presents the Alliance with a make-or-break moment is, unsurprisingly, not publicly embraced by NATO governments or Alliance officials. And it is certainly true that the Alliance has a history of institutional survival, notable for the ability of Allies to live with intramural tensions. It may fairly be assumed that its involvement in Afghanistan, whatever the outcome, will not result in its liquidation. But NATO's Afghanistan mission has brought home the strains between the ambitious political aspirations that the Alliance has long proclaimed and the kinds of military missions that its members are capable and prepared to undertake. Put more bluntly, NATO's experiences in mounting and sustaining operations in Afghanistan have provided a reality check, pointing not only to the possibilities but also the limitations of NATO's contribution to international peace and security outside the Euro-Atlantic area. The latter include familiar difficulties relating to burden-sharing, the absence of political consultations among Allies, generation of forces and maintenance of defence expenditure to match new ambitions. At a deeper level, they include questions about the unity of political purpose and the clarity of strategic direction required to sustain global engagement in an environment bereft of the certainties that kept the Alliance together for much of its history. There is also the issue, often neglected in debates about

NATO's post-Cold War evolution, of how the wider world (a category ranging from major powers outside the Alliance, notably Russia, China and India, to international organisations and looser groupings of states) is likely to view a Western Alliance committed, in the words of its secretary-general, 'to address security challenges at their source, whenever and wherever they arise'.[3]

Against this backdrop of uncertainty and tensions, it is necessary to reassess what can realistically be expected from NATO. Much can be learnt from the manner in which the Alliance has responded to changing strategic circumstances since the Cold War, and the constraints, internal and external, that have impinged on its activities and are likely to continue to do so. Particularly informative are the attempts to 'modernise' or 'transform' the Alliance, the need for which was highlighted by NATO's Kosovo campaign in 1999 but which only got underway in earnest in 2002. Central to the narrative is a disconnect between NATO's configuration for major combat operations and the broadening of its actual portfolio into humanitarian, stability and wider peacekeeping operations and activities. The policy confusion stemming from this disconnect has done little to bestow the Alliance with the type of relevance initially sought through the transformation process. Even one of the more impressive outcomes of transformation on paper, the NATO Response Force (NRF), lacks a clear purpose and has yet to be used for other than permissive humanitarian endeavours.

The NRF lacks a clear purpose

Given its strengths and weaknesses, it may be both more realistic and more valuable for NATO to concentrate its efforts on the development of what are still demanding stabilisation and wider peacekeeping tasks, rather than pursue an unlikely role in the US-led 'war on terror' or in high-intensity war. At the same time, NATO's Afghanistan campaign has brought home the difficulties and constraints of assuming a global role in complex stability operations. These difficulties are not insurmountable, but will require a more clear-eyed and realistic understanding of what it takes to project stability beyond the NATO homestead and the adoption, should political will and capability prove insufficient, of more modest but still important military tasks that Alliance members are able to undertake. It would also involve drawing up a new Strategic Concept that brings the broader and more exalted political purposes of the Alliance into closer alignment with its actual military missions and capabilities.

The search for relevance

NATO's deepening engagement in southeastern Europe in the 1990s, like the process of eastwards enlargement, was ultimately about resolving unfinished Cold War business and the consolidation of security in Europe. The element of common interest on the part of Alliance members was still considerable and explains why collective action was possible. Even so, NATO's activities in the Balkans frequently revealed severe strains and acute tensions over appropriate policy. NATO involvement on the ground had also been marked by highly uneven levels of commitment and exposure to risk among Allies. It was this ambiguous record that explains the widely shared sense among Allies at the time of NATO's 50th-anniversary celebrations in Washington in April 1999 that change was now urgently required if the Alliance were to remain relevant. The most concerted effort to ensure such relevance came in the form of 'transformation', a US-driven attempt to modernise the Alliance's Cold War structures and endow it with the capabilities and assets thought to guarantee its continued centrality into the twenty-first century.

The course of transformation

The ever-expanding scope of NATO operations in the 1990s revealed a growing mismatch in defence capabilities between the United States and its European allies. By the time of the Kosovo operation, only the United States possessed the advanced capabilities necessary to conduct the campaign as desired.[4] The campaign therefore sat badly with the US military, which felt politically constrained by Alliance members that were unable to bring much to the table in terms of assets.

The weakness of NATO Europe was ascribed to its disinvestment in the defence sector in the 1990s. Alliance members, including the United States, had sought to cash in on the 'peace dividend' presumed to flow from the collapse of the Soviet Union.[5] The drop in defence spending was shared across the Alliance, but its effect was felt in Europe rather than the United States, whose budget, even in 2000, eclipsed that of all NATO's European members combined by $295bn to $163bn, and whose 1,483,000-strong armed forces outnumbered the largest military in NATO Europe, that of Turkey, by 690,000 troops. Moreover, NATO Europe's military was configured for territorial defence rather than power projection; the general lack of strategic air- and sealift capabilities meant that Alliance operations conducted further afield would rely heavily on US assets. This posed a serious problem for the United States, which more than other Alliance members saw NATO's future as a global security actor rather than one restricted to contingencies within or on the periphery of its treaty-defined area of interest.

In the aftermath of the Kosovo intervention, questions began to surface regarding the viability of this lopsided Alliance: to Washington, NATO's future came to be tied to the ability of its European partners to counteract their declining defence budgets and fill the 'capability gaps' exposed in Kosovo. This backdrop informed the subsequent effort at NATO modernisation, the Defence Capabilities Initiative. Endorsed at the Washington Summit in April 1999, the initiative laid out 59 targets to be met, spread across five areas: mobility and deployability; sustainability; effective engagement (meaning, roughly, technology and defence equipment); survivability; and interoperable communications.[6] Spearheaded by then US Secretary of Defense William Cohen, the initiative reflected Washington's interest in NATO developing capabilities for major combat operations and its conviction, not shared across the Alliance at this point, that NATO had, in Senator Richard Lugar's words, either to 'go out of area or go out of business'.[7]

The initiative did not get far in fulfilling the vision of NATO modernisation. It suffered from a lack of enforcement mechanisms and its effects, already limited, were spread across the entire European defence posture.[8] Many of its deficiencies were corrected with NATO's second effort at modernisation, the Prague Capability Commitments. Rolled out during NATO's Prague Summit in 2002, the commitments focused on similar capabilities as in the Defence Capabilities Initiative, but were now tailored and country specific, and given target dates for implementation.[9]

The Prague Summit saw the introduction of a second transformation initiative: the NRF. A brainchild of then US Secretary of Defense Donald Rumsfeld, it was designed as a 25,000-strong, European-dominated combined force, deployable worldwide in a minimum of five days, either as a spearhead or a stand-alone force, and sustainable for a period of 30 days.[10] It would be a catalyst for transformation and a focal point for the Prague commitments: troops committed would train together and gain familiarity with advanced capabilities. As troops rotated through the force, such experience would be spread across the European force structure.[11]

NATO Europe has, since Prague, had some success in developing new defence capabilities. In broad terms, different European NATO countries have taken the lead in specific areas such as airlift, sealift and defence against chemical, biological, radiological and nuclear weapons, and achieved much by pooling their resources in intergovernmental consortia.[12] The momentum behind the implementation of the Prague commitments was such that a 2006 NATO press kit was able to claim that 'by the end of 2008, over 70 per cent of the 460 or so commitments made by Allies will have been fulfilled' and that 'most of the remainder will be completed by 2009 and beyond'.[13] The veracity of this statement is difficult to corroborate as most progress reports are classified, yet while the available evidence is mixed, important headway has been made. The most evident sign of progress was the November 2006 declaration that the NRF had reached full operational capability. At the Riga Summit, the NRF was presented as comprising a 'brigade-size land component with forced-entry capability; a naval task force including a carrier battle group, an amphibious task group and a surface action group; and an air component capable of 200 combat sorties a day'.[14]

Enduring challenges

Despite these accomplishments, NATO has not escaped talk of irrelevance and crisis, the same language that prompted the transformation process. To a degree such talk is misinformed of the progress made since 1999 and the time required for what is, after all, an inter-governmental alliance to commit itself to and carry through on reforms. But important problems remain. NATO's transformation was never grounded in an Alliance-wide agreement on future roles and missions. The absence of a clear and shared vision of the Alliance's purpose has resulted in a disconnect between capability development and the requirements of current and likely future operations, and has done little to displace the underlying political differences plaguing the Alliance, problems accentuated in the aftermath of the 11 September 2001 attacks.

The political vacuum in which transformation has occurred helps explain the limited progress of both the Defence Capabilities Initiative and the Prague Capability Commitments. Certainly, the latter initiative has experienced more success in impelling NATO Europe to develop new capabilities, but the transformation process as a whole remains hamstrung by critical unanswered questions: what missions is the Alliance prepared to undertake and where? By skirting these fundamental questions, the Alliance never arrived at a convincing blueprint for transformation and the process has not achieved the European buy-in necessary for its success. While some European nations failed to see why they should invest limited resources in 'generation-after-next' defence systems, others wanted NATO to remain focused on its treaty-defined area and resisted the push toward expeditionary capabilities.[15] The enduring divisiveness explains in part why combined European defence spending decreased from 2.17% of gross domestic product in 1996 to 1.77% in 2006 and why, of 1.8 million personnel in the combined armed forces of the EU, only 10% are 'deployable' in the broadest sense of the term.[16]

'Transformation' has not made NATO more useable for war-fighting

Just as transformation could not, in itself, provide NATO with a new *raison d'être*, it has not made the Alliance more useable for future war-fighting. In short, capability development has not, and will not, displace the political constraints that come with fighting as an Alliance. First, since decisions in all key NATO bodies are reached by consensus, the political process involved in approving a combat operation is still likely to be prohibitively time-consuming, an issue revealed by a NATO war game held in October 2003.[17] And, as analyst Michael Mihalka notes, 'even for those countries that do not need parliamentary approval for short-term deployments, such as

France, there remain questions as to whether UN authorization is required', an authorisation that 'may be slow in coming, if it comes at all'.[18] Many within the US government will reject the notion of the UN Security Council carrying a potential veto over future NATO operations, but for Europe, particularly after the Iraq War, coercive action without UN authority will be a very hard sell.

Even when the need for action is agreed upon, the constant search for consensus among 26 member states will severely undermine the effective conduct of combat operations. During the Kosovo intervention in 1999, the US government and military derided the NATO air campaign as 'war by committee', where the political reservations of each member state had to be taken into account before action could be taken. This is a main reason why, when NATO countries have engaged in major combat operations in recent years, it has been outside the Alliance, often through a US-led coalition of the willing. In the immediate aftermath of the 11 September attacks, Washington was glad to accept NATO help in patrolling US airspace, a largely symbolic gesture, but when it came to planning and conducting more serious combat operations in Afghanistan, it declined the offers of assistance made by its NATO Allies.[19] For the United States the first priority in Afghanistan, as in Iraq, was to defeat the enemy, defined within the context of a 'global war on terror', not to provide NATO with an opportunity to prove its relevance, particularly as the latter objective would often come at the expense of the former. And, as illustrated in both campaigns, the United States really needed no help from NATO in conducting the initial major combat phase of operations.

Pushing in the wrong direction

Transformed or not, NATO's future role in major combat operations may be limited. Current and recent operations corroborate this finding: continued peacekeeping in the Balkans; a military training mission in Iraq; a naval patrol mission in the Mediterranean; logistical support to the African Union force in Darfur; humanitarian assistance in the aftermath of the Katrina hurricane and the 2006 Pakistan earthquake; and a large-scale stabilisation effort in Afghanistan. Yet even against this background, the transformation process has remained firmly focused on major combat operations, revealing a lack of appreciation for the political and military requirements of NATO's recent, ongoing and, in all likelihood, future operations. This too helps explain the limited success of transformation in bestowing relevance to the Alliance and in modernising European armed forces.

The conventional slant to the transformation process was a natural product of its origins, as the militarily superior US force sought to shape the European armed forces in its own image. While technologically advanced and certainly more deployable than its European counterparts, the US military has historically focused almost exclusively on achieving and maintaining conventional primacy, that is, domination against adversaries shaped and operating like itself. In contrast, it has often struggled against irregular or non-state adversaries, and in operations requiring more than the destruction of military targets.[20] Grounding NATO's transformation in this strategic culture was likely to replicate this narrow specialisation across the Alliance.

> *The Alliance read too much into the consensual nature of 1990s peacekeeping*

NATO's virtually uninterrupted institutional experience withy peacekeeping during the 1990s in Bosnia, Kosovo and Macedonia might have been expected to have made a mark on the Defence Capabilities Initiative and the Prague commitments. However, while official NATO documents typically acknowledged the importance of these types of campaigns, their complexity was often downplayed.[21] Much like the US military of the time, the Alliance read too much into the consensual nature of the peacekeeping operations of the 1990s and failed to consider that future stability operations might present altogether more serious challenges.[22]

It did not help that NATO transformation was conceived during the United States' own transformation era, in which it was heavily influenced by its apparent ability to defeat most adversaries through precision-guided munitions and other high-tech capabilities. When the Defence Capabilities Initiative was endorsed in 1999 the requirements for military effectiveness were informed by the major military operations of the preceding decade:

Iraq, Bosnia and Kosovo. Particularly within the United States, these campaigns were viewed as validating investment in the emerging technology of the Revolution in Military Affairs: primarily precision-guided munitions, but also advanced communications technology and surveillance and reconnaissance systems. By the time the Prague commitments were endorsed in 2002, the US military was one year into an Afghanistan campaign interpreted within its senior echelons as a resounding vindication of its transformation programme. In Washington DC, the initial rout of the Taliban by horse-mounted US special-operations forces calling in precision air-strikes was taken to epitomise the promise of transformation. These advanced conventional capabilities, it was reasoned, could defeat not only traditional adversaries but also, as President George W. Bush put it, 'shape and then dominate in an unconventional conflict' fought against insurgents and terrorists.[23]

The US intellectual foundation for NATO's process of transformation is perhaps most evident in the reforms made to the NATO command structure. At the Prague Summit, NATO officially replaced the Atlantic Command with the Allied Command Transformation (ACT), which was to guide Alliance modernisation. The new command was co-located in Norfolk, Virginia with the US Joint Forces Command (JFCOM), stood up in 1999 to drive the US military's own transformation. The ACT commander was also to double-hat as the commander of JFCOM. Gradually, the terminology of US force transformation was adopted in NATO circles: 'network-centric warfare', 'effect-based operations' and, of course, 'transformation' itself.

Particularly since the US-led invasion of Iraq in 2003, much scorn has been poured on the US military's faith in transformation and the way in which it blinded Pentagon planners from considering the need to 'win the peace' as well as the war. As the US military itself has learned, wars are today more ill-defined and 'irregular' affairs, involving adversaries concealed among civilian populations, executing hit-and-run attacks, and dispersing to avoid becoming likely targets for precision-guided munitions. In places where NATO has already been involved, the distinction between war and peace has become blurred, a defining feature, many say, of contemporary conflict. Accordingly, the types of operations that NATO will have to conduct, assuming it maintains an active operational role, will require different capabilities and a different understanding of war from what has to date been advanced through NATO transformation.

While the US military is learning important lessons from its campaigns in Iraq and Afghanistan, the course of NATO transformation since 2002 remains fundamentally unchanged, continuing to focus predominantly on decisive combat operations.[24] This is worrying; even if Afghanistan proves to be the only large-scale NATO attempt at 'state-building' in such a contested environment, future land-based campaigns will call for similar skill sets and combinations of forces: military police, linguists, engineers, civil-affairs specialists, medics and construction teams, all of whom will require specific training. Given the increased frequency of stability operations since the end of the Cold War and the global trend toward urbanisation, not to mention NATO's comparative superiority in conventional combat and the attractiveness and effectiveness of asymmetric tactics to potential adversaries, when NATO ground troops are again deployed they will most likely face challenges not too far removed from those encountered in Afghanistan: how to operate amongst a civilian population, how to train indigenous forces and how to build government capacity.

Some European countries do foresee a larger role in stability operations and have adapted their militaries accordingly. As part of its conversion to an all-volunteer force, the Italian army has designed its brigades for dual use in combat support and stabilisation and recovery missions.[25] Germany has also assigned 70,000 of its troops to stability operations, creating a sustainable force of 14,000, though it is doubtful whether these units would be available for missions in non-permissive environments. These initiatives are, however, exceptions to the norm under which virtually all readily available European NATO forces are configured for major combat operations.[26] NATO militaries will thus need to refit conventional troops for stability operations as and when necessary, a practice that unnecessarily complicates their employment and which is often insufficient.

NATO should acknowledge stability operations and wider peacekeeping missions as a profitable and perhaps Alliance-saving niche for NATO Europe, or for NATO as a whole. Making such missions the basis of its transformation is, however, likely to meet resistance, mostly because there is no consensus as to whether these are the operations the Alliance should undertake. While capabilities for stability operations would be less costly and complicated than for major combat operations, and while these capabilities would also have a greater likelihood of being used, stability operations suffer from an undeserved reputation for being somehow less glamorous than climactic war-fighting. Many within Europe would view a focus on stability operations as an admission of military weakness while, in the United States, such a specialisation would likely be perceived as free-riding, contributing on the margins yet demanding the rights of full Alliance membership. For all this, the relevance so fervently sought through transformation would be better achieved if NATO embraced and prepared for the types of operations it currently struggles to conduct, rather than the unlikely conventional wars for which there is both insufficient will and capacity.

A symptom of malaise

The NRF is in some ways a remarkable achievement of NATO transformation: proposed in 2002 and declared operational in 2006, its evolution demonstrates NATO's ability to agree and adapt swiftly to new demands. It provides the Alliance with a focal point for modernisation, a standing sizeable force and a capability to respond forcefully and on short notice to emerging crises worldwide. At the same time, the force is also victim of unquestioned assumptions regarding the types of capabilities most needed in today's strategic environment. While NATO documents claim that the NRF is 'capable of carrying out the full range of Alliance missions', it is optimised for short-notice combat operations, a mission it is unlikely ever to undertake.[27]

Conventional combat operations are, first, exceedingly rare for the Alliance. More importantly, the lengthy political process necessary for the North Atlantic Council to authorise the use of force undermines the ability of the NRF to deploy quickly, one of its chief selling points. The deployment of AWACS aircraft in the immediate aftermath of 11 September was both rapid and largely unproblematic, but it is doubtful whether a forcible intervention involving ground troops into a non-NATO country could be launched as quickly or as seamlessly. The issue is not only one of political differences of opinion; a number of NATO members still resist the very idea of out-of-area engagements, a split that would further limit the scenarios in which the NRF might be used.

Should the need for an intervention arise, there are also strong arguments against sending the NRF. Beyond the difficulties of achieving agreement to deploy, it is doubtful whether NATO Europe will have the capabilities to get the job done. So far, development of the NRF has, according to US analyst John Schmidt, been 'hampered by the continuing inability of European allies to devote the resources required to acquire key logistical capabilities, such as strategic lift, or to train and equip sufficient numbers of combat troops to U.S. standards'.[28] The continued lack of strategic sea- and airlift capabilities is particularly critical, as it undercuts the NRF's ability to mobilise without significant US support and within the five-day target period. It is also uncertain whether this shortfall will be addressed in the near future, given the at best uneven investment in the defence sector within NATO Europe.

If the NRF is unlikely and perhaps also unable to fulfil its intended purpose, what could be its fall-back uses? The discussion is ongoing and shows the lack of unity among NATO members. So far, the NRF has been used twice, both times in humanitarian endeavours. It first deployed in September 2005 to the US Gulf Coast to deliver assistance to the victims of Hurricane Katrina. Later that year, it deployed to Pakistan to provide relief to the survivors of the 8 October earthquake there. The larger-scale Pakistan operation in particular, involving tactical airlift, command and control, engineering units and field hospitals, was critical in saving many lives and in enabling a more effective relief effort.[29] At the same time, even such a benign and well-intentioned deployment sparked tensions within NATO, with some members arguing that humanitarian operations were not the anticipated function of the NRF – that it should not become 'an arm of the International Red Cross'.[30]

The Pakistan operation saved many lives

A second possible function of the NRF is as a catalyst for transformation, to develop a heightened combat capability within NATO Europe. While this is an important aim, there are underlying problems. Firstly, such a function might simply reinforce already-existing problems with transformation. Secondly, troops in the NRF would already need sufficiently advanced capabilities, seldom the case among the armed forces of NATO Europe.[31] Thirdly, with NATO struggling to find enough troops to conduct operations in Afghanistan, it is illogical to keep those associated with NRF in training simply to help them as far as possible to transform. An alternative, suggested by Jamie Shea, is to consider the NRF 'not only as a tool for experimentation but also as a real fighting force that can be used when NATO is under pressure – for instance, as a reserve in Afghanistan'.[32] This and similar proposals have elicited little or no support from major European Allies.[33] Absent such a course, however, nations reluctant to contribute to ongoing operations, particularly in Afghanistan, have been accused, off the record, by senior NATO officials of seeking to 'hide out' in the NRF to avoid deployment.[34] This was not the outcome Rumsfeld intended when he proposed establishing the force at the Prague Summit in 2002.

International peace and security

NATO transformation has not displaced the uncertainty and divisions within the Alliance over its role in the post-Cold War world. Hopes that more sophisticated capabilities, a changed command structure and new rapid-reaction forces would, in themselves, bestow the Alliance with a clear function and new relevance were ill founded, in part because the pursuit of these transformational initiatives was conducted with little consideration of whether, when and where they were to be used. Most fundamentally, the transformation process never reconciled the divergences in opinion across the Alliance as to whether it should remain a collective defence organisation concerned about Russia or other neighbourhood threats, or a global-security actor conducting operations far from its traditional North Atlantic homestead. These divergences have, if anything, increased in recent years, with Eastern European members in particular expressing concerns about the continued need to deter and defend against security threats stemming from Russia, whether cyber-attacks such as those against Estonia in April 2007, threats over energy security, or more traditional assertions of military power and influence. Over the past three years in particular, Russia's determined effort to reassert, often crudely and provocatively, its claim to great-power status has led to a deterioration in relations with the West and exposed growing divisions within the Alliance over how best to respond and the priority that ought to be placed on such efforts.

NATO has paid insufficient attention to the requirements of stability and wider peacekeeping operations it has increasingly undertaken. As its experiences in the Balkans in the 1990s showed, the Alliance holds many assets which would be valuable in such operations, ranging from logistics and strategic-lift capabilities to headquarters functions and intelligence assets. Yet the demands of stability operations, conducted in complex environments where other actors may be reluctant or unable to operate, will often be more arduous. While reconstruction activities, the provision of basic services and the establishment of governance are tasks that, ideally, are best conducted by civilian agencies, the frequent inability of the latter to operate in insecure conditions has forced NATO troops to assume responsibility for such areas alongside the provision of security, and may well do so again.

The way forward for NATO may be to embrace stabilisation and wider peacekeeping tasks more openly as a 'core business'.[35] This would involve developing its own capacity to conduct such missions and exploring, in concrete ways, how the Alliance can assist other multilateral bodies in mitigating some of the more persistent weaknesses and vulnerabilities of large-scale peace operations, most of them now under UN auspices.[36] NATO's post-Cold War record and distinctive characteristics suggest five areas where the Alliance has already made a difference, but could make a greater one.

The first is providing or assisting with the organisation, management and running of headquarters in the field, a major weakness of UN-led peace operations. An example is the use of elements of the mobile core of Northern Army Group (NORTHAG) headquarters in support of UN forces in Bosnia in the early 1990s.[37] Following reform of its force structure, NATO now has six High Readiness Forces Headquarters at its disposal which, in theory, might form nuclei around which larger multinational operations could be based.

A second is providing or coordinating strategic lift capacity to facilitate more rapid deployment. This may include the coordination of lift through established movement-control structures such as the new NATO Movement Coordination Centre for strategic lift established in July 2007, or it may involve more direct involvement, as in the assistance given to African Union peacekeepers rotated in and out of Darfur since 2005.

A third is providing or assisting with logistics support, tactical mobility and other specialised units. In July 2005 the International Crisis Group explored the option of deploying a NATO bridging force to Darfur, drawing upon the NRF and NATO's obvious strengths in 'planning, command and control and logistic support'.[38] Although the proposal was unlikely for political reasons ever to go very far, it was an interesting example of how NATO could, political circumstances permitting, play a supportive role for other organisations. With the UN relying increasingly for troop numbers on the contributions made by poorer and developing countries, the traditional shortage of enabling or specialist capabilities and resources in UN operations has been further exacerbated.[39] Again, NATO assets and expertise may act as much-needed force multiplier.

NATO's contribution to the post-communist transition was significant

A fourth area involves training, mentoring and assistance with security-sector reform.[40] The collapse of Yugoslavia into violence in the early 1990s showed that the passing of the Cold War would not necessarily translate into a continent-wide era of order and stability. Systems of communist control might have crumbled with surprising speed but the transition to stable, pluralistic and market-oriented regimes would have to be actively assisted. NATO's contribution to this transition, which involved security-sector reform broadly conceived, was not insignificant and has probably been underestimated. One aspect was the development of partnership programmes which, although sometimes ridiculed for their lack of substance, nonetheless assisted the delicate process of transition within the militaries of former Warsaw Pact countries. NATO has continued its security-sector reform and capacity-building role in the Balkans, is providing training in Afghanistan and Iraq, and is exploring similar roles for other organisations outside Europe. The need to build credible, accountable and effective indigenous capacity in war-torn countries through training, mentoring and assistance requires more systematic attention than it has received in Afghanistan or other peace and stability operations. It has even been suggested that NATO should consider the creation of a dedicated 'Military Advisory Force'.[41]

A final area involves providing quick-reaction forces to assist peace operations in force protection, meeting direct challenges to a mandate or, if required, for extraction purposes. Such forces would in principle play a role similar to that of the French-led EU force deployed in *Operation Artemis* in eastern Congo in 2003 to prepare the ground for an expanded UN force (MONUC). In early 2000, a robust British force deployed to Sierra Leone in *Operation Palliser* and helped prevent the collapse of the fledgling UN mission there. Absence of such robust forces has often proved the Achilles heel of major peace operations, making them vulnerable to sudden deteriorations in the operational environment.

Though the Alliance may form an important and valuable part of international solutions to specific security challenges by working alongside and in support of other actors, it cannot provide such solutions on its own. There are two basic reasons. Firstly, NATO is a military alliance and, while the threat of and use of force may be appropriate in certain circumstances, to be effective military force must serve wider political purposes and be employed alongside other instruments. As NATO Secretary-General Jaap de Hoop Scheffer has noted, 'transforming for stabilisation operations is not "just" a new capability initiative ... it is about developing a "new mission model" that successfully integrates the Alliance's actions with those by international actors'.[42] A second reason involves legitimacy: NATO lacks widespread international legitimacy of the kind commanded by the UN, however flawed the world body's ability to deliver may be in other respects. The North Atlantic Committee did bypass the UN Security Council over Kosovo in 1999, but this is generally seen, particularly among NATO's European members, as a matter of regret and an exception to be avoided. Outside the North Atlantic area, NATO continues to be viewed as serving a distinctive Western agenda. Indeed, in many quarters (witness statements from groupings such as the Non-Aligned Movement and the Group of 77) the Alliance is essentially seen as an instrument of US hegemonic policies. This view has only been reinforced since 11 September 2001; while NATO emphasises its role in bringing reconstruction and development to Afghanistan, the vast majority of UN member states see it merely as an extension of the US 'war on terror'. This widespread perception has formed the backdrop to all discussions about possible roles for NATO outside its core area, whether in Lebanon in 2006 or in Darfur in 2004–06. As Jacques Chirac observed in summer 2006 when the Alliance was contemplating a peacekeeping role in southern Lebanon, 'NATO is perceived, whether we like it or not, as the armed wing of the West in these regions, and consequently, in terms of its image, NATO is not the right organisation here'.[43] NATO's own rhetoric and public diplomacy have often done little to counter the blanket association of NATO with US policies. Thus, when NATO's secretary-general spoke of the readiness to meet 'security challenges at their source, whenever and wherever they arise', the obvious connection made outside NATO was with the US doctrine of pre-emption and the notion of preventive wars, of which the invasion of Iraq in 2003 is seen as a major manifestation.

It follows that the Alliance needs not only to be more honest and realistic about its comparative advantages and limitations, but also to develop more meaningful relationships with other multinational organisations. NATO is already working alongside other actors in many places, but the scope for deepening ties is, judging from Afghanistan, considerable. Relations with the EU, for example, remain fraught with tension.[44] This is not just a challenge for NATO. Many bodies, not least the UN, are deeply and instinctively distrustful of the Alliance, wishing to keep it at arm's length while hoping to tap into its assets and resources. It was the UN Secretariat, not NATO, which held out against a more substantive and meaningful agreement on practical cooperation than the anodyne and vague Joint Declaration on UN–NATO Secretariat Cooperation signed in September 2008.[45] As long as this tendency persists there will be obstacles to the development of the Alliance as an instrument at the service of the wider international community.

The advent in January 2009 of a new US administration, whose appeal and popularity outside the United States is in striking contrast to that of its predecessor, may offer a window of opportunity for forging more effective multilateral arrangements to address issues of international security, arrangements in which NATO can and should play an important part. The reintegration of France into NATO's military command, under a French president more inclined toward transatlantic cooperation than his predecessor, may also provide the political space and opportunity for progress to be made, particularly when combined with the occasion of NATO's 60th anniversary. Expectations of a new dawn must, however, be tempered. The muted response among NATO's European members to calls from the new US administration in early 2009 for an increased effort in Afghanistan shows that the issue is not simply one of European disagreements with the deeply unpopular administration and policies of G.W. Bush.[46] Absent an unlikely new grand consensus at the 2009 summit, the best that may be hoped for NATO's 60th anniversary is not an agreement to do more, but to do less: a scaling back of NATO ambitions in line with its political will and military capability.

Acknowledgements

The article is a shorter and substantially revised version of a paper entitled 'Whither NATO?' prepared for the Center for International Cooperation (CIC) in New York in 2008.

Notes

1 International Council on Security and Development, *Struggle for Kabul: The Taliban Advance* (London: MF Publishing, 2008), pp. 5–6. See also Antonio Giustozzi, *Koran, Kalashnikov and Laptop: The Neo-Taliban Insurgency in Afghanistan* (London: Hurst, 2007); and, for a more recent assessment, Antonio Giustozzi, 'The Pygmy who turned into a Giant: The Afghan Taliban in 2009', in 'Afghanistan: Now You See Me?', *IDEAS Strategic Update* SU001, March 2009.

2 Private interviews, NATO Brussels, June 2007.

3 Jaap de Hoop Scheffer, 'Managing Global Security and Risk', address given at IISS Global Strategic Review, Geneva, 7 September 2007, http://www.nato.int/docu/speech/2007/s070907a.html. Similar language was used in the Final Communiqué of the Ministerial Meeting of the North Atlantic Council in Reykjavik, held on 14 May 2002, which stated that NATO 'must be able to field forces that can move quickly to wherever they are needed, sustain operations over distance and time, and achieve their objectives'.

4 That is, a campaign of aerial bombardment and not a ground invasion, which in strictly military terms would have been far more effective in achiev-

ing the central aim of halting 'ethnic cleansing' operations by Former Republic of Yugoslavia security forces. Over the skies of Kosovo and Belgrade, the US military delivered '90 per cent of the precision-guided munitions' and provided '100 per cent of NATO's jamming capability, 90 per cent of the air-to-ground surveillance, and 80 per cent of the air refuelling tankers'. Robert Bell, 'Transformation Scorecard', *NATO Review*, no. 1, Spring 2005, p. 22.

5 From the mid 1980s to 2000, the average allocation made by NATO countries to the defence sector decreased from 3.18% to 1.99% of gross national product. See Data Analysis Section, *NATO–Russia Compendium of Financial and Economic Data Relating to Defence* (Force Planning Directorate, Brussels, 18 December 2006), http://www.nato.int/docu/pr/2006/p06-159.pdf; *SIPRI Yearbook 2002* (Oxford: Oxford University Press, 2002), ch. 7.

6 Frank Boland, 'NATO's Defence Capabilities Initiative: Preparing for Future Challenges', *NATO Review*, no. 2, Summer 1999, pp. 26–8.

7 Richard Lugar, 'NATO: Out of Area or Out of Business: A Call for US Leadership to Revive and Redefine the Alliance', Presentation to the Open Forum of the US Department of State, 2 August 1993.

8 Hans Binnendijk and Richard Kugler, 'Transforming European Forces', *Survival*, vol. 44, no. 3, Autumn 2002, p. 126.

9 For details of these objectives see 'Prague Capabilities Commitment (PCC)' at http://www.nato.int/issues/prague_capabilities_commitment/index.html.

10 See Public Information Office, 'Fact Sheet: NATO Response Force', March 2005, http://www.1gnc.de/history/history2005/nrf/LoRes NRF Mar05 BR.pdf.

11 This function was laid out by NATO Secretary-General Jaap de Hoop Scheffer in a joint press conference on the NRF with General James L. Jones, SACEUR, on 13 October 2004; see http://www.nato.int/docu/speech/2004/s041013b.htm. See also Jeffrey P. Bialos and Stuart L. Koehl, *The NATO Response Force: Coalition Warfare through Technology Transfer and Information Sharing* (Washington DC: Center for Technology and National Security Policy, National Defense University, 2005), p. v.

12 The progress includes Norway and Denmark's efforts to augment European strategic sealift capabilities; the commitment of seven European NATO partners to acquire Airbus A400M aircraft for European strategic airlift; the acquisition and pooling of three to four C-17 aircraft by another consortium of 14 NATO states (and Sweden); a charter arrangement by another group of 15 NATO countries for Antonov 124-100 aircraft from Ukraine; and the leasing of tanker aircraft by a consortium of nations led by Spain. See Carl Ek, *NATO's Prague Capabilities Commitment*, CRS Report for Congress RS21659 (Washington DC: Congressional Research Service, 22 July 2008), p. 3. See also NATO Press Release, 'Riga Summit Declaration', 29 November 2006, http://www.nato.int/docu/

pr/2006/p06-150e.htm; and NATO Parliamentary Assembly, *Progress on the Prague Capabilities Commitment*, November 2005.

13 See NATO Riga press-kit document, November 2006, pp. 5–6.

14 NATO Updates, 'NATO Response Force Declared Fully Operational', 29 November 2006, http://www.nato.int/docu/update/2006/11-november/e1129c.htm.

15 Marco Overhaus, 'Transatlantic Co-operation and the Future of NATO', *Foreign Policy In Dialogue*, vol. 8, no. 25, October 2008, pp. 22–3.

16 For the respective statistics, see International Institute for Strategic Studies, *European Military Capabilities: Building Armed Forces for Modern Operations* (London: IISS, 2008), p. 93; and Tim Bird, 'The European Union and Counter-insurgency: Capability, Credibility, and Political Will', *Contemporary Security Policy*, vol. 28, no. 1, April 2007, p. 192.

17 Peter Spiegel, 'War Game at Nato Talks Highlights the Need for Quick Deployment', *Financial Times*, 10 October 2003.

18 Michael Mihalka, 'NATO Response Force: Rapid? Responsive? A Force?', *Connections*, vol. 4, no. 2, July 2005, p. 79.

19 As argued by Senator Lugar in a speech given only months after 11 September: 'Rightly or wrongly, the legacy of Kosovo has reinforced the concern [within the US] that NATO is not up to the job of fighting a modern war'. See Richard G. Lugar, 'NATO'S Role in the War on Terrorism', US–NATO Missions Annual Conference, Brussels, Belgium, 18 January 2002. See also John R. Schmidt, 'Last Alliance Standing? NATO after 9/11', *The Washington Quarterly*, vol. 30, no. 1, Winter 2007, pp. 97–8, 103–104.

20 Frederick W. Kagan, *Finding the Target: The Transformation of American Military Policy* (New York: Encounter Books, 2006).

21 See Henning-A. Frantzen, *NATO and Peace Support Operations, 1991–1999: Policies and Doctrines* (New York: Routledge, 2005), pp. 2–3, 5, 78–81.

22 David Ucko, *The New Counterinsurgency Era: Transforming the U.S. Military for Modern Wars* (Washington DC: Georgetown University Press, 2009), ch. 3.

23 George W. Bush, 'President Speaks on War Effort to Citadel Cadets', Charleston, South Carolina, 11 December 2001.

24 No major transformation initiative has been issued since the Prague commitments in 2002, which therefore continue to inform the course of transformation. Nor have NATO Summit communiqués since Prague recognised any need to broaden transformation or build capabilities for a wider range of missions. The one exception to this trend is a sentence in the Riga Summit communiqué of 2006, which alluded to an 'initiative … ensuring the ability to bring military support to stabilisation operations and reconstruction efforts in all phases of a crisis'. NATO, 'Riga Summit Declaration', 29 November 2006, http://www.nato.int/docu/pr/2006/p06-150e.htm, para. 24. The initiative has not informed subsequent capability development nor received much institutional attention.

25 Hans Binnendijk and Richard Kugler, 'Needed – A NATO Stabilization and Reconstruction Force', *Defense Horizons*, no. 45, September 2004, p. 3.

26 *Ibid.*

27 NATO, *NATO Transformed* (Brussels: NATO, June 2004), p. 10.

28 Schmidt, 'Last Alliance Standing', pp. 98–9.

29 Julianne Smith et al., *Transforming NATO (...Again): A Primer for the NATO Summit in Riga* 2006 (Washington DC: Center for Strategic and International Studies, 2006), p. 30.

30 Statement of a member of the French mission to NATO, as quoted in Smith et al., p. 30. See also 'NATO Summit Talks End on a Sour Note', *New York Times*, 30 June 2004.

31 Smith et al., *Transforming NATO*, p. 59.

32 Jamie Shea, 'A NATO for the 21st Century', *Fletcher Forum for World Affairs*, vol. 31, no. 2, Summer 2007, p. 51.

33 David Brunnstrom and David Morgan, 'NATO Allies Offer Limp Response to U.S. Afghan Call', Reuters, 19 February 2009.

34 Interview with senior NATO officials, Brussels, summer 2007.

35 One proposal for doing so is outlined in C. Richard Nelson, *How Should NATO Handle Stabilisation Operations and Reconstruction Efforts?* (Washington DC: Atlantic Council, September 2006).

36 A successful (and perhaps therefore rarely mentioned) operation in which NATO operated closely and effectively alongside the EU and the OSCE was *Operation Essential Harvest* in the Former Yugoslav Republic of Macedonia in 2001 in which the Alliance undertook to support local disarmament and weapons collection.

37 At the time, NATO offered a much larger contingent than the UN was prepared to accept.

38 See International Crisis Group, *The AU's Mission in Darfur: Bridging the Gaps*, Policy Briefing no. 28 (Brussels: ICG, 2005), pp. 12–13.

39 This is not, of course, a comment on the quality of troops provided by developing countries, which has varied greatly from case to case and has often been excellent.

40 This role is also highlighted by Shea, 'A NATO for the 21st Century', pp. 52–3.

41 Daniel Korski and Michael Williams, 'Creating a NATO Military Advisory Force', *World Defence Systems*, no. 17, November 2008, pp. 148–51.

42 Cited in Nelson, *How Should NATO Handle Stabilisation Operations and Reconstruction Efforts?*, p. v.

43 'Interview with Jacques Chirac, President of the French Republic, for "Le Monde" Newspaper', 26 July 2006, available at http://www.elysee.fr/elysee/elysee.fr/anglais_archives/speeches_and_documents/2006/.

44 See Judy Dempsey, 'German General Giving Up on Afghan Mission', *International Herald Tribune*, 12 September 2007.

45 'Joint Declaration on UN–NATO Secretariat Cooperation', Annex to DSG (2008) 0714 (INV), 23 September 2008.

46 See Craig Whitlock, 'Afghanistan Appeal May Temper European Allies' Ardor for Obama', *Washington Post*, 6 February 2009.

France and NATO

Jeremy Ghez and F. Stephen Larrabee

The new French White Paper on defence and national security, released in June 2008 after months of internal debate, jettisons a number of precepts and policies that have dominated French defence thinking since the mid 1960s.[1] The most controversial change announced is President Nicolas Sarkozy's initiative to return France to NATO's integrated military command, from which General Charles de Gaulle withdrew the country in 1966. Sarkozy's decision should bring significant security benefits both for France and NATO. It not only removes an important irritant that has hindered good relations between the United States and France but also opens up new possibilities for improving US–European cooperation more broadly. Cooperation between NATO and the EU in particular should become easier.

However, France's return to fuller integration in the Alliance faces a number of obstacles and could still falter. Sarkozy's plan faces opposition at home, even from within his own party. Much depends on the approach of the new Obama administration as well. The last attempt at reintegrating France collapsed at the eleventh hour due to inadequate preparation and mismanagement at the top on both sides, leaving a legacy of suspicion and mistrust that exacerbated US tensions with France and Europe for the better part of a decade. Thus, how well the Obama administration manages this issue will be an important test of its diplomatic skill and ability to forge a new security partnership with Europe.

Jeremy Ghez is a doctoral fellow at the Frederick S. Pardee RAND Graduate School. **F. Stephen Larrabee** holds the Corporate Chair in European Security at the RAND Corporation.

Survival | vol. 51 no. 2 | April–May 2009 | pp. 77–90 DOI 10.1080/00396330902860819

Creeping reintegration

Although Sarkozy's decision to promote France's return to NATO's integrated command appears to reverse a key tenet of Gaullist thinking, it represents less a rupture with de Gaulle's policy than the culmination of a process of 'creeping reintegration' that has been quietly going on since the early 1990s.

In the initial period after the end of the Cold War, France saw little need for NATO and favoured a diminished role for the Alliance and the United States in European security. When it became clear, however, that Europe was not capable of managing the Bosnian crisis on its own, President François Mitterrand gave the green light for combined operations between French and NATO forces and increased 'deliberative participation', on a selective basis, in meetings of NATO defence ministers and the Alliance's Military Committee.[2] He also agreed that the French forces in the Eurocorps could be put under NATO operational control in times of crisis.

This process of creeping reintegration intensified under President Jacques Chirac. Chirac came very close to achieving France's full reintegration into the Alliance in 1996–97. Indeed, had he been a bit more modest in formulating his conditions for France's return, his efforts might well have succeeded. However, Chirac's price for agreeing to full reintegration, European command of Allied Forces Southern Europe (AFSOUTH) in Naples, was regarded by the Clinton administration as too high and the deal ultimately collapsed.

Behind the scenes, however, French cooperation with NATO on a practical level quietly increased. France is today the largest contributor to the NATO Response Force and participates in all major Alliance expeditionary operations, including Kosovo (KFOR) and Afghanistan (ISAF). As François Heisbourg has noted, by the end of Chirac's final years in office, French cooperation with NATO, from a military, strategic and operational perspective, had developed to the point where France could be seen as a de facto member of the integrated command.[3]

A number of developments contributed to this growing rapprochement. The first was Europe's broad failure in managing the conflict in the former Yugoslavia. This failure made clear that the United States and NATO were still necessary to maintain Europe's collective-defence capabilities and to address the post-Cold War security challenges that France initially thought Europe could manage on its own. French leaders concluded that confronting these challenges required more engagement with the United States and NATO, not less.

This conclusion was reinforced by Washington's reluctance to commit ground troops to peacekeeping operations in the Bosnian conflict. Whereas initially French officials had worried about constraining US hegemony in Europe, after Bosnia they became increasingly concerned about the prospects of US disengagement and a weakening of America's commitment, as the focus of Washington's strategic attention began to shift to addressing security challenges beyond Europe's borders.

As memories of the Cold War faded, France's decision to remain outside the NATO military structure made less and less political and military sense. On the one hand, it prevented France from exerting influence within the Alliance commensurate with its contribution to NATO military operations. On the other, it sowed suspicion and distrust of French political ambitions and made it harder for France to gain support among its European allies for its broader foreign-policy goals in Europe, especially the strengthening of the European Security and Defence Policy (ESDP).

Enlargement changed the dynamics and balance within both NATO and the EU

The enlargement of NATO and the EU also contributed to France's re-evaluation of its relationship with the Alliance. Enlargement changed the internal dynamics and balance within both organisations. The addition of seven new EU members with a strong Atlanticist perspective made it much harder for France to pursue its European agenda. The new Eastern European members tended to side with the United States on many security issues, as their strong support for the US invasion of Iraq in 2003 underscored. Contrary to French expectations, they were not willing to sit quietly in the corner like well-behaved schoolchildren and obediently follow the lead of their French elders. Their action served notice that the old EU led by France and Germany was dead.

After 1999, moreover, it became increasingly clear that a stronger European defence policy could not be built without the United Kingdom and that the British government, even under 'Europhile' Tony Blair, was not ready to sacrifice its close ties to Washington on the altar of a more independent ESDP. This forced France to adjust its ambitions for European defence in ways that were more compatible with British views.

Finally and most importantly, it became clear that a strong ESDP could not be built in opposition to the United States and NATO. This was one of the key lessons of the Franco-American dust-up in spring 2003 over the French-led proposal to create a separate EU planning cell at Tervuren (a suburb of Brussels). This effort met stiff US resistance and was also opposed by many of France's European allies, especially Great Britain, as well as the new EU members from Eastern Europe, who feared it would weaken NATO.

By the end of Chirac's tenure in office, it was clear that French security policy was in need of a major overhaul. France's influence in Europe was waning, and its refusal to participate in NATO's integrated command was hindering the achievement of broader French objectives.

Sarkozy's decision to promote France's reintegration into NATO's military command is not an end in itself but part of a wider effort to update and modernise French defence and security policy and is closely tied to the goal of building a stronger and more autonomous ESDP. In Sarkozy's eyes, ESDP and NATO reintegration are closely linked. As he stressed in his speech to the US Congress in November 2007, 'the more European defense is achieved, the more France will be resolved to take its place in NATO'.[4] His decision to bring France back into the integrated command reflects a recognition that Paris cannot achieve its broader foreign-policy goals in Europe without rapprochement with NATO and the United States. If France does not adopt a more favourable view towards NATO, the Eastern European countries and other Atlanticist members of the Alliance, especially the United Kingdom, are unlikely to support France's effort to strengthen ESDP.

Sarkozy, however, has set limits on France's integration. He has insisted that France will maintain control over the sending of French troops in all military operations; that it will not put its troops under NATO control in peacetime; and that France's nuclear weapons will remain under national control.[5]

At the same time, Sarkozy has promoted a stronger ESDP as a guarantee of Europe's ability to act independently from the United States. Thus, while the French president has been careful to present NATO and ESDP as complementary rather than rival alternatives,[6] one of his key conditions for France's reintegration into NATO is likely to be a greater willingness by the United States to accept the EU's right to act independently in certain circumstances.

France is also likely to press for a reform of NATO structures and procedures: French officials argue that the organisation's command structure needs to be streamlined. On this, they face opposition not from the United States or United Kingdom, but rather the smaller members of NATO, who will be forced to give up much-coveted posts in any command-structure reform.

By joining the military command, Sarkozy hopes to increase France's influence within the Alliance so that it is at least commensurate with its military contribution. But after being outside the integrated command for over 40 years, reintegration will pose a number of serious challenges. One is staffing. If France rejoins the Alliance's integrated command, Paris will need to increase the number of personnel assigned to NATO nearly ten-fold. This will require finding personnel to fill about 800–1,000 slots. At the moment, France lacks the money and qualified personnel with a sufficient knowledge of English and NATO's internal workings and procedures to fill these posts. Thus, France's re-entry into the Alliance's military command is likely to be a gradual process.

The broader European context

France assumed the presidency of the EU on 1 July 2008. Sarkozy initially intended to use France's presidency to promote an ambitious European defence agenda and relaunch ESDP. However, the Irish rejection of the Lisbon Treaty in June 2008, the Russian invasion of Georgia and the growing global economic crisis forced Sarkozy to reshape his agenda. While France continued to give ESDP high rhetorical priority, French ambitions had to be scaled back.

Moreover, giving ESDP strong new momentum may be difficult. The Czech Republic, which took over the EU presidency after France, is one of the most vocal eurosceptics in the union and is unlikely to give ESDP high priority. In addition, the fate of the Lisbon Treaty remains unclear. Much depends on the outcome of the second Irish referendum, likely to be held in late 2009. A year ago the outlook for ratification looked bleak. With the onset of the global economic crisis, however, public attitudes in Ireland have begun to shift. Recent polls show that more than half the population now supports ratification of the treaty, with one-third opposed (compared to 53% opposed in the May 2008 referendum).[7]

In the event that the Lisbon Treaty is not ratified, France may push for closer security and defence cooperation through the formation of small groups of member states, or 'pioneers', who desire to develop closer cooperation in advance of the other members. There has been a growing trend toward this type of cooperation in the EU in recent years. The Schengen zone was initially formed by a small group of countries who wanted to remove border controls and thereafter expanded to include more member states. The euro zone provides another example of such cooperation; it initially included 11 members and today comprises 16 of the EU's 27.

Brown has little appetite for new European defence proposals

France would like to see this type of cooperation extended to the defence area. But pursuing such a project could face resistance from Great Britain. British Prime Minister Gordon Brown is less of a Europhile than Blair. He has been badly weakened, moreover, by a series of mishaps and policy failures, which have provoked growing disenchantment with his leadership, even within his own party. Under assault from all sides and facing the possibility of elections in 2009, Brown has little appetite for new European defence proposals.

Faced with the British government's lack of enthusiasm, French officials openly concede that there is little prospect for a 'second St Malo', that is, a Franco-British summit devoted to relaunching ESDP. Bilateral defence cooperation will continue but securing British support for a new push to strengthen ESDP in the near future seems unlikely. Indeed, many French officials feel the real obstacle to strengthening ESDP today lies in London and not Washington, a problem that can only grow if the eurosceptic Conservative Party wins the next election.

Nor can Sarkozy expect strong support from Berlin for an ambitious new effort to relaunch ESDP. Franco-German cooperation has lost the warmth and centrality it enjoyed under Chirac and German Chancellor Gerhard Schröder. On the surface an attempt is made to give the appearance of amity, but behind the smiles the relationship is marred by suspicion and a scarcely concealed rivalry for leadership of Europe. This rivalry is reinforced by different political styles. Sarkozy's hyperactivity and tendency to launch initiatives without prior coordination with his EU partners, especially Berlin, has irritated Chancellor Angela Merkel, who favours a more methodical and consultative style of diplomacy.[8] In addition, Paris and Berlin are at odds over a number of substantive issues, including nuclear power, energy and climate change and the role of the European Central Bank.

In the defence area, Germany continues to punch well below its weight. Defence spending remains at only about 1.27% of GDP, considerably lower than that of France and Britain.[9] This limits Germany's ability to play a leadership role both within NATO and on matters related to European defence. In addition, there is growing concern in the Bundestag about committing German troops to peace operations abroad, as highlighted by Berlin's unwillingness to participate in the French-led mission in Chad. Hence, Sarkozy cannot count on Germany to pick up the slack created by Blair's departure and Brown's more reserved approach to European defence.

Finally, France's effort to strengthen ESDP is regarded with reserve by the new EU members from Eastern Europe. While they support ESDP, they do not want a stronger European defence policy to come at the expense of weakening NATO or damaging relations with the United States. Moreover, many are still smarting from Chirac's criticism in the run-up to the Iraq invasion that they would have been better off to have 'remained silent' instead of supporting the United States.[10] Although Sarkozy has stated that the days are over when French presidents will lecture the East Europeans on how they should behave, his effort to woo them during the French presidency has done little to dispel East European suspicions about France's long-term goals.[11] He recently added fuel to the fire by suggesting that the Czech Republic, the current holder of the rotating EU presidency, was not up to the job of leading Europe and urging that France's automobile manufacturers close down their plants in Eastern Europe in return for state aid, a remark that infuriated Czech Prime Minister Mirek Topolanek.[12]

None of this is to suggest that ESDP will lose its importance to the French government. But it will be hard for Sarkozy, or any other European leader, to give ESDP serious new momentum until the fate of the Lisbon Treaty is resolved. Moreover, Europe faces the danger of a deepening recession. Dealing with the global financial crisis is likely to be a top priority for European leaders in the months ahead, overshadowing other issues. The downturn is also likely to reduce the money available for defence.

The domestic context

Sarkozy's plan for NATO reintegration has provoked strong opposition among the Socialists. Louis Gautier, former defence adviser to Prime Minister Lionel Jospin, and former Defence Minister Paul Quilès have attacked the proposal, arguing that it weakens France's commitment to European defence. The plan has also been attacked by members of Sarkozy's own party.[13] Former Prime Minister Alain Juppé, a close Chirac ally, has charged that the decision represents a one-sided concession for which France has received nothing in return.[14]

The impact of this opposition should not be exaggerated, however. The Socialists are deeply divided and in political disarray. Sarkozy has a strong parliamentary majority and has been able to push through a number of unpopular domestic reforms, including legislation rescinding the 35-hour work week. At the end of September, he won parliamentary approval for maintaining the French presence in Afghanistan.[15] Finally, the French public does not really care that much about NATO reintegration. Thus, domestically Sarkozy has a fairly large field for manoeuvre.

Another concern is the reaction of the military. The reforms outlined in the 2008 White Paper have sparked considerable discontent within some parts of the French military, especially the army, which has been hardest hit by the extensive personnel cuts and base closures called for in the paper.[16] Shortly after the White Paper's release, a group of French officers published an anonymous article in the French daily *Le Figaro* charging that Sarkozy's defence initiatives would produce unchallenged British leadership over European defence, weaken France's military capabilities and reduce its ability to influence NATO's decisions. France, they warned, would be reduced to playing 'in the same league as Italy'.[17]

But these concerns do not extend to Sarkozy's plans for France's reintegration into NATO. The French military have traditionally supported closer ties to NATO and favoured France's reintegration into the Alliance's military command. The main opposition to France's reintegration has generally come from the Foreign Ministry, which tends to be a bastion of Gaullist orthodoxy. But the ministry is a secondary player on defence matters. Moreover, Foreign Minister Bernard Kouchner strongly supports Sarkozy on this issue.

A potentially more serious problem could be the impact of French engagement in Afghanistan. The Afghan mission is not popular in France and in recent months public discontent has visibly increased. The Afghan mission is also not popular with the French military, who feel it lacks a clear strategy and eats up funds that could be better spent on modernisation. So far Sarkozy has been able to separate French engagement in Afghanistan from the issue of France's return to NATO. But this may become harder if the security situation in Afghanistan continues to deteriorate and France suffers heavier casualties. There is a danger that the two issues could become conflated in the public mind.[18]

Challenges for the Obama administration

The United States has a strong interest in the success of French defence reforms, especially the country's closer cooperation with NATO. France's expected return to the Alliance's integrated command removes one of the most important remaining obstacles to better US–French relations and opens up new possibilities for improving cooperation between the EU and NATO, especially in the field of crisis management.

France's reintegration, however, will raise a number of potentially controversial issues. Among these is the question of which command or commands

France will receive. This is a sensitive issue and affects the distribution of posts and influence within the Alliance. Given that the 1996–97 negotiations collapsed over this issue, it needs to be handled with diplomatic tact. Recent press reports suggest that the issue may be close to resolution: the United States has reportedly agreed that French officers could have responsibility for Allied Command Transformation in Norfolk, Virginia, which is in charge of preparing the Alliance's long-term vision and doctrine, and also for the Alliance's command post in Lisbon, which is the headquarters for the NATO's Rapid Reaction Force.[19] If confirmed, this agreement could pave the way for France's full return to NATO and allow Sarkozy to defuse the charge by domestic critics that France's reintegration was a one-sided concession to the United States for which he received nothing in return.

The most important factor affecting France's return to the integrated command, however, is likely to be the US attitude toward ESDP. To deflect domestic criticism, both from the opposition and from parts of his own party, Sarkozy needs to be able to demonstrate that France's return to the military structure of the Alliance brings concrete benefits and does not represent a weakening of France's commitment to European defence. French officials will therefore be looking for signs of a more open and flexible attitude toward ESDP on the part of the United States.

A more positive approach toward European defence is in the US interest

A more positive approach toward ESDP and European defence is in the US interest. It would not only facilitate France's reintegration into NATO but would promote closer cooperation with the EU and help break down the firewalls that have developed between the two organisations. Until very recently, the United States has been wary of ESDP, fearing that it could lead to unnecessary duplication and undermine NATO. However, with France reintegrated into NATO's military command these dangers are likely to diminish. France should be less inclined to try to block or limit NATO's involvement in crisis-management operations.

US fears that ESDP will supplant or weaken NATO are exaggerated, especially now that France is evincing a more positive attitude toward the latter.

Neither London nor Eastern Europe will allow ESDP to weaken NATO or develop in an anti-NATO direction. And France knows that it cannot afford to lose British support if it is to achieve a robust ESDP.

The United States has an interest in having a strong European partner that can help address new threats and challenges. If the EU is going to play an effective role in helping to manage crises, it needs to be able to act independently of NATO in some limited instances, especially during crises such as those in Chad or the Democratic Republic of the Congo, in which the United States does not want to get involved. These instances are likely to be relatively limited in number and scope. If a serious crisis were to arise that threatened Western interests, the United States would almost certainly get involved, though it might not take the lead.

The EU has a number of civilian capabilities that NATO lacks and which are needed in the stabilisation and reconstruction phases of peace operations. Thus, closer cooperation and coordination between NATO and the EU is essential for effective crisis management. France's return to the Alliance's military command should make this cooperation easier, reducing the sense of competition and rivalry between NATO and the EU that has hindered cooperation in crisis management in the past.

This does not mean that France and the United States will see eye-to-eye on all issues. Differences could arise over two issues in particular. The first is the question of the creation of an EU planning capacity. This perennial source of friction between Washington and Paris came to a head at the so-called 'chocolate summit' between France, Germany, Belgium and Luxembourg in April 2003. France's proposal for the establishment of an EU planning capacity at Tervuren provoked strong US (and British) opposition, and Paris was eventually forced to modify the proposal. The issue, however, is far from dead. France's White Paper calls for the strengthening of a permanent and autonomous European capacity for strategic planning.[20] New tensions could be sparked if this issue is not carefully managed.

Fortunately, the situation today is quite different from the one that existed in 2003. The row over Tervuren arose in the context of growing US–French differences over Iraq and a perception that Chirac was trying to establish ESDP as a rival or counterweight to NATO. Today, however, US–French relations are on the mend. Sarkozy sees NATO and the EU as complementary, not rivals. France's return to the military wing of NATO should reduce the sense of suspicion and mistrust on both sides and make the establishment of an EU planning capacity less contentious and easier to manage.

A second area where policy differences with Paris could emerge is over space policy. Sarkozy has indicated that forging a clear EU space policy is a high French priority. France is backing a proposal to place independent ground-based space-surveillance assets in Germany, France and elsewhere in a network that would eventually be expanded to give Europe a space-monitoring capability alongside of that of Russia and the United States. The European Space Agency is expected to propose that the member governments spend €100 million over three years to coordinate the existing ground-based systems. The goal is to build a rudimentary space-surveillance network, for civil and military users, to give Europe a measure of autonomy.

In the past, the United States has opposed such efforts on the grounds that they were expensive and duplicated US efforts. If France rejoins the NATO military command, however, this issue may prove less contentious, and it may be easier for the United States to accept a greater degree of European autonomy as long as US, EU and NATO space policies are closely coordinated.

The question of NATO's geographic scope could also be contentious. France has traditionally sought to limit NATO's geographic range and has been one of the chief critics of a 'global NATO'. US efforts to intensify the Alliance's ties to countries outside Europe, such as Australia, Japan and South Korea, could face French resistance. Nor is France alone on this issue. Its concern is shared by a number of other NATO allies, including many of the new members from Eastern Europe.

France is also likely to take a sceptical approach to further enlargement of the Alliance to Ukraine and Georgia. This is one of the areas where German and French views and interests closely coincide. Both governments are concerned about the impact of further enlargement on relations with Russia and oppose giving Membership Action Plans to Georgia and Ukraine at this time, a view shared by many other NATO members as well. While generally supportive of Georgian and Ukrainian membership, the Obama administration is unlikely to give it high priority at a time when it faces so many other first-order challenges on which it needs allied support. Thus, enlargement is not likely to be a source of major controversy between Paris and Washington in the near future, though differences could develop over the longer term.

* * *

France's return to the Alliance's integrated military command is an important watershed. It removes an important source of transatlantic discord and tension and should make cooperation between NATO and the EU easier. Contrary to the fears expressed by French critics, Sarkozy's decision does not signal the death knell of the European defence project, but just the opposite. With France fully integrated into the Alliance's military command, the United States will be more relaxed about the development of ESDP and less worried that it will develop into a rival of NATO. This will make it easier, not harder, for European defence to advance.

Notes

1 *Défense et Sécurité nationale: Le Livre blanc* (Paris: Odile Jacob, 2008). For an English version see 'The French White Paper on Defence and National Security', Présidence de la République, June 2008, available at http://ambafrance-uk.org?New-French-White-Paper-on-defence.html.

2 For details on Mitterrand's attempted rapprochement with NATO see Robert P. Grant, 'France's New Relationship with NATO', *Survival*, vol. 38, no. 1, Spring 1996, pp. 58–80.

3 'Livre blanc sur la defense: Deux des auteurs s'expliquent', *Le Monde*, 19 June 2008.

4 Nicolas Sarkozy, 'Renewing the French–American Alliance', speech before the Congress of the United States of America, 7 November 2007.

5 France is thus unlikely to participate in the Alliance's Nuclear Planning Group. 'La France gardera une liberté d'appréciation totale', *Le Monde*, 18 June 2008.

6 The new French White Paper states: 'There is no rivalry between NATO and the European Union, rather complementarity. We need both to manage threats and crises. These realities lead us to favor the full participation of France in the military structures of the Atlantic Alliance.' 'Les priorités du Livre blanc sur la défense', *Le Monde*, 18 June 2008.

7 Stephen Collins, 'Major Swing in Favor of Lisbon Treaty as 51%

Would Now Vote Yes', *Irish Times*, 16 February 2009.

8 Merkel was particularly irritated by Sarkozy's initiative for a Mediterranean Union, which was launched without prior consultation with Berlin and seemed to duplicate the EU's Barcelona Process. Her reservations killed the initiative before it could get off the ground. The decision to fold the initiative into the Barcelona Process was largely a result of active behind-the-scenes German diplomacy.

9 *The Military Balance 2009* (London: Routledge for the International Institute for Strategic Studies, 2009), p. 447.

10 See '"New Europe" Backs EU on Iraq', BBC, 19 February 2003, http://news.bbc.co.uk/1/hi/world/europe/2775579.stm.

11 Henri de Bresson et Arnaud Leparmentier, 'Sarkozy poursuit à Varsovie son offensive de charme en Europe centrale', *Le Monde*, 25 June 2008.

12 Ben Hall and Jan Cienski, 'Czechs act on "Protectionist' Paris', *Financial Times*, 10 February 2009.

13 Jean-Michel Normand, 'Le PS dénonce des "conclusions définies par une logique budgétaire"', *Le Monde*, 18 June 2008.

14 Françoise Fressoz, 'Le scud d'Alain Juppé contre la politique de défense de Nicolas Sarkozy', *Le Monde*, 20 June 2008.

15 For details, see Laurent Suply and Charlotte Menegaux, 'La Mission française en Afghanistan est prolongée', *Le Figaro*, 22 September 2008, http://www.lefigaro.fr/politique/2008/09/22/01002-20080922ARTWWW00600-fillon-defend-l-engagement-en-afghanistan.php.

16 For details, see '14 Juillet: grogne dans les rangs', *Le Monde*, 13–14 July 2008; 'Mailaise in den französischen Streitkräften', *Neue Zuercher Zeitung*, 7 July 2008, http://www.nzz.ch/nachrichten/wissenschaft/malaise_in_den_franzoesischen_streitkraeften_1.775178.html.

17 The 'Surcouf' group, 'Livre blanc sur la défense: une espérance déçue', *Le Figaro*, 19 June 2008, http://www.lefigaro.fr/debats/2008/06/19/01005-20080619ARTFIG00011-livre-blanc-sur-la-defense-une-esperance-decue.php.

18 The death of ten French soldiers in August 2008 caused a national outcry and sparked a vivid debate about France's ties to NATO, putting Sarkozy in a tough position. The strong public reaction highlighted the sensitivity of the Afghanistan deployment and is one of the reasons why Sarkozy has been circumspect about responding to US requests to send more French troops to Afghanistan.

19 Natalie Nougayrède, 'Paris finalise sa pleine réintégration dans l'OTAN', *Le Monde*, 5 February 2009. See also Ben Hall and James Blitz, 'Command Accord Presages French Return to NATO', *Financial Times*, 5 February 2009.

20 *Défense et Sécurité nationale*, p. 90.

Russia and the West

Eugene Rumer and Angela Stent

After a turbulent decade in transatlantic relations, the 2008 US presidential election has raised hopes for improved ties between Europe and the United States and a more constructive approach to dealing with some of the more troubling issues facing the Alliance. Speaking at the Munich Security Conference in February, US Vice President Joe Biden promised closer cooperation with America's allies and re-engagement with Russia. Perhaps the greatest foreign-policy challenge on the European continent is how to achieve a more productive relationship with Russia while developing policies toward other former Soviet states that would be true to European and US values and advance European and US interests.

The August 2008 war between Russia and Georgia was the culmination of 17 years of tensions between Russia, its neighbours and the West about the future of Eurasia. The conflict has shown that building a more productive relationship with Russia will be impossible without closer coordination between America and Europe. The war also demonstrated that the US commitment to Europe is still a critical component of European security and cohesion. As the Allies embark on the search for a reinvigorated Russia policy, they will have to rethink the premises of earlier policies. They will also have to confront head-on the differences between the way much of Europe views Russia and how it is perceived in Washington. If they cannot

Eugene Rumer is a Senior Fellow at the Institute for National Strategic Studies, National Defense University, Washington DC. **Angela Stent** is Professor of Government and Director of the Center for Eurasian, Russian and East European Studies at Georgetown University and a Senior Non-Resident Fellow at the Brookings Institution.

Survival | vol. 51 no. 2 | April–May 2009 | pp. 91–104 DOI 10.1080/00396330902860835

resolve these differences, or at least agree to disagree on some issues, it will be difficult to craft an effective and unified Western policy. Moreover, they will also have to respond with care to the mixed signals emanating from Moscow.

End of an era?

For the United States, the Russian–Georgian war marked the end of a phase in East–West relations, that began with the blossoming of perestroika in the Soviet Union, gained momentum with the collapse of Communism in Eastern Europe and eventually the Soviet Union itself, survived the turbulence of the Yeltsin years and regained momentum early in the Bush–Putin era. For nearly two decades, US policy toward Russia was guided by a commitment to integrate Russia into the West and a belief that the new Russia sought a genuine partnership with the West. The war and its aftermath sent the United States back to the drawing board, seeking to redefine the relationship with a different Russia than it had initially anticipated.

Three consecutive US administrations, of Presidents George H.W. Bush, Bill Clinton and George W. Bush, built their policies toward Europe, Russia and other former Soviet states on the premise that Europe's old divisions would eventually be erased. Russia and the former parts of the Soviet empire would join Europe whole and free, at peace with itself and its neighbours, projecting stability and prosperity far beyond its borders. American leaders assumed Russia's own transformation would move it closer to the West. The Clinton administration espoused the theory of liberal internationalism: that democratic states are more productive and reliable partners than authoritarian countries and that a purely interest-based relationship had its limits. It also encouraged Russia to adopt a rapid transition to a market economy through 'shock therapy' which, it believed, was the only way to ensure a democratic transition.

Western Europeans started off with rather different expectations. Geographic proximity and a long shared history inclined them to believe in a much longer timetable for Russia's transformation. Their own economic history made them sceptical of a rapid transition to a market economy via shock therapy. Their expectations for quick change in Russia were more modest than Washington's and their timetable for Russia's Western integration much longer. The newly independent states in Central and Eastern Europe and the Baltic had a more sceptical view about whether Russia was willing or able to integrate into Euro-Atlantic structures, but they were in no position during the 1990s to set the agenda with Russia as they themselves rushed to join the West.

When the USSR collapsed there was enormous relief that, with the exception of the local wars that produced today's frozen conflicts and the Chechen war, it fell apart peacefully. Yet the absence of conflict meant the West never had to engage Russia and its new neighbours in a focused, systematic discussion of how Russia's relations with the former Soviet states could be regulated and how the newly independent states defined their interests. In the 1990s Russia's relations with its neighbours fluctuated as they all emerged from the rubble of the Soviet Union. Meanwhile, the United States and Europe embarked on selective engagement with Russia's neighbours, focusing on security and energy interests.

Although expectations from the beginning differed, the United States and its European allies sought to construct Europe's new security architecture with Russia as its easternmost pillar, and the gap between the old NATO and Russia was over the course of nearly two decades gradually filled by new members of the Alliance. NATO's eastward progression was not intended, Alliance leaders reassured Moscow, against Russia, but designed to expand the zone of stability, security and prosperity toward it. New structures were created to include Russia: the NATO–Russia Council and its precursor NATO–Russia Permanent Joint Council, the EU–Russia Partnership and Cooperation Agreement, and Russian participation in the G7 and G8.

> Russia opposed NATO enlargement from the beginning

Russia opposed NATO enlargement from the beginning. Since Mikhail Gorbachev's time, Russian leaders, and some in the West, have insisted that in return for the USSR assenting to a united Germany joining NATO the participants in the 2+4 talks that negotiated German unification promised that NATO would not expand 'one inch'.[1] This forms a central element of the Russian narrative about how the West ignored Russian interests in the 1990s, forcing Moscow to accept an agenda in which it had no say or had already rejected. It became clear as the 1990s wore on that American assumptions about Russia's development trajectory were unrealistic. Yet a changed Russia was eventually expected to occupy its rightful place in the transatlantic community and become a key member, an integral part, eventually embracing its values and its interests.

The alternatives to engagement were too difficult to contemplate. What were the options for dealing with Russia other than partnership or a return to the Cold War? Both the United States and Europe faced so many challenges, ranging from European Union expansion to the 'war on terror', that neither was prepared for military, ideological and economic competition with Russia. As a result, the expectation of Europe whole and free with Russia as an integral part persisted.

War in Georgia

The war in Georgia exacerbated tensions between Russia and the West. The overall Western goal had been to shore up the independence and viability of Russia's neighbours. A core goal of Vladimir Putin's foreign policy, and Dmitry Medvedev's, however, has been to restore Moscow's influence in its neighbourhood and roll back the American and European presence in Eurasia. Nevertheless, the war also highlighted the differences between the United States and key European allies. Washington pointed to a long chain of Russian actions prior to the war, including deployment of troops to Georgia's separatist regions, violations of Georgian airspace, discrimination against ethnic Georgians in Russia, and trade sanctions on Georgian goods, arguing that this left no doubt that the war was a continuation of a deliberate Russian policy. The goals of that policy are well known: restoration of Russia's sphere of influence or 'privileged interests', as President Medvedev called it in the aftermath of the war;[2] an end to NATO's eastward expansion; and recognition on the part of the West that Russia is a great power that has to be treated as an equal, with interests that need to be respected. Many EU members (although not the newest ones) believed that Georgia was equally, if not more, culpable than Russia. Although they were dismayed by what they viewed as a disproportionate Russian response, they were more sympathetic than Washington to the Russian version of events.

The August war highlighted that some NATO members do not share the US view of what constitutes legitimate Russian interests. While many in Washington have argued that Russia's neighbours have every right to pursue a Euro-Atlantic orientation, including membership in NATO and the EU, the consensus in Berlin and Paris (albeit not in Warsaw or Tallinn) is that Russia will inevitably have a *droit de regard* in the former Soviet space and that there are limits to how far the West can venture into this area without provoking a Russian reaction that could threaten Western interests. Although the EU lacks a comprehensive policy on Russia and its neighbourhood, the EU's reactions to the Georgia crisis differed considerably from those of the George W. Bush administration and the two main US presidential candidates, Senators John McCain and Barack Obama.

The European drive to engage Russia immediately to seek a compromise solution to the conflict reflected the different stakes America and Europe have in their relations with Russia. For Europeans, Russia is a large, sometimes awkward and difficult neighbour, with whom they are fated to live side by side and with whom they must interact on a sustained basis. Engagement and partnership are the only option. Europe and Russia have become increasingly interdependent economically, especially in energy, and Europe is projected to become increasingly dependent on imports of Russian natural gas over the next decade.[3] The EU and Russia are linked by a robust network of political, human and commercial ties.

The more distant United States, in contrast, has at best enjoyed a selective partnership with Russia. The Obama administration has made it clear it hopes that the positive aspects of the relationship – arms control, counterterrorism, counter-proliferation – will work better on its watch than they have in the last eight years. Biden explained at the Munich Security Conference in February that the pledge to 'press the reset button' in US–Russian relations involves cooperation on some common interests and agreement to disagree on others, a view rather different from the EU's commitment to pursue a broad-based strategic partnership.

Formula for a new Europe?

Moscow understands the differences between the US and European perspectives and has pursued policies that reinforce them. Even before the Georgia war, Medvedev's first major foreign-policy speech in Berlin in June 2008 included a sweeping but vague proposal to redesign the entire Euro-Atlantic security architecture on the basis of each country's 'naked' national interests.[4] Reactions in the United States to this ambitious and amorphous proposal ranged from polite puzzlement to outright dismissal. However, the Germans immediately responded that this was an issue on which Europeans should engage Russia, and other countries have followed suit.

Reactions ranged from polite puzzlement to outright rejection

Medvedev's idea can be traced to the 1954 Soviet proposal for an all-European security framework agreement. Subsequent iterations of that scheme, particularly the one that led to the 1975 Helsinki agreement, contained persistent themes which some Russian spokesmen have described as key elements of the current appeal. Securing a sphere of influence, legitimising post-1945 borders and promoting economic ties between Europe's two halves were the Kremlin's key goals in negotiating the Helsinki accords. But the accords also contained provisions – the 'Basket Three' – intended to foster closer humanitarian ties and greater social contacts between the two halves of Europe. Despite early concerns that the accords would legitimise the Soviet occupation of Eastern Europe, they played a decisive role in undermining the very gains Moscow had tried to consolidate, and contributed to the fall of the Iron Curtain. The Conference on Security and Cooperation in Europe, created as a result of the Helsinki accords, became the key forum for the West to engage the Soviet Union on human rights.

After the collapse of communism and the emergence of post-communist states, the renamed Organisation for Security and Cooperation in Europe (OSCE) expanded its activities to include a new Office of Democratic Initiatives and Human Rights. Its election-monitoring activities have become increasingly controversial in many of the post-Soviet states, including Russia, and it did not monitor the 2007 Duma elections or the 2008 presidential election. In recent years, Russian officials and Kremlin-connected pundits have hinted that Russia might withdraw from the OSCE, now viewed in Moscow as an instrument for the West to act against Russian interests.

The Medvedev proposal appears to be an attempt to create a 'son of OSCE' without the Basket Three provisions for democracy-building, a system in which Russia, Europe and the United States would be equal partners, but which does not concern itself with the internal organisation and politics of members states. In an October 2008 speech at Evian, France, Medvedev criticised the 'NATO-centric' approach to European security and then offered several basic principles on which a new security treaty should be based: inadmissibility of the use of force in international relations; guarantees of 'equal security'; and the impossibility of one state or international organisation having 'exclusive rights' to maintain peace and stability in Europe.[5]

This Russian idea could gain momentum in 2009, if only because it is a significant vehicle for the Kremlin to advance its claim that after the Georgia war Europe needs a new security paradigm, and that the West needs to treat Russia as an equal partner in setting the new agenda. In the absence of an active joint US–European effort to engage Russia on this issue, the Russian proposal could create further tensions within the alliance, especially if Moscow pursues bilateral diplomacy with select European capitals. Versions of the Russian proposal circulating in some European capitals call for countries to sign a renunciation-of-force agreement and for reiteration of the principles on which the United Nations is based. Some versions envisage the creation of a UN Security Council-type directorate made up of the larger European states that would run this new Euro-Atlantic organisation, reinforcing the impression that, for many of the Russian foreign-policy class, the nineteenth-century Concert of Europe remains an attractive model.

Sceptics on both sides of the Atlantic argue that Russia is trying to dilute NATO and the OSCE, and that Moscow's ultimate aim is to supplant these organisations with a new Euro-Atlantic security treaty legitimising its sphere of influence. Even if Russia does not succeed in getting rid of the organisations, Moscow could divide the Alliance sufficiently to weaken the core transatlantic security institutions.

But the lack of specificity in the proposal offers an opportunity to think creatively about how to engage Russia more productively on these matters. This engagement and any new agreement it produced could moderate the brittle nature of Russia's relations with many of its Western interlocutors, and could ensure that Russia becomes a stakeholder in a more stable and secure Europe. If it convinced Russia that the West was treating it as an equal, it could diminish the strength of the narrative that the West has ignored Moscow's interests in Europe. Not engaging seriously with the Kremlin on its initiatives would be irresponsible.

Three issues that cannot wait

Russia could play a substantial role over three issues that require urgent Allied attention: how to deal with the Euro-Atlantic aspirations of Ukraine and Georgia; the Iranian nuclear programme; and the war in Afghanistan.

Ukraine and Georgia. After the December 2008 NATO ministerial meeting, NATO membership is not on the cards for either country in the foreseeable future. But both countries will need a perspective that enables them to pursue their aspirations of security, stability and prosperity in Europe.

The Alliance is facing a difficult choice: What to do with Ukraine and Georgia? On the one hand, pressing on with NATO membership plans for these states is unacceptable for some key European countries, most notably Germany, because of concern about the effect of enlargement both on NATO's future effectiveness and on relations with Russia. But having reiterated their commitment to an 'open-door' policy on numerous occasions, and having agreed in April 2008 in Bucharest that Georgia and Ukraine would one day join NATO, the Allies do not have the option of turning their backs on them now. Retreating in the face of Russian threats would further undermine NATO credibility, but pressing on with membership plans could split the alliance and render it incapable of action.

Since the end of the Cold War, NATO membership has been treated as an informal stepping-stone toward membership in the European Union. Both Ukraine and Georgia have declared their interest in joining the EU, but neither has received much encouragement from Brussels. A clear signal from Brussels to Kiev and Tbilisi that membership is part of their future if they embark on the path of domestic transformation and stay the course (along with a generous assistance package) could offer a realistic way out of the current impasse. Russia has never treated EU expansion with the same hostility and resentment it has shown toward NATO enlargement.

Iran. US and European relations with Russia are also strained by their different approaches to Iran. While Russia does not want Iran to acquire nuclear weapons, it does not assign the same urgency to this issue as do the United States and Europe. Russian views on Iran involve a different set of interests at stake than those of the United States or Europe. They reflect a very different geography, recent history and distant past, threat assessment, economic concerns, and overall worldview. For Moscow, Iran is an important commercial partner and a key entry point into Middle East and world politics. Russian analysts view Iran's nuclear ambitions primarily as intended to guarantee Tehran's independence and sovereignty in the face of a threat from Washington; they can even sympathise, having in their view suffered devastating setbacks in the 1990s and given up major geopolitical gains in the last century under pressure from the United States. Moscow sees US–Iranian rapprochement as probably marginalising Russia and perhaps making Russian–Iranian relations quite competitive, as the two would compete for the same lucrative European energy market. The status quo suits Russian interests by elevating Moscow's role in the international arena due to its special relationship with Tehran.

The status quo suits Russian interests

Nevertheless Russia does not want to see Iran get the bomb. The record of Russian–Iranian diplomacy suggests that Moscow lacks the influence to persuade Tehran to accept a compromise on its nuclear programme; Russian participation in a resolution of the dispute will likely be necessary but not sufficient for success. A deal with Iran is more likely to emerge from negotiations between the United States and Iran than from an effort on the part of Russia to 'deliver' Iran. Recent US statements about direct engagement with Iran and an apparently favourable response from Tehran are a promising beginning. The possibility of linking US deployment of missile defences in Europe to progress on the resolution of the Iranian nuclear issue could serve as an incentive for Russia not to act as a spoiler. Reviving earlier Russian proposals for reprocessing Iranian spent fuel at a joint Russian–Iranian facility in Russia could be a further incentive.

Afghanistan and Central Asia. The most urgent issue operationally on the Alliance's agenda with Russia is Afghanistan or, more precisely, getting there from anywhere. Afghanistan has emerged as the crucial test of NATO's will and skill to meet a twenty-first-century security challenge.

Moscow has long maintained it shares an interest with the United States and Europe in securing Afghanistan and preventing the Taliban from returning to power. Instability in Afghanistan could easily spill over into Central Asia, which Russia considers to be in its zone of privileged interests, and thence into Russia proper. In recent years drugs from Afghanistan have flowed through Central Asia into Russia and beyond, and Russian officials have complained about the toll this traffic has taken on their country. In 2008 Russia and NATO signed an agreement to facilitate NATO access to Afghanistan by opening the Russian transportation network to NATO's supply trains (including lethal goods), though important details have yet to be finalised.

But Russia has not always played a supporting role in the Alliance's efforts in Afghanistan. While endorsing the goal of a stable Afghanistan and pledging its support for NATO, Moscow has taken a series of contradictory steps that suggest clear limits to its willingness to cooperate. In 2005, a Russian-inspired Shanghai Cooperation Organisation declaration included an appeal to the United States to commit to a schedule to withdraw from Central Asia. In 2009, according to news reports, Russia made a generous offer of grants, loans and debt forgiveness to Kyrgyzstan in exchange for expelling the United States from the Manas air base, which serves as a key hub for US and Allied operations in Afghanistan.[6] These steps have had a negative impact on NATO's operations in Afghanistan and reputation in the region.

While Moscow wants a stable Afghanistan, it is not prepared to accept a permanent US presence or enhanced US influence in Central Asia. Russia has a strong interest in maintaining its hold on the region, where, its leaders think, it has far more at stake than the United States or Europe. But the situation in Central Asia is changing. Russia is no longer the hegemon in the region and China plays a more important role in its economic development and political fortunes. Central Asian countries have shown considerable diplomatic skill navigating the treacherous waters between Russia, China, Afghanistan and Iran while maintaining a careful balance in their ties to Washington. For NATO, engaging Russia in a dialogue about Afghanistan and Central Asia is not tantamount to leaving the region to Moscow's mercy, merely an acknowledgment that Russia still plays a major role in the region.

Toward a transactional relationship

The situation involving Russia, Afghanistan and Central Asia reinforces the fact that, despite some common interests between America, Europe and Russia, this relationship falls considerably short of a strategic partnership. Rather, Russian policy with respect to US access to Central Asia points to a transactional relationship, involving quid pro quos and bargains, which can serve as a useful model for rebuilding US and European relations with Russia. It would call for Washington and its allies to define and rank their interests and engage Moscow in a dialogue about common concerns or competition and mechanisms for addressing them or managing differences where their priorities conflict or do not coincide. This option does not assume Russian cooperation on the basis of shared interests, but rather seeks to develop a bargaining mechanism whereby the parties could manage their relations on a quid pro quo basis. Nor should it be mistaken for a grand-bargain-style policy that would call for the United States to trade off Georgia for Iran, or NATO expansion for steady gas supplies to Europe. On the contrary, a transactional relationship calls for smaller-scale compromises aimed at devising mechanisms for managing differences, not doing away with them in one broad sweep; it does not imply abandoning long-standing goals, but rather setting priorities and sticking to them.

The United States and Europe share interests in Russian respect and support for the nuclear non-proliferation agenda; restraint in dealing with states such as Iran, Syria, Venezuela; restraint in the conventional arms trade; respect for the territorial integrity, sovereignty and strategic independence of Russia's neighbours; constructive participation in global financial markets; sustained and expanded flow of oil and gas to world markets; and domestic political transformation toward a state that respects the rule of law, as Medvedev has often promised. In the absence of a strategic partnership with Russia, the United States can work with Europe to set priorities among these goals and negotiate agreements with Russia.

Russian integration with the West, however, remains a long-term issue, one it is not clear the majority of Russians favour. The Russian people and their government will ultimately have to decide whether they want to continue to develop on a trajectory that differs markedly from that of the United States and Europe. The West has limited influence over this issue, but it can take measures to lessen the prospect of further conflict in the post-Soviet states and negotiate with Russia on the important international challenges we collectively face. The task of pressing the reset button in East–West relations promises to be arduous.

Acknowledgements

The authors have benefited from discussions with members of the working group on US policy toward Russia supported by the Carnegie Corporation of New York. The authors alone bear responsibility for the contents of this article.

Notes

1 Angela Stent, *Russia and Germany Reborn: Unification, the Soviet Collapse and the New Europe* (Princeton, NJ: Princeton University Press, 1999), ch. 5; James A. Baker III, 'Russia in NATO?', *Washington Quarterly*, vol. 25, no. 2 (Winter 2002), pp. 95–103.

2 President Medvedev's interview with Channel One television, 31 August 2008, http://www.kremlin.ru/eng/text/speeches/2008/08/31/1850_type82912type82916_206003.shtml.

3 *Securing the Future: Making Russian-European Gas Interdependence Work* (Cambridge, MA: Cambridge Energy Research Associates, 2007), ch. 4.

4 Dmitry Medvedev's speech to the Deutsche Gesellschaft für Auswärtige Politik, 5 June 2008, http://www.kremlin.ru/text/appears/2008/06/202133.shtml.

5 President Medvedev's speech at the 8 October 2008 World Policy

Conference, Evian, France, available at http://www.kremlin.ru.

6 Clifford J. Levy, 'Poker-Faced, Russia Flaunts its Afghan Card', *New York Times*, 21 February 2009, http://www.nytimes.com/2009/02/22/weekinreview/22levy.html.

The Roots of Germany's Russia Policy

Christopher S. Chivvis and Thomas Rid

For many American observers, Germany's reaction to Russia's August 2008 invasion of Georgia left something to be desired. German Chancellor Angela Merkel was relatively slow to denounce the invasion, and when she did so she took a position that was less strong than many in Washington would have preferred. After the crisis, German Foreign Minister Frank-Walter Steinmeier sought to maintain the warmest possible relations circumstances would permit, pushing to reinstate the NATO–Russia Council as quickly as possible. German politicians across the political spectrum stood behind him. For many in the United States, Russia's invasion had primarily damaged Russia itself and hastened a trend toward Russian 'self-isolation', as then-US Secretary of State Condoleezza Rice put it in the *Frankfurter Allgemeine Zeitung*.[1] Many in Germany agreed with this analysis, but for most German observers Russian self-isolation was something to be avoided at all costs, a potentially disastrous development for the post-Cold War European order.

It would be too simplistic to contrast a confrontational US policy toward Russia with wobbly-kneed German capitulation. But the responses that Russia's invasion of Georgia evoked in Washington and Berlin pointed to deeper differences that have been apparent for some time, as in the debate over NATO enlargement or US plans to deploy missile-defence installations in Eastern Europe. Within Germany itself, there is an uncanny degree of consensus when it comes to Russia policy. It can be difficult to find major

Christopher S. Chivvis is an Associate Political Scientist with the RAND Corporation in Washington DC. **Thomas Rid** is Calouste Gulbenkian Fellow at the Center for Transatlantic Relations at Johns Hopkins University's School of Advanced International Studies.

 DOI 10.1080/00396330902860850

differences between not only the main political parties, but also the major social and economic interest groups. Social Democrats, Greens, post-communists and conservatives might differ in their rhetoric on Russia, but in substance they share many of the same views, and these are very different from those that predominate in the US foreign-policy establishment. Indeed, Merkel's delayed reaction to Russia's invasion of Georgia was only the latest manifestation of Germany's emerging *Russlandpolitik* – a policy that is itself a manifestation of the broader trends in German foreign policy since the end of the Cold War.

The nature and logic of Germany's Russia policy is not well understood in Washington, and too often portrayed in wishful or simplistic terms. To fully understand German policy, one must go beyond the tired clichés about Germany's dependence on Russian energy to the deeper historical, political, economic and cultural forces that have shaped Berlin's evolving relationship with Moscow. As Russia regains significance in the transatlantic relationship, finding common ground between Berlin and Washington over Russia policy will grow more important, especially given Germany's central role in the European Union. At the same time, it may grow more challenging.

Germany's new *Russlandpolitik*

Germany's geographical position as the largest country in Central Europe has for centuries encouraged Berlin to pursue a policy of balancing between East and West. Even after the Second World War, some West German leaders favoured a policy of neutrality in the Cold War as a shortcut to German reunification. They were defeated, however, by the pro-NATO, Atlanticist orientation of Konrad Adenauer's conservative Christian Democratic Party. West German economic power was brought fully to bear on the Atlantic side of the East–West standoff. Even Willy Brandt's *Ostpolitik* of the late 1960s and early 1970s was firmly anchored in the principles of 'Western integration'.

When the Cold War ended, Atlanticism was at its apogee under Helmut Kohl's conservative government. It seemed destined to become a fixture of German foreign policy, and many US observers hoped that a rejuvenated, reunified Germany would now assert itself in favour of transatlantic ideals with renewed vigour and authority. In retrospect, however, the staunch

Atlanticism of the late Kohl era now seems more of a hangover of the Cold War than any indication of Germany's post-Cold War foreign-policy trajectory. Indeed, it masked the real impact of reunification on German foreign policy and retarded full recognition of that impact in the United States. For many Germans, reunification marked the beginning of a process of broader European reunification in which Germany was no longer the edge of the West, but the centre of a pan-European space that stretched from the Atlantic to the Urals. This new Europe, for better or worse, included, or at least overlapped with, Russia, which became a close neighbour – even an odd member of the European family. Germany's *Russlandpolitik* was reconsidered and reassessed in this context.

The contours of Germany's new policy first began to emerge in the late 1990s, when the Social Democrats returned to power. At that time, the prevailing comity in the broader East–West relationship under Russian President Boris Yeltsin made the warming German–Russian relationship less remarkable. By 2003, however, the new closeness of the relationship became more apparent when Chancellor Gerhard Schröder chose to split with the United States over the Iraq War, siding ostentatiously not only with France, but also Russia. For a time, this choice appeared to have more to do with the war itself than German–Russian relations, and those who hoped for a return to the Altanticism of the Kohl era could argue that Schröder's stance would prove ephemeral – all the more so given Schröder's close personal ties to Russian President Vladimir Putin. As the immediate fallout of the Iraq War dissipated, however, and Schröder eventually left office, Germany continued to seek warm relations with Moscow, even as the US–Russia relationship deteriorated. This trend was all the more striking given that Schröder's successor, Angela Merkel, was both heir to the staunchly Atlanticist party of Adenauer and Kohl and an East German – a leader hardly inclined to romanticise a common Communist past.

Merkel was hardly inclined to romanticise a common Communist past

To be sure, Merkel is critical of aspects of Russia's past as well as its present domestic evolution. But under her chancellorship, the diplomatic distance between Berlin and Moscow has continued to decrease – especially if measured against the near standstill in US–Russian relations during the final years of the Bush administration. US critics noted Merkel's decision to continue plans for the Baltic Nord Stream pipeline, which, in carrying Russian gas to Western Europe, would circumvent the states in Russia's old 'sphere of influence' to the East, rendering Poland and the Baltic states more isolated in terms of energy supplies and more vulnerable to Russian energy manipulation. Meanwhile, Russian objections encouraged German resistance to the planned US missile shield, and Merkel led the charge against American plans to offer Georgia and Ukraine NATO Membership Action Plans at the Alliance's 2008 Bucharest Summit.

In part, Germany's pro-Russian orientation can be attributed to the fact that Merkel is the head of a Grand Coalition, and her foreign minister, Steinmeier, was Schröder's former chief of staff. Stenmeier, himself now running for chancellor, clearly seeks to continue the tradition of Brandt's *Ostpolitik*, which he has explicitly tried to reinvigorate.[2] Nevertheless, the differences between the parties over how to deal with Russia are smaller than one might expect. For example, opposition to a third round of NATO enlargement in the wake of the August 2008 crisis has intensified across the German political spectrum. The Social Democrats' foreign-policy spokesman, Gert Weisskirchen, argues that past rounds of NATO enlargement had a negative effect on the evolution of Russia's internal politics.[3] On the conservative side, leaders doubt that a NATO commitment to Georgia or Ukraine could be credible, and worry that moves toward NATO enlargement would now be interpreted as a direct challenge to Russia, inviting more problems.[4] German Conservatives and Social Democrats both also express reservations about missile defence. Even some of the most staunchly pro-American politicians in the Bundestag have been critical. 'The American plans are right and important', said Hans-Ulrich Klose, a conservative-leaning Social Democrat and co-chairman of the foreign-relations committee, 'but in the implementation, Washington did not take Moscow's sensitivities into account enough. The Russians feel humiliated.'[5]

In general, whereas US leaders have tended to view Russian proclamations of alarm at NATO's enlargement or missile defence as political grandstanding, German leaders have tended to interpret Russia's reactions as signs of deeper, and more dangerous, Russian discontent with the way the post-Cold War European political order has developed. They do not think Russian fears are justified, but they do worry that Russia's sense of insecurity could pose a more serious problem if it encourages Russia's leaders to behave even more erratically.

All this is not to say that there are no differences between the German political parties. On the hawkish end of the spectrum is Eckart von Klaeden, the foreign-policy spokesman of the Conservative parliamentary group, who dismisses the Social Democrats' views of Russia as 'misty-eyed' and 'driven by post-Soviet phantom pain'.[6] In general, the Conservatives tend to be more willing to criticise Russia than their Social Democratic counterparts. Yet, on Russia, fundamental differences between the parties can be hard to find, especially when their views are compared with the consensus view in the United States.

One noteworthy development is the re-emergence, at least in some circles, of the idea of *Äquidistanz*, or equidistance, between Moscow and Washington. While the idea remains controversial, it is not without its proponents. 'It is Germany's strong interest that its partnership with Russia is at least on the same level as Germany's partnership with United States', says Martin Schulz, a Social Democratic member of the European Parliament and one of the party's foreign-policy leaders. He adds, 'Equidistance means same distance. I would prefer same proximity.'[7] Similarly, Peter Struck, Gerhard Schröder's former minister of defence and now head of the Social Democratic parliamentary group argued in 2007 that 'Germany should have the same proximity to America on the one hand and Russia on the other hand'.[8] As one might expect, straightforward statements of support for a policy of equidistance are even more common on the German far left. Wolfgang Gehrcke, foreign-policy spokesman of Die Linke, the newly established left-wing party in Germany's state and federal governments, believes that the policy of 'equidistance' will gain momentum.[9]

Of course, none of these leaders would deny the towering significance of Germany's close economic ties to the United States. And many German politicians and opinion leaders, including those cited above, remain vocal critics of the general direction of Russian domestic policy in recent years. Nevertheless, they do want to see the German–Russian relationship in all its dimensions treated as a high priority. By contrast, for many observers in the United States, the end of the Cold War also meant the end of Russia as a major power and the beginning of an era of US – or at least Western – primacy. The significance of Russia in US foreign policy was thus downgraded, a trend accelerated by the post-11 September focus on the Muslim world. For most Germans, however, the end of the Cold War only returned Russia to its pre-Soviet status as a great power, in the European system at least, and hence a priority in German foreign policy.

Explaining the relationship

The factor most commonly taken to be the driving force in contemporary German–Russian relations is energy, especially natural gas. Across the political spectrum, German politicians have two overriding fears when it comes to Russian gas: firstly, that Moscow will continue to threaten Ukraine's gas supplies, and thereby the supplies of some members of the European Union; and secondly, that Russia may not be able to meet Europe's demand for gas over the medium term. The second concern weighs at least as heavily as the first, if not more so, though the intensity of the January 2009 Russian–Ukrainian gas dispute was serious and damaged Russia's image across the political spectrum in Berlin.[10]

Russia's significance as a reliable energy supplier across Germany and Europe is not in question. Germany is Europe's largest importer of gas. It is also Russia's largest market for gas, followed by Italy and Ukraine.[11] 20% of Russia's natural-gas exports and 10% of its oil exports flow to German households and industrial centres. In the near and mid-term future, it will be impossible to satisfy Germany's growing hunger for energy without Russian gas supplies. Although gas imports from other parts of the world – North Africa, for example – are likely to grow, and Russia's share likely to fall, Germany will still need Russian gas to meet its basic energy requirements.[12] Given that some 37% of the gas burned by German consumers is of Russian origin, the general public's sense of vulnerability to Russian manipulation is likely to remain significant.

The security of Russia's future supply is uncertain, however, and this increases German unease. Russia has long been the world's leading producer of natural gas, and, according to current estimates, is home to the world's largest natural-gas reserves, with about 1,680 trillion cubic feet.[13] But Russia has growing energy needs of its own. It is second only to the United States in natural-gas consumption, having consumed some 16.2tr cubic feet in 2005, and more than half of Russia's electrical energy is generated from natural gas, a high figure for a modern industrial country. (In Germany, the equivalent figure is 10%.[14]) Russia sells its gas at a significant discount on domestic markets as well as in some former Soviet states, such as Ukraine and Belarus. This encourages higher levels of domestic energy consumption, discourages consumer energy efficiency and increases pressure on Russian reserves.[15] During an exceptionally cold winter in 2006, Russia's industrial centres had difficulty meeting their own energy needs. Meanwhile, the financial crisis and falling gas prices have hit Russian energy producer Gazprom hard. There is reason to doubt that the company's development of new natural-gas fields, such as on the Yamal Peninsula or the Shtokman field in the Barents Sea, will remain on budget and on schedule. The company's market capitalisation has fallen by three-quarters, and its foreign debt has risen to more than $49 billion.[16] All of this will impede badly needed investment in infrastructure.

Russia has growing energy needs of its own

In these circumstances, Gazprom has been forced to rely on gas from the Caspian region to meet its contracts in Europe. But Turkmen gas production could itself decline, and suppliers such as Kazakhstan may have difficulty filling the gap. If Russia's own economy continues to grow, even at a more moderate rate than it has in recent years, domestic demand will rise, and the risk of production shortages will become real. Keeping pipeline pressure up during future winters, without interruptions, will be a challenge. This poses a real problem for Germany and other European consumers of Russian gas.

Thus, Germany's medium-term concern is not so much that Russia will once again seek to cut gas supplies to Europe temporarily, as it did in January

2009, but rather that Russia may not have the production capacity to supply Europe's gas in the long term. This concern diminishes the relevance of potentially malevolent Russian intentions. Russian gas supplies are thought to be in danger not for political reasons, but on account of inefficiency and lack of investment in the energy sector. Given that European demand is expected to grow by about 40% in the next two decades,[17] it seems essential, from the German perspective, to strengthen ties with Russia if only to encourage needed investment in energy, gain levers for the liberalisation of Russian energy markets, and help make Russia's domestic consumption more efficient. In other words, Germany's aim is not just closer diplomatic relations to appease Russia and protect German households from the 'energy weapon'; Germany seeks a real deepening of its influence in the development of Russia's energy sector.

Russia as a market

The energy issue must be placed in the broader context of Germany's evolving relationship with Russia and viewed, in particular, alongside Germany's search for profitable new export markets. Germany's long-standing economic strategy of maintaining relatively high wages through exports of high-quality, value-added industrial goods and expertise requires that German businesses perpetually seek new markets. During the Cold War, this strategy was maintained in part by European integration and the growth of global trade through the GATT process. In the post-Cold War era, the extension of European integration to growing economies in central and Eastern Europe, along with a new wave of globalisation, allowed Germany to continue this model, despite the challenge of integrating less efficient East German firms into the West German economy at an overvalued exchange rate.

The growth of the Russian economy over the last eight years promises new opportunities for German exports. Russia had real GDP growth of over 7% in 2006 and over 8% in 2007.[18] German–Russian trade has grown apace, with Russian imports from Germany more than doubling between 2005 and 2007, from $99bn to $200bn.[19] Although the diversity of German exports to Russia has increased, industrial machinery is still by far the largest segment and represents more than 40% of German exports. (Automobiles represent 14%.[20]) Germany's exports to Russia constitute more than 13% of total Russian imports by volume, making Germany the world's largest exporter to Russia.[21] As Germany's exports to Russia have grown, German businesses have developed valuable expertise and contacts within Russia, which German business leaders would prefer not to see go to waste.

When it comes to investments, the picture is somewhat more complex. In 2007, Russia became both a major recipient and source of foreign direct investment.[22] Before the financial crisis, Russia received only a small share (4%) of the EU's total outward foreign direct investment, but still came in ahead of China.[23] From the Russian perspective, EU investments are crucial, and German investment in Russia is larger than US investment. Powerful German corporations including E.ON, Volkswagen, Bosch and Siemens are among the major investors.

Germany's trade and investment flows to Russia are small when compared with the volume of goods and capital exchanged between Germany and the United States, but it is the growth potential of the relationship with Russia that attracts many German businesses. After decades of neglect, Russia's industrial infrastructure is in dire need of new investment and machines. With an increasingly wealthy Russia, large and medium-sized companies in export-oriented Germany find themselves in a good position to meet this growing demand, even if it is temporarily stifled by the current economic crisis.

These economic interests foster a mutual recognition of interdependence between the two countries. More importantly, they encourage German industry to lobby for good relations with Russia. This factor was almost completely absent during the Cold War, when German business was focused almost exclusively on European and especially US markets; Germany's conservative foreign policy was oriented accordingly. Now, the Christian Democratic and Liberal parties, the parties with the closest ties to German industry, are evolving from Cold War anti-communist sceptics into pragmatic Russophiles who see the former Soviet Union as a promising target for capitalist expansion.

Geopolitical determinants

Although economic factors are significant, it would be too easy to conclude that Germany's emerging *Russlandpolitik* is driven entirely by political economy. Energy and exports are no more important than geopolitics and a range of historical factors that have shaped not just Germany's approach to Russia, but Germany's entire post-Cold War foreign-policy culture.

Geopolitics, understood in the literal sense as the politics of geography, has always been fundamental to the German–Russian relationship.[24] Russia's proximity to Germany is a matter of fact that has influenced German policy toward the Kremlin for centuries, regardless of the political ideology of the Russian regime. Outside observers can easily underestimate the significance of the fact that Berlin is only 1,600 kilometres from Moscow – closer than Madrid. Across the party spectrum, advisers and politicians agree that having Russia at Germany's doorstep is important. 'We just don't have an ocean between us and Russia', says Niels Annen, a young Social Democratic member of parliament and foreign-affairs expert.[25]

Geographical proximity has political consequences. From Berlin, Russia not only feels close, it also seems enormous. Russia's vastness is a second geopolitical fact that Germany and other European states have been forced to grapple with since the time of Peter the Great. Off the record, most German politicians will agree that Russia is, to put it bluntly, more important than the smaller states in the Soviet Union's former sphere of influence, which are already 'on safe shores' and thus do not require as much special treatment as Russia.

The weight of history

Geopolitics is also at the root of the two nation's complex historical relationship, which continues to weigh heavily on politics today. For one, a large part of the German political class feels a 'historical responsibility' to Russia. The extent to which the legacy of National Socialism and the Holocaust still influence German foreign policy and political culture in general should not be underestimated. The process of *Vergangenheitsbewältigung*, or coming to terms with the past, continues, and this affects the German–Russian relationship. During the Second World War, more than 10.6 million Soviet soldiers perished, one-third of them in German captivity. The number of Soviet civilian fatalities was even greater, with estimates ranging from 11.4m to well over 15m. As the Green Party's leading Russia expert, Marieluise Beck, put it, anybody who does not understand what German historical responsibility means should visit the memorial in St Petersburg that commemorates the city's siege, during which more than 1.2m civilians were starved to death by the Wehrmacht.[26]

The past can make it difficult for German leaders to take positions that appear aggressive toward Russia. They tend to exhibit, as do others in Europe, though to a lesser degree, a strong preference for engagement and cooperation. 'Historical guilt [*Schuld*] vis-à-vis Russia makes it an imperative for us to be markedly restrained, particularly regarding [Russia's] internal condition', says Beck.[27] Germany's deep-rooted emphasis on its 'historical guilt' is, of course, the counterpart of Berlin's supreme confidence in the moral superiority of its policy, especially evident when it comes to broader transatlantic discussions of how best to cope with Russia.

> Soviet leaders' cooperative approach to German reunification left a lasting impression

History has also shaped contemporary Germany's overwhelmingly positive perception of *Ostpolitik*. Brandt's decision to reach out to the Soviet Union and Eastern Europe in the late 1960s offers a basic model of how to promote change within authoritarian regimes, and in Russia in particular. As Germany emerges from its Cold War shell, it is hardly surprising that the memory of one of its most successful Cold War policies has an impact, as does the overwhelmingly positive view of the process of European integration, which also implies that relations between states can be transformed through economic interdependence.

Many German leaders absorbed a different set of lessons from the end of the Cold War than their counterparts in Washington. The peaceful and generally cooperative approach of Soviet leaders to German reunification left a lasting impression in Germany, where Mikhail Gorbachev and Boris Yeltsin are viewed as having played especially constructive roles.[28] Some politicians in Berlin also believe that an implicit promise not to enlarge NATO was part of the post-war settlement. While many Germans staunchly supported the first two rounds of NATO enlargement, that round was accompanied by parallel enlargement of the European Union. Proposals to enlarge the Alliance further, well beyond the EU, are viewed with more suspicion.

This historical relationship has created a Germany that is deeply concerned about what happens inside Russia, both economically and socially. The consensus is that Russia needs gradual and steady political and economic modernisation. Germany (and its allies) can either help or hinder this process, but it cannot remain ambivalent or allow Russia to experiment with its own path. 'Russia does not act out of a position of strength, it acts out of a position of weakness', says Weisskirchen. The country's grim demographic outlook and falling life-expectancy figures, failing health and education systems, and high levels of alcohol abuse, HIV infection, domestic and public violence and environmental pollution all point in one direction: Russia is in dire need of an 'efficiency revolution' to reverse the social decay rooted in the country's faltering economic and industrial base. Many Germans believe that their country can be a catalyst for this revolution, indeed, that it has a historical responsibility to play this role, if only to help avert a Russian version of Germany's early twentieth-century descent into nationalism and militarism.

Cultural ties

Cultural ties also matter, and those between Russia and Germany go back centuries. Catherine the Great was a German noble, born in Stettin. Her father held the rank of a Prussian general, and her marriage to Peter III was a symbol of Prussian–Russian friendship. German generals, including Carl von Clausewitz, fought with the Czar's armies against Napoleon, and when Nicholas I died in 1855, the headline in the German newspaper *Kreuzzeitung* read, 'Our emperor is dead'.[29] Russian support made Otto von Bismarck's unification of Germany possible before and after 1870, and the chancellor praised Russia as a 'natural historical and intimate ally'.[30]

In the nineteenth century, German writers and thinkers were especially fascinated by Russia and the 'mythical' Russian soul (*die russische Seele*): deep, sensual, melancholic and patriotic. The widespread idea that Germans and

Russians shared a *Seelenverwandschaft* (relationship of souls) captured a specific self-image of German intellectuals and artists, who longed for a more authentic and genuine life in contrast to the industrialisation and orderly, disciplined processes of capitalist Germany. For Friedrich Nietzsche, Russia was the antithesis of 'European particularlism and nervousness'.[31] The popularity of Russian music and culture continued into the twentieth century and can be seen to this day: in a recent poll, 64% of Germans agreed that Russia had a 'great cultural tradition'.[32]

Russia's Cold War occupation of East Germany has imparted a special character to contemporary Russian–German cultural ties. Not all East Germans have a benign view of the Soviet occupation (Angel Merkel, for one, clearly doesn't) and criticism of East Germany's former political regime can be stark. But Russia's 40-year occupation of half of Germany has resulted in a more pro-Russian perspective than in many other countries once under the Soviet yoke; the fear of Russian aggression that characterises the political culture in so many East European states is absent in the former East Germany. The reasons for this are complex and rooted in German history and self-perception as well as in the special position of East Germany in the communist bloc.

> *Charlottenburg is popularly known as 'Charlottograd'*

Today, more than a million people of Russian origin live in Germany, although they are mostly not organised politically. Russian migration to Germany has reached levels last seen in the early 1930s. Charlottenburg, one of Berlin's largest boroughs, is popularly known as 'Charlottograd' thanks to its large Russian population. One of the city's trendiest night clubs for the past few years has been Russendisko, and Berlin's gallery scene in downtown Mitte is bustling with Russian artists and customers.

The lasting desire to 'understand' Russia and put its actions into perspective is even evident in the German reception of the recent book-turned-blockbuster-movie, *Anonyma*. The film tells the story of a German woman raped by Russian soldiers in war-ravaged Berlin. When it appeared in Germany, many critics noted that a film with such a horrific theme could easily have portrayed the Russian soldiers as cruel and barbaric, but it did not, suggesting the deeper, more tragic nature of the German–Russian relationship.[33] This says much both about the way Germany sees Russia and the way it sees itself.

Against this backdrop it is unsurprising that many Germans want close ties to Russia, and vice versa. A recent poll by the Institut für Demoskopie in Allensbach, one of the largest German polling firms, found that only 5% of Germans see Russia as 'hostile', the same number that think the United States is hostile. Less surprisingly, perhaps, only 2% of Russians see Germany as hostile, while 65% see the United States as hostile.[34] When asked how much cooperation they desire with other countries, 56% of Germans want closer cooperation with the United States, while 45% would welcome close cooperation with Russia. The links are particularly strong for the 'generation of '68', many of whom are important figures in Berlin today.

Toward a transatlantic approach to Russia

In the aftermath of the Cold War, many American observers expected that the new Germany would more or less follow in the strong Atlanticist tradition of the old West Germany and its Conservative leadership in particular. A rejuvenated, reunited Germany is now seeking a more prominent role in international affairs, but its foreign policy is evolving away from the staunch Atlanticism that predominated during the Cold War. Even conservative Germany is no longer the bastion of Atlanticism it once was. Two decades after the fall of the Berlin Wall, Germany unquestionably sees the United States as a crucial ally, but also sees Russia as an inevitable partner for the stability of the European order.

When it comes to Germany's *Russlandpolitik*, the bottom line for most German leaders is that the isolation of Russia is unacceptable and must be avoided at all costs. Isolating Russia would deprive the West of its few remaining economic levers over Russian policy and leave Europe and the United States with only cruder means of influencing Russian behaviour. Meanwhile, Russian nationalism and even militarism could accelerate. 'We need a stable Russia', argues Heinrich Kreft, a senior diplomat and foreign-policy adviser to the Conservative parliamentary group. 'Policies that strengthen the hawks in the Kremlin should be avoided.'[35] Others might add that a strong Russia is a better partner than a weak Russia, and that Russia could eventually turn into a security threat for Europe precisely on account of its weaknesses; Russian narcotics trafficking and modern slave trade are just two of the many problems that already affect countries beyond Russia's borders. From this perspective, saving Russia is the only option. The sense that Germany has become Russia's last strong link with the West only intensifies German concern, driving German leaders to redouble their efforts to maintain good relations.

NATO enlargement, in this light, is not a priority for Germany. 'For most Germans, NATO is history,' says Niels Annen. There are 'no more emotional ties' to the Atlantic Alliance.[36] Annen, of course, is far too intelligent to dismiss the broader German–American bilateral relationship in all its political, economic and cultural dimensions. His statement comes across more as an observation of political fact by an astute politician than any normative statement of his own aspirations for Germany. It suggests a real dilemma for US policymakers: a hawkish policy toward Moscow designed to cater to East European fears might ultimately strengthen Berlin's proponents of *Äquidistanz*. Needless to say, this could also hurt the transatlantic relationship, and the common interest shared by countries on both sides of the ocean in seeing Russia emerge from its current precarious condition without unacceptable costs to its neighbours or the world.

Although there will inevitably be ups and downs in German–Russian relations, the fundamentals of German policy toward Russia seem unlikely to change anytime soon. Anyone who seeks to strengthen transatlantic cooperation in the future will need to take this into account. The prospects for cooperation may be improving, however. When US–Russian relations soured in the later years of the Bush administration, this resulted in a certain degree of German accommodation toward Russia as Germany sought to avoid Russia's isolation. By contrast, if the Obama administration pushes the 'reset button' on US–Russia relations, as Vice President Biden has promised,[37] and demonstrates to its German allies that it recognises German concerns and interests in Russia, Germany may find it easier to take a tougher line with its eastern neighbour. Serious transatlantic discussions over issues of common concern – Russian energy supplies, Russia–NATO relations, and, above all, the probable impact of the current economic crisis on Russia's future – are strong imperatives for a more coordinated transatlantic approach.

In the end, of course, Germany and the United States can only do so much to affect Russia's future direction. Mutual suspicion and latent hostility could still complicate a reorientation of US policy. Moreover, even as US policy changes and the outlook for a new transatlantic consensus over Russia improves, there is no guarantee that the Russia problem will be resolved. This will depend as much on Moscow as on Washington or Berlin.

Acknowledgements

The authors extend their thanks to those who kindly agreed to be interviewed for this article. Thanks also to Steve Larrabee, Sabine Fischer and Sumona Guha for their incisive comments on earlier drafts.

Notes

1 According to Rice, the United States would aim 'to make it clear to Russian politicians that their decisions send Russia down a one-way-street into self-inflicted isolation and international irrelevance'. Condoleezza Rice, 'Russland isoliert sich selbst', *Frankfurter Allgemeine Zeitung*, 23 September 2008.

2 Steinmeier, in direct reference to Egon Bahr's '*Wandel durch Annährung*' ('change through rapprochement'), the cornerstone of *Ostpolitik*, coined the phrase '*Wandel durch Verflechtung*' ('change through interdependence'). Markus Wehner, 'Steinmeiers Moskauer Karte', *Frankfurter Allgemeine Zeitung*, 24 September 2006, p. 8.

3 Interview with Gert Weisskirchen, Berlin, 23 September 2008.

4 Andreas Schockenhoff, quoted in Ralf Beste et al., 'Wandel durch Bestürzung', *Der Spiegel*, 25 August 2008, p. 24.

5 Hans-Ulrich Klose, quoted in Ansgar Graw, 'Die Russen fühlen sich gedemütigt', *Die Welt*, 4 June 2007.

6 'Von Klaeden: Russland und Europa entfernen sich immer weiter voneinander', Deutschlandradio, 28 April 2007; 'Moskaus Doktrin ist geprägt von postsowjetischem Phantomschmerz', interview with Eckart von Klaeden, *Die Welt*, 9 September 2008.

7 Martin Schulz, quoted in 'Die Russland-Versteher', *Frankfurter Allgemeine Zeitung*, 20 May 2007, p. 6.

8 Peter Struck, 'Schäuble ärgert mich ziemlich', *Frankfurter Allgemeine Zeitung*, 6 May 2007, p. 7.

9 Interview with Wolfgang Gehrcke, Berlin, 24 September 2008.

10 Jonas Grätz and Kirsten Westphal, 'Ende gut, alles gut?' *SWP Aktuell*, 3 January 2009.

11 Bernard A Gelb, *Russian Natural Gas: Regional Dependence*, CRS Report for Congress RS22562 (Washington DC: Congressional Research Service, 5 January 2007).

12 On Russia's need for customers, see Andreas Goldthau, 'Resurgent Russia? Rethinking Energy Inc.', *Policy Review*, no. 147, March 2008.

13 International Energy Agency (IEA), *Key World Energy Statistics 2008*, http://www.iea.org/textbase/nppdf/free/2008/key_stats_2008.pdf; Energy Information Administration (EIA), 'Country Analysis Brief: Russia', May 2008, p. 8.

14 EIA, 'Country Analysis Brief: Russia'.

15 Russia itself is the largest 'customer' of Gazprom, which produces 85% of Russian gas. The company is obliged, by law, to service a growing domestic market in Russia at prices that are a mere 15–20% of international market rates. Foreign markets, therefore, are a crucial source of cash for the company, particularly in times of tight capital markets and lower energy prices.

16 Andrew E. Kramer, 'Gazprom, Once Mighty, Is Reeling', *New York Times*, 29 December 2008.

17 The US Energy Information Administration estimates that Europe's natural-gas consumption will grow from 19.3 trillion cubic feet in 2005 to 27.2tr cubic feet in 2030. Energy Information Administration, 'International Energy Outlook 2008', DOE/EIA-0484 (2008), June 2008, http://www.eia.doe.gov/oiaf/ieo/nat_gas.html.

18 OECD, *OECD Economic Outlook*, EO84, 25 November 2008, available at http://www.oecd.org/.

19 Bundesagentur für Außenwirtschaft (BFAI), 'Wirtschaftsdaten kompakt: Russische Föderation', November 2008. http://www.ahk.de/fileadmin/user_upload/BFAI_-_Wirtschaftsdaten_Kompakt/Russland.pdf.

20 *Ibid.*

21 *Ibid.*, p. 2.

22 OECD, *OECD Investment Policy Review: Russian Federation*, 2008, p. 9.

23 *Ibid.*

24 The term 'geopolitics' is frequently used today to mean something like 'world politics' or 'international political strategy'. An earlier, more precise meaning refers to the fundamental role that geography has played in shaping international politics. This usage was common in the writings of early twentieth-century figures such as Halford Mackinder in 'The Geographical Pivot of History', *Geographical Journal*, vol. 23, 1904, pp. 421–37.

25 Interview with Niels Annen, Berlin, 24 September 2008. Similarly, when asked what matters most about Russia for Germany, a Russia expert in the planning staff of the Ministry of Defence simply pointed to the tiny distance between Moscow and Berlin on a map.

26 Interview with Marieluise Beck, 28 September 2008.

27 *Ibid.*

28 On this point, see Alexander Rahr, 'Germany and Russia: A Special Relationship', *Washington Quarterly*, vol. 30, no. 2, Spring 2007, pp.137–45.

29 Peter Brandt, 'Das deutsche Bild Rußlands und der Russen in der

modernen Geschichte', *Jahrbuch für europäische Prozesse*, vol. 1, 2002, pp. 42–70.

30 *Ibid*.

31 *Ibid*., p. 26.

32 When asked to name the ten most significant Russian personalities of all time, Germans named several cultural figures including Leo Tolstoy, Fyodor Dostoyevsky and Pytor Tchaikovsky. Renate Köcher, 'Das Russlandbild der Deutschen – das Deutschlandbild der Russen', Institut für Demoskopie in Allensbach, 18 September 2008, p. 11.

33 See Andreas Kilb, 'Kitsch und Vergewaltigung: "Anonyma"', *Frankfurter Allgemeine Zeitung*, 22 October 2008.

34 Köcher, 'Das Russlandbild der Deutschen', p. 3.

35 Interview with Heinrich Kreft.

36 Interview with Niels Annen.

37 Vice President Joe Biden, 'Speech at the 45th Munich Security Conference', 7 February 2009, http://www.securityconference.de/konferenzen/rede.php?menu_2009=&menu_konferenzen=&sprache=en&id=238&.

Serbia's Choice

Elizabeth Pond

Suddenly, Serbia's anti-Western exceptionalism has faded. After almost five years during which ultranationalists set the political agenda, pro-Europeans in Belgrade now hold power and accord top priority to joining the European Union. To this end the new Belgrade government is even tempering to a degree its quest to restore the sovereignty over Kosovo that strongman Slobodan Milosevic forfeited a decade ago to NATO intervention and subsequent United Nations stewardship. The shift is incomplete and the way it is playing out is conferring some new legitimacy on the extreme Radical Party nationalists. Nonetheless, it is real enough to alter the dynamic of Serbia's internal and external politics.

The turnaround is a tribute to the single most successful foreign policy of the European Union: the attraction of its soft power to make a growing arc of neighbours want the kind of democracy and market economy the EU wants, even if this requires painful reforms. It is a notable about-face for a nation whose leaders a short year ago threatened, if Kosovo declared independence, to turn its back on the EU, encourage next-door Republika Srpska to secede from Bosnia-Herzegovina, cut off Kosovo's electricity supply, trigger a mass exodus of the roughly 120,000 remaining Serbs in Kosovo, or even send Serbian armed forces back into the province that NATO forced Belgrade to evacuate in 1999.[1]

That was then, this is now. At last we are witnessing the birth of a 'normal, boring, democratic' Serbia, as Ivan Vejvoda, executive director of

Elizabeth Pond, a Berlin-based journalist, is the author of *Endgame in the Balkans* (Brookings, 2006).

Survival | vol. 51 no. 2 | April–May 2009 | pp. 123–136 DOI 10.1080/00396330902860868

the Balkan Trust of the German Marshall Fund, put it as early as last May.[2] The harbinger of transformation he perceived was a tiny shift in votes in yet another early election. The transformation was anything but predetermined. As neighbouring states rushed down the EU path, this land of 22 million in the heart of the Balkans held out the longest in refusing to become a 'normal, boring' state. It cherished its exceptional history as the heroic regional hegemon before and after its half-millennium of Ottoman subjugation from the fourteenth to the nineteenth century. It expected to lead again as Communist Yugoslavia disintegrated after the end of the Cold War; Milosevic successfully mobilised popular support for the use of force to carve a Greater Serbia out of Croatia and Bosnia in the early 1990s.[3]

After Milosevic lost his last war, in Kosovo, and the democratic opposition unseated him by votes and street protests in 2000, reformist Prime Minister Zoran Djindjic and his Democratic Party (DS) did pursue a pro-European policy for two years and two months. But Djindjic was assassinated in 2003, and nationalist fundamentalists again set the tone. The Radicals, who coveted an even larger Greater Serbia than did Milosevic in the 1990s, won repeated pluralities in parliamentary and local elections and thrice came within a whisker of voting in their presidential candidate, Tomislav Nikolic.

Vitriolic campaign

The climax of Radical influence seemed to arrive in early 2008; the increasingly strident Vojislav Kostunica, prime minister and leader of the Democratic Party of Serbia (DSS), deserted his long-time DS ally in the 3 February presidential run-off, then manoeuvred to break up the fractious eight-year coalition of the democratic centre altogether to form a new hard-line nationalist majority with the Radical and Socialist parties.

In the vitriolic Serbian general-election campaign that quickly followed Kosovo's declaration of (EU-supervised) independence on 17 February, mainstream media in Belgrade once more idolised as Serb heroes the war-crimes fugitives Ratko Mladic and Radovan Karadzic, respectively the military and political leader of the Serb forces that carried out the 1995 Srebrenica massacre. Kostunica and the Radicals beat a single-issue drum: punishing Kosovo and the European Union for Kosovo secession. Only one party leader, Cedomir Jovanovic, head of the Liberal Democratic offshoot of the DS, showed any sympathy for self-determination for the 90% majority Kosovar Albanians, given that Milosevic's security forces in 1999 had murdered 10,000 and ethnically cleansed a staggering 1.4m out of the 2m Albanians in the Serbian province.[4]

The European Union made repeated gestures in 2008 to strengthen the hand of the DS and President Boris Tadic, who succeeded Djindjic as its leader. The EU and the United States first arranged for Kosovo to delay its declaration of independence until after the Serbian presidential run-off to help Tadic again edge out Radical Tomislav Nikolic by 2.3% of the vote. Brussels promised future visa liberalisation for Serbs, and signed (but did not ratify) the EU–Serbian Stabilisation and Association Agreement that had been in limbo for two years over Serbia's failure to arrest Mladic. Above all, the European Union scrupulously avoided linking the issues of Kosovo's status and eventual EU candidacy for Serbia.

Not so Kostunica and the Radicals, who thundered that 'Judas' Tadic's support for signing the agreement, after Brussels had orchestrated Kosovo's independence, constituted treason. Should Kostunica succeed in forming a new anti-European parliamentary majority with the extreme nationalists, their rhetoric signalled, the new government would impeach Tadic, boycott the EU and revive Russian patronage. Or, more darkly, it suggested that Tadic would be murdered, on the pattern of the Djindjic assassination.

Tadic never contested the substance of the Kosovo issue

In the 2008 campaign Tadic never contested the substance of the Kosovo issue. Since Djindjic's death he too had vehemently demanded restoration of Serbian rule over Kosovo, both out of conviction and as a tactical manoeuvre to keep Kostunica in the centrist coalition as long as possible. Tadic differed from his hardline rivals, however, by categorically ruling out the use of force and shifting the debate from the ideological and political to the legal arena. He further contended that the disagreement should not block Serbia's integration into the EU, and that it was precisely through joining the EU and influencing its policies from inside that Serbia would be able to reclaim its former province.

This last argument appealed to a public that overwhelmingly resented the loss of Kosovo but longed to become rich and safe by joining the European Union. At the very least, it appealed to some key marginal voters. On 11 May the pro-European bloc Tadic cobbled together drew 38.4% of the vote, slightly more than the parties had previously garnered separately, and for the first time in four and a half years snatched the parliamentary plurality from the Radicals. The Radical Party increased its popular vote by 66,000, but dropped to 29.4% on a slightly higher turnout than in 2007. The Radicals, whose leader Vojislav Seselj daily denounced Croats, Bosniaks and unpatriotic Serbs from his war-crimes trial at The Hague, owed their gains in part to defections from Kostunica's DSS, which fell five points to an impotent third-place 11.6%.

As expected, Kostunica, the Radicals and the Socialists began immediate talks to form a government. It was at this point that Vejvoda issued his prophecy of a 'normal, boring, democratic' Serbia, though sceptics dismissed him as an incorrigible optimist. Serbs doubted the awkward government he foretold, a coalition of the remnants of Milosevic's authoritarian Socialist Party with the Democratic Party, could ever be forged. True Democrats would rebel at colluding with their party's nemesis. True Socialist believers would rebel at joining forces with the DS 'traitors' who had sent Milosevic to stand trial at The Hague.

Some European observers contended that, while Tadic talked the good European talk, he was far too passive, letting himself be pushed around by the ultranationalists.[5] Even as the DS–Socialist flirtation advanced, the knowledgeable Deutsche Welle network expected this 'temporary alliance' to fall apart within months.[6] There seemed far too little change in the election results to challenge pro-Western journalist Dejan Anastasijevic's gloomy pre-election warning that 'instead of moving towards the EU, Serbia seems to be on the fast track towards isolation, and even renewed conflict over Kosovo. What's more, Milosevic's nationalist ideology and his policies have been rehabilitated and incorporated into the political mainstream.'[7]

Yet by July Vejvoda's counter-intuitive alternative won out, thanks to the defection of the Socialists and their critical 7.6% of the vote. Younger Socialist leaders, who since the death of Milosevic in 2006 had yearned to end their pariah status, seized Tadic's offer of the posts of first deputy prime minister, interior minister, energy minister and parliamentary speaker, along with seats on the boards of lucrative state-run firms. During the two months of Democratic–Socialist bargaining, the wannabe Socialist moderates lobbied Greek and Spanish Socialists for future membership for their party alongside the DS in the impeccably democratic Socialist International. Domestically, they dissuaded their own party's old guard from mounting a party coup against them. Tadic then added a few tiny parties to the mix for a DS-led majority in parliament.

The difference was electrifying. Two weeks after the new coalition took office in July a security team boarded a bus near Belgrade and captured Radovan Karadzic, the former Bosnian Serb political leader and for a dozen years the Hague Tribunal's second-most-wanted fugitive. Significantly, the Socialists in government did not object, in accordance with the detailed coalition agreement, even if they were quick to point out that the police under Socialist First Deputy Prime Minister and Interior Minister Ivica Dacic played no role in the arrest. Even more significantly, street demonstrations in Belgrade called by the Radicals to protest 'the dictatorship of President Tadic' and Karadzic's extradition to the tribunal drew only 10,000 instead of the anticipated 300,000.[8]

The issue of Kosovo had finally been overplayed. Abruptly, it lost its salience. The era when chauvinists could rally pensioners, war refugees and other losers from the post-1989 democratisation and globalisation appeared to be over. Fatigue with lost wars and constant political mobilisations that put no bread on the table was setting in.

Challenges

The odd-couple government faces four unknowns: the longevity of the coalition, its capacity to tame the security services, its skill at reconciling its EU and Kosovo policies, and the global financial crisis.

On the face of it, this should be the first Serbian government since the defeat of Milosevic to serve a full four years and have the strength to act decisively. Structurally, the partners seem to be locked in embrace. The DS leads in opinion polls. The Socialists recognise the Democrats as the coalition's senior partner, endorsing the DS drive for European integration and acquiescing in the corollary pledge to track down Mladic – key planks that distinguish the Socialists from their former soulmates in the Radical Party. Indeed, the Socialists are totally dependent on the Democrats. Their lurch toward the centre has alienated enough of their former constituents to drop them below the 5% minimum needed to win parliamentary seats in a new election.[9] If they are to rally new, younger voters, they must stay in office long enough to show their pro-European policy can produce jobs and raise living standards. So too must Tadic's Democrats, however hard this will be in the global financial crisis. The economically liberal technocrats in the G17 Plus Party have no alternative coalition to jump to, and the coalition's smaller partners would not lightly forfeit the perks of office, including patronage appointments to the boards of public firms.

The Socialist example, moreover, helped break up the Radical Party. For several years Nikolic, as the top Belgrade deputy of the absent Seselj, had been softening the edges of his chief's scorn for the European Union. The final split came last September, when Seselj reversed overnight, behind Nikolic's back, the decision of Radical MPs to join in approving signature of the Stabilisation and Association Agreement. Moving toward the centre, Nikolic placed the EU on a par with Russia as a strategic partner for Serbia, and tacitly signalled he was sublimating the Radicals' goal of a Greater Serbia. As the Radicals' three-time presidential candidate quit the party, he took with him the country's best local-party network and a score of MPs, conveniently misplacing the mandatory blank resignation letters they had signed on taking their seats. Posters for his infant Serb Progressive Party quickly went up all over Belgrade. By early November the party was already outpolling the remaining Radicals two-to-one in opinion surveys.[10]

Nikolic's mutiny strengthened the hand of the Democrats

Initially, Nikolic's mutiny strengthened the hand of the Democrats. It moved the political centre of gravity toward moderation. For a few months it made Nikolic both Tadic's most formidable rival and a potential ally for the president should the Socialists be tempted to flex too much muscle inside the government. Nikolic publicly offered the DS ad hoc support depending on the issue at hand. The opposition Radicals and DSS acknowledged the new political balance after they called for a vote of no confidence shortly before Christmas, then had to abandon it for lack of support.

The Radicals could neither dislodge the government nor set the political agenda. They could and did, however, become a powerful spoiler through the use of filibusters, procedural challenges and cascades of legislative amendments. These delaying tactics repeatedly postponed budget approval and adoption of the minimum set of laws the European Union has pressed for if Belgrade wants to win visa-free travel for Serbs within the EU any time soon. The 2009 budget to cope with the financial crisis and ensure a €300m World Bank loan and €402m International Monetary Fund standby arrangement was passed only 90 minutes before the 30 December deadline. In the absence of an approved budget the government's quarter-by-quarter 'temporary financing' in the new year would have been capped at 2008 levels.

The Radicals' price for the last-minute withdrawal of 115 budget amendments was high: requiring the DS to join ostentatiously in stripping the Progressive Party of chairmanships and memberships of parliamentary committees. Nikolic charged that the Radicals also received €2m for dropping the amendments, an accusation denied by both Democrats and Radicals.

In the words of one pro-European Serb observer, the Democrats' surrender to the Radical 'blackmail' amounted to an 'informal coalition' with the party's old foes. It forced Tadic to 'all but burn his bridges with Nikolic' and sowed doubts about the government's staying power. More importantly, it broke the long-standing DS taboo against letting the Radicals gain political power. In the jostling three Progressive MPs defected back to the Radicals. And Nikolic himself is again courting both the Radicals and the DSS, calling for new elections, while trying to build a single strong opposition to Tadic under his own leadership.

Moreover, the observer continued, the DS dalliance with the Radicals, along with its inability in the financial squeeze to deliver on promises of funding for allies, has slackened discipline within the government and left the DS open to 'being blackmailed by its coalition partners'. The Socialists, without informing their partners in advance (since both the Democrats and

G17 Plus have ties to global tobacco giants) introduced a bill on excise taxes giving Serbian cigarette manufacturers the same breaks that multinationals enjoy; three MPs from small coalition parties also voted with the opposition to pass the excise tax.[11]

Other intramural coalition feuds have also made the headlines. Economics Minister and Deputy Prime Minister Mladjan Dinkic from G17 Plus has complained publicly about a 'crisis of authority' in the government, with ministers overridden by unnamed outsiders and 'certain members of public company boards [voting] against the decisions of their own government'.[12] The Socialists, siding with the Serbian Orthodox Church, are unravelling a coalition deal previously struck with the small Social Democratic League of Vojvodina to extend Vojvodina's regional autonomy.[13] And in a dust-up between two DS reformers, Defence Minister Dragan Sutanovac fired Army Chief of Staff Zdravko Ponos for airing in public complaints from the officer corps about poor equipment and other issues. General Ponos, Serbia's first Sandhurst graduate and deputy chief or chief of staff since 2005, was largely responsible for professionalising the military and cleaning up the murky security forces that, among other exploits, had protected Mladic from arrest until at least 2002.[14] In the tense year preceding Kosovo's declaration of independence, he was also credited with having helped avert any Serbian exercise of force through discreet contacts with NATO commanders of the Kosovo Force (KFOR), who made clear the United States' and Europe's red lines.[15] These NATO–Serbian military contacts were broken off in summer 2008 and have not been resumed.

The issue of whether the Belgrade government will be able to tame its security services translates primarily, in the eyes of the EU, into the simple question of whether Serbia can find and arrest Mladic, the 'most wanted' of the two remaining war-crimes fugitives who have evaded arrest for more than a decade. Until he is extradited to The Hague, the EU's long-standing precondition for ratifying the Stabilisation and Association Agreement, the Netherlands will veto further advance of Serbia toward EU membership. The failure of too lightly armed Dutch troops to prevent the 1995 Srebrenica atrocity has seared the Dutch conscience. The contention of today's Serbian democrats that they had nothing to do with the massacre, and even deposed Milosevic themselves, carries no more weight with the Dutch than does the argument that Germans born after Hitler bear no responsibility to atone for his sins.

Many European officials believe that the old army and security networks that harboured Mladic have been significantly weakened. They attribute this success in part to the conviction and jailing of senior officers of the elite Red Berets for the 2003 murder of Djindjic and disbanding of this unit, in part to gang warfare that liquidated the notorious Arkan and other paramilitary commanders, and to the persistence from 2005 to 2008 of then Chief of Staff Ponos in cleaning up the army. They await proof that these rogue networks have been neutralised: the arrest of Mladic or archival evidence, still withheld from Hague Tribunal prosecutors, that Mladic is no longer in Serbia. And they are uncertain about how much power is still wielded by various other gangs that spun off from Tito's secret police, flourished during the heyday of smuggling under international sanctions against Milosevic, and then turned to freelance protection rackets and ad hoc or organised crime. The lack of spectacular assassinations and revelations of high-level political–criminal collusion in recent years may suggest that these networks have shrunk into ordinary criminal bands.[16] And the arrest of Karadzic three days after Tadic replaced the Milosevic-era head of the intelligence service with his own appointee suggests that Tadic and the DS, rather than Dacic or old Milosevic allies, will increasingly control the secret services.[17] But no outsider knows for sure.

Kosovo and the EU

The trickiest balancing act for the nine-month-old Serbian government will, of course, be reconciling the two policies it is now according top priority: fast EU integration and 'preservation' of Serbia's old 'territorial integrity'.[18] So far the government has successfully managed to fend off DSS and Radical accusations of treason in dealing with Kosovo even as it has achieved a wary détente with Europe on the issue. Yet the tacit fallback of the government, as veteran observers characterise it, of its claim to sovereignty over all of Kosovo to manoeuvring for de facto partition of Serb-majority northern

Kosovo, offends not only the Radicals, the DSS and the Serbian Orthodox Church, but also the EU and the fledgling Kosovo government.

In its quest for EU integration, Belgrade is proceeding with unilateral implementation of the Stabilisation and Association Agreement prior to its ratification. This involves passing the remaining two-thirds of 89 essential bills on rule of law, corruption, organised crime and migration; lowering tariffs for the bulk of imports from the EU; and pushing ahead with reforms that the government regards as crucial for Serbia's modernisation in any case. It entails as well renewed efforts by G17 Plus technocrats to steer investments into legitimate economic rather than political projects. In return for these measures Belgrade hopes, with or without extraditing Mladic, to win visa-free travel in the EU for its nationals by early next year, along with EU candidate status. Serbs have already benefited concretely from EU associations through emergency German and Hungarian deliveries of fuel after Russia suspended pumping gas through Ukraine last winter.

The Kosovo issue greatly complicates EU–Serbia relations and the forging of common EU foreign policy. In its own contorted way, the European Union does have a common Balkan policy. Although five of its 27 members have not recognised Kosovo's sovereignty, the largest and oldest members settled on Kosovo independence as the least-worst course a year ago; the five holdouts did not veto this decision, and most are consenting participants in the EU's supervisory rule-of-law EULEX mission in independent Kosovo. As defined by EU High Representative for Foreign Policy Javier Solana, the agreed aim of EU crisis management in the region is 'to create a space for politics to work. But functioning politics is one thing that foreigners cannot provide; only the locals can do that.'[19]

The EU conviction that only locals, and not outsiders, can establish 'functioning politics' explains its patient reliance on soft power and institutional improvisation as Brussels waited out the nine months in 2008 during which Belgrade's rejection of EULEX deployment in northern Kosovo made the region a paradise for smugglers of everything from fuel to the bulk of heroin that crosses EU borders and granted implicit license to Serb gangs to intimidate any isolated EULEX officials who might appear.

The threat was real enough. A year ago Serb rowdies in northern Kosovo responded to Kosovo's declaration of independence by burning down Serbia–Kosovo border posts, hounding international officials out of the north, firing automatic weapons and heavy-duty grenades at KFOR soldiers, and killing one Ukrainian UN policeman. The EU has no military bodyguards of its own; for protection of its civilian EULEX personnel it depends entirely on public order. It was therefore relieved when Belgrade finally agreed at the end of November to EULEX deployment in the north and promised it a permissive environment. The first EULEX teams took up positions north of the Ibar River on 9 December.

The compromise document that smoothed the way for Belgrade's 'yes' was a report on Kosovo by UN Secretary-General Ban Ki Moon, endorsed by the Security Council. The text consisted of classic diplomatic fudge. Thus, Belgrade reads the UN circumlocutions as EULEX 'neutrality' on whether Kosovo is independent and as Western assent to perpetuating the Serbian 'parallel structures' that ruled northern Kosovo de facto during the decade of post-war UN administration of Kosovo. The Serbian government is content for the moment to cooperate with EULEX in squeezing out Radical and DSS machine bosses in northern Kosovo and collecting millions of euros in unpaid fuel taxes, but it has every intention of eventually replacing these networks with its own appointees. EULEX sees its operation, especially in monitoring the constitutional guarantee of minority Serb rights both in heartland Albanian Kosovo and in its northern tip, as resting on an invitation from the independent government in Pristina. The EU interprets the UN language as a variant of the 1972 détente treaty in which West and East Germans first acknowledged each other's existence and began meeting face to face, while continuing to dismiss each other's legitimacy. Similarly, the EU is now cajoling Serbian and Kosovo officials to agree to disagree on Kosovo's status and talk directly to solve pragmatically the technical problems of interaction between Serbs and Albanians. In the EU vision these contacts should in the medium term detoxify ethnic hostility and in the long term socialise both sides into the EU's post-national credo of making borders increasingly irrelevant in a common EU space. Stressing the contrast between the two views, Doris Pack, chairwoman of the European Parliament's Delegation for

Relations with Southeast Europe, flatly calls on Belgrade 'not to hinder the development of [Kosovo] and not to support a parallel structure'.[20]

Despite these contrary interpretations, the compromise language has already had a striking impact in averting escalation in the most violence-prone part of Kosovo, the Serb-majority northern segment of the ethnically divided city of Mitrovica on the Ibar River. If past patterns had been repeated, Serb and Albanian hardliners, and the mafias that cooperate across ethnic lines, would have shattered the slow confidence-building of moderates by igniting ethnic clashes to start a new spiral of revenge and retaliation.

The compromise language has had a striking impact in averting escalation

Indeed, the EULEX police, judicial and customs mentors quickly encountered a rash of low-level brawls that contrasted with the overall ethnic peace in 2008. But arson of Albanian shops, the stabbing of a young Serb, and other incidents never flared up into large-scale riots. Serbian plainclothes agents quickly broke up groups of Serb troublemakers as they began forming. Joint patrols of EULEX executive police and Kosovo police, including both Albanian and Serb officers, backed by highly visible combat-ready KFOR peacekeepers, restrained Albanian hotheads and provocateurs. And, for the first time, the more responsible media in Serbia and Kosovo did not treat the disturbances as spontaneous ethnic eruptions, but instead asked pointedly which mafias were instigating them and why.

By February 2009, EULEX customs officials reopened, for registration of transit goods, if not yet for collection of tariffs, the two border posts that had been burned down a year earlier. Concurrently, Serbian officials began manning two other posts on the 'administrative line' between Kosovo and Serbia proper. EU judges commenced their first trial against a Kosovo Albanian, for the murder of an Albanian civilian in 1998, and started to work through the decade-long backlog of untried criminal cases. And Belgrade's Kosovo and Metohija Ministry, greatly helped by the local knowledge of the two moderate Kosovo Serbs at the top, Minister Goran Bogdanovic and Albanian-speaking State Secretary Oliver Ivanovic, progressively sidelined some of the old regime's nastier enforcers.

Much could still go wrong. Mladic could continue to evade capture and block Serbia's road to EU integration. Sluggish efforts to pass laws required for advancement toward EU membership could drag on. Political disarray within the governing coalition could mount and once again force premature elections. The financial crisis that is shrinking growth and the dinar, as well as foreign investment, bids on further privatisation, and the payoffs that lubricate politics, could also depress living standards and sour voters on the democratic centre. Belgrade's success in ostracising Kosovo officials in international forums could backfire and help bring about a Serbian nightmare of a virtual Greater Albania, as Tirana increasingly represents Kosovo interests and hosts Kosovo diplomats in Albanian embassies in states that do not recognise Pristina. The creative diplomatic ambiguity on display so far could tip over into destructive ambiguity; Serbia and the EU's perceived common interests in cleaning out northern Kosovo smugglers could be overshadowed by acrimony over partition.

Yet, when measured against the aftermath of conflict in Iraq, Afghanistan or the Congo, this particular situation looks almost idyllic. The post-Yugoslav cycle of hate and revenge in the Balkans has been reversed, the mass killing halted. Serbia after Milosevic, and after the murder of Djindjic, was not destabilised. In 2009 politics in Belgrade has moved beyond the radical nationalists' anti-European stew of hubris and special sense of victimisation. The transformative power of the European Union is working, however messily. Today's conjunction of Serbia's reassertion of a European identity and EU patronage for Balkan states that want to leap from nineteenth-century blood-and-soil chauvinism to post-nationalist rule of law offers a rare opportunity.

Notes

1 For the best single account of the international negotiations leading up to Kosovo's declaration of independence on 17 February 2008, see Marc Weller, *Negotiating the Final Status of Kosovo*, Chaillot Paper no. 114 (Paris: European Institute for Security Studies, 2008), http://www.iss.europa.eu/uploads/media/cp114.pdf.

2 Public statements by Vejvoda and author's interviews with him, including at the Bosch Foundation, Berlin, 2 June 2008.

3 This reading of the dynamics of the wars of Yugoslav succession in the 1990s is based on the legal truth established in convictions at the International Criminal Tribunal for the Former Yugoslavia at The Hague. For a narrative presentation of the court's premises, see James Gow, *The Serbian Project and Its Adversaries* (London: Hurst, 2003).

4 See *ibid.* and Independent International Commission on Kosovo, *Kosovo Report* (Oxford: Oxford University Press, 2000), p. 304.

5 Author's interviews with European diplomats in Serbia and EU member states.

6 'Serbiens neue Regierung als Bündnis auf Zeit', Deutsche Welle, 10 July 2008, available at http://www.dw-world.de/.

7 Dejan Anastasijevic, 'What's Wrong with Serbia?', European Stability Initiative, 21 May 2008, http://www.esiweb.org/pdf/dejan_anastasijevic-what-is-wrong-with-serbia_april-2008.pdf.

8 Nenad Pejic, 'Serbia's Second Chance To Embrace The West', RFE, 30 July 2008, available at http://www.rferl.org/.

9 'Poll: 61% Support EU Entry', B92 Radio/TV, 4 September 2008; available at http://www.b92.net/eng/.

10 'Poll: DS leading with 40 percent', B92, citing *Vecernje novosti*, 6 November 2008. The Strategic Marketing poll gave the Progressives 20%, the Radicals only 10%.

11 Interview with author.

12 'Dinkic Warns of "Crisis of Authority" in Government', B92, 26 December 2008.

13 'Ruling Socialists Turn against Vojvodina Statute', B92, 7 February 2009.

14 Daniel Williams and Rade Maroevic, 'Serbs Admit that Officials Aided War Crimes Fugitive', *Washington Post*, 28 March 2006, p. A20; 'Ljajić Dismisses Mladić speculation', B92, 19 January 2009.

15 Author interviews with KFOR and diplomatic sources.

16 For what is still one of the best thumbnail descriptions of the evolution of UDBA operatives into undisciplined paramilitary and criminal gangs, see Center for the Study of Democracy, *Partners in Crime: The Risk of Symbiosis between the Security Sector and Organized Crime in Southeast Europe* (Sofia: CSD, 2004), available at www.csd.bg. On ordinary police, the Belgrade daily *Borba* warns that the police chief and some 700 staff members in the Interior Ministry continue to be holdovers loyal to the old DSS interior minister. 'DSS Still Running Interior Ministry', B92, 18 February 2009.

17 For a brief description of the Security and Information Agency (BIA), see Aleksandar Vasovic, 'Serbia's Secret Service Comes out of the Shadows', BIRN, 31 July 2008, http://balkaninsight.com/en/main/analysis/12189/.

18 'Jeremić: Serbia to Battle on Two Fronts', B92, 4 January 2009.

19 Javier Solana, 'Five Lessons in Global Diplomacy', *Financial Times*, 21 January 2009, p. 11.

20 'EP to Adopt Kosovo Resolution on Thursday', B92, 4 February 2009.

The Political Consequences of Climate Change

Paul F. Herman Jr and Gregory F. Treverton

The conventional wisdom on climate change and security affairs features resource wars, weak states toppling, and trickles of immigrants turning into torrents. Over the medium term, however, climate change is not likely to involve simple causality and a stark, one-to-one correspondence. Climate impacts may be all but imperceptible for states already beset with acute ongoing problems, such as Afghanistan, North Korea and Zimbabwe. And they may be surprisingly tolerable for long-arid states, such as Saudi Arabia and Iran, whose entire histories have involved adjusting to inhospitable climates.

For most states climate change tends to be under the radar, intersecting with and exacerbating existing difficulties such as economic weakness, infrastructural shortcomings, communal strife, weak governance and tenuous political legitimacy, often with spillover effects beyond borders. Climate impacts are manifold, diffuse and of systemic consequence in the aggregate. Well-governed states may be better positioned to adapt than states in the developing world, but even the most privileged nations will not get off scot-free.[1]

There is increasing awareness and appreciation of direct climate changes in the form of mean surface temperature and patterns of precipitation as well as the secondary physical impacts on the earth's natural systems. But

Paul F. Herman Jr is Program Director, Transnational Issues, National Intelligence Council Long-Range Analysis Unit. The views expressed herein are his and not necessarily those of the NIC or the US government. **Gregory F. Treverton** is Director of the RAND Corporation's Center for Global Risk and Security. His most recent book is *Intelligence for an Era of Terror* (forthcoming).

 DOI 10.1080/00396330902860876

the more intangible third-order socio-political and institutional effects have not been fully appreciated.[2] It is only by adding in an accounting of these indirect effects, which bear on security, that a full evaluation of global climate change and appropriate responses can be made.

Physical changes, social responses

Rising temperatures and water anomalies, like droughts or floods, bear on the availability of natural resources such as pasture, agricultural produce and drinking water.[3] Relative scarcity can lead to either cooperation or competition among affected groups, but it is competition that drives the social effects of most concern. This competition, disruptive enough, occurs between urbanites and displaced rural dwellers moving to cities, as has been seen in many parts of the world, such as South Asia. When cities do not have the resources to accommodate new arrivals, many will aim to move on to more prosperous countries. This can lead to human tragedy for migrants stuck outside various cordons and fences, recriminations on sending countries for not securing their borders, and ugly nativist backlashes in destination countries.

Another fault line for competition among domestic groups involves distinct regional entities, such as Saharan–Maghrebi divides within North African countries. And competition takes place between clans and ethnic groups as well. Already-weak central governments will be strained by the loss of revenues, new welfare demands, and the upsetting of traditional political balances. Official responses to hard-hit areas are likely to be perceived as inadequate, sometimes stoking pre-existing feelings of marginalisation and discrimination. Central incapacity and local grievance may prompt insurrection in the underserved hinterlands in areas such as parts of the Near East. Conversely, autonomy movements in wealthier portions of beleaguered countries could arise, as may already be happening in some Andean countries. Poorer states further weakened by climate-induced stress will fare poorly keeping some order.

It is tempting to be complacent, if not dismissive, of the relatively modest climate-induced sea-level rise – measured in centimetres – expected in the coming decades. But small amounts can make a big difference. Computer modelling shows, for example, that an 18cm rise in sea level would claim 10% or more of the vast freshwater marsh in Florida's Everglades National Park.[4] Nor is saltwater contamination of freshwater resources simply a matter of rising seas crossing the beach and spilling into wells. It is rather a function of short-sighted drainage and pumping practices on shore combined with dense and increasingly heavy saltwater columns offshore. Saltwater intrusion from rising sea levels is already contaminating underground water sources in Israel, Thailand, small island states in the Pacific, Indian Ocean and Caribbean, and in some of the world's most productive river deltas, such as the Yangtze and Mekong.[5] Moreover, even small rises in sea level cause the interface between salt water and fresh water at river mouths to move inland.[6] Perhaps the most damaging effect of that movement is the die-off of freshwater vegetation which would otherwise serve to clean and oxygenate the river, as well as form a buffer against storm surges and flooding.

Perceptions of impending inundation will probably do more to trigger human actions than actual sea-level rises. In an era of global, accessible communications, reports of scientific results – frequently garbled or out of context – can quickly animate individuals or groups. People may move before they get permanently wet, taking major storms as foreshadowing of the worst. With nine of the 38 countries in the world with more than a tenth of their populations living less than a metre above sea level in the Caribbean, for example, contingency planning in Washington will be necessary well before the metre mark is reached.[7] Changes in extreme weather events, too, are among the most serious challenges to societies in coping with a changing climate.[8] Both the United States and China suffered unusually heavy weather-related damages during 2008.[9] By May the United States was on pace to experience the deadliest year of tornado activity ever, and much of the Midwest was under water.[10] China went through a paralysing freeze, devastating earthquake and debilitating floods. While specific weather events, such as America's 2005 Hurricane Katrina or Myanmar's 2008 Cyclone Nargis, cannot be attributed to global warming, they are consistent with emerging scientific evidence. The burden endured around

People may move before they get permanently wet

the world in recent years may indicate what a future with more frequent and intense weather events could look like, all the more so as the value of national infrastructure damaged by intense weather continues to increase.

Extreme weather events tend to be thought of as civil disasters rather than national-security threats. Such events very rarely physically destroy a country's seat of power or economy, or trigger regime-threatening revolts.[11] But extreme weather events do exemplify the manifold, diffuse, and aggregate systemic nature of climate effects. The US floods of spring and summer 2008, for example, were not the root cause of global food insecurity, but they both symbolised and exacerbated the problem. By mid June grain prices and livestock futures reached or approached record levels, and parts of the swollen Mississippi River were closed to foodstuff-conveying barge traffic. The resulting food inflation affected not just US consumers but dozens of countries that import US grain.[12] National security is even more directly affected when enormous fires, such as those in Greece and Australia in the last several years, require mobilising the military.

Political impacts and institutional developments

Climate-change impacts, especially in the form of water availability, will colour relations among regions, states and institutions. China, for example, has large-scale plans to divert water from major southern rivers to its drier north. This, along with existing Chinese dams on the Mekong and declining water from lower snow and glacial melt, would diminish water that would otherwise flow down the Mekong River, vastly reducing its flow through Vietnam, and creating grave economic hardship for people in the Mekong Delta who rely on this resource for fishing and agriculture. It is hard to imagine Chinese–ASEAN amity under such circumstances, and easy to imagine conflict among downstream countries that fight each other because they cannot take on China. These tensions need to figure in any assessment of future East Asian institutional architectures and regional conflict-resolution mechanisms.

Another example, albeit of lower probability, would be a revived border dispute between Russia and China in the Far East. Climate change is projected to force more people in China than in any other country into a condition of water scarcity, while Russia is projected to have the most delivered from such scarcity.[13] Moreover, as the world's factory, and with a growing and acquisitive middle class, China's demand for raw materials and commodities is voracious. This could prompt Beijing in the decades ahead to press a claim to secure control of the Amur River and tributaries, as well as the rich natural-resource base north of the Amur in land once controlled by China.

Alternately, or perhaps in conjunction, Chinese labourers and traders might on their own move into an increasingly temperate, habitable and commercially active Russian Far East. Such a process could culminate in a situation that Moscow would perceive as intolerable, for a Chinese invasion of sorts already looms large in Russian imaginings.[14] Demographically, Russia's population in the Far East is dwindling, creating a perception in Moscow of both a tenuous Russian grasp on the territory, and a pull dynamic for enterprising or dissatisfied Chinese. At the same time, climate could provide one more reason for migration from the South Caucasus and Central Asia into Russia, pushing the country's politics in a rightward, xenophobic direction. Both processes – a direct state claim and an undirected immigration flow – could lead to a confrontational border clamp-down. This, in turn, would dampen prospects for Sino-Russian cooperation across the board, including their leadership condominium over Central Asia's strategically important Shanghai Co-operation Organisation.

Chinese labourers and traders might move into an increasingly temperate Russian Far East

Climate change is likely to also have an effect on the capabilities and range of activities of existing state actors and institutions. Western European states will need to spend considerable amounts in the coming decades on mitigating and adapting to climate change within their own countries, on recent European Union entrants to the east, around the Mediterranean basin, and globally through various funding mechanisms. So will other economically advanced states such as Japan, Australia and the United States. This new spending could come at the expense of traditional system-maintenance tasks, such as extending development assistance and countering nuclear-, biological- and chemical-weapons proliferation, money laundering, and trafficking of all sorts. If so, international priorities themselves could become more precarious. A real revival in nuclear power, driven in part by climate change, would reconfigure debates over nuclear proliferation.

Climate change is also likely to spur normative deterioration in certain national contexts. Where temperature rise and water scarcity causes a decline in subsistence agriculture, the result may be increased reliance on drug crops, which require less water and cultivation. And as agriculture suffers, the extraction of energy resources and other raw materials takes on increased importance. Such exploitation of resources, instead of more broad-based economic development, fosters corruption and internal conflict over who controls resource flows.

Long before the recent food riots in Haiti, Egypt and elsewhere it was becoming clear that the intersection of warming, water scarcity, high energy and petrochemical-fertiliser prices, and the switch from agricultural to biofuel crops were creating food insecurity. While traditional reliance on the power of the market would suggest that once the world's farmers get the right price signals, food-supply problems will right themselves, there may be ground for believing this is no longer the case, the recent drop in commodity prices notwithstanding. As Laurie Garrett points out,

> the crisis that is unfolding is a fundamental, structural change in the world food supply and agricultural production, clearly linked to rising energy costs, climate shifts, and the emerging Asian middle class. Unless the food crisis is addressed at that level, starvation and malnutrition will become enduring features of the global landscape, sparking instability and anxiety for decades to come.[15]

Food insecurity is increasing in a number of places already riven by civil conflict, such as Sudan, Afghanistan, Gaza and Somalia. With populations closer to the edge of starvation and demise, the utility of food as a domestic weapon rises. Relief supplies of food will be increasingly attacked, seized or destroyed. International institutions such as the United Nations and its

World Food Programme, already struggling for adequate resources, will have to retrench under dangerous conditions, raising further questions about the efficacy of such multilateral organisations and programmes. Over the long term, countries with hungry, malnourished, sick populations will be unable to build the human capital necessary to escape protracted destitution.

Another interstate dynamic triggered by climate change involves maritime boundaries. Rising sea levels threaten to swamp some low-lying islands which currently serve as baselines on which maritime borders are fixed.[16] There are, for example, more than 200 islets, rocks and reefs dotting the shallow banks of the South China Sea basin. While barely above, or even below, the high-tide mark at present, these define nations' exclusive economic zones (EEZs) and thus are important legally, politically, economically and strategically. Nearer the poles, especially in the Arctic, melting sea ice and emerging rock outcrops might prompt new territorial claims and extended EEZs. Ambiguous maritime boundaries and competing claims will become more contentious as off-shore resources become more valuable due to coastal erosion and loss, demographic pressure and resource overuse on land. And as sea temperatures change, fisheries too may change, and new tensions arise over fishing areas.

Climate negotiations and global order

Finally, climate change may also impel the creation of new international institutions, just as it is making clear that others are brittle and inflexible. Most obviously, a future multilateral arrangement to lower CO_2 emissions could involve an International Energy Agency-type organisation to monitor national commitments and perhaps censure those in gross non-compliance. The UN Framework Convention on Climate Change already is supported by a secretariat in Bonn that does some of this monitoring. Beyond that, some observers have concluded that greenhouse-gas mitigation will eventually involve global-scale geo-engineering, such as implanting reflective materials in the upper atmosphere.[17] States are unlikely to cede to other states a unilateral right to tamper with the atmosphere, so should mitigation efforts come to such extremes, trustworthy multilateral regimes would be necessary.

In the nearer term, there are great hopes, especially in Europe, that a multilateral agreement to put the brakes on CO_2 emissions will be completed by the end of this year to supersede the 1997 Kyoto Protocol, which expires in 2012. Some observers argue that the United States occupies a favourable pragmatic or centrist position between climate purists, typified by many states in Western Europe, and a heterogeneous group of developing countries that are wary of taking on binding commitments lest they turn out to reflect economic competition masquerading as environmental pretence. If the United States were arbitrating between the most developed and developing states this centrist position would indeed be a fulcrum.

Yet the US position could turn out to be a double bind instead. What the most developed states want from Washington, substantial cuts in national emission levels, is also what the developing world wants. And what the developing world also wants, liberal financial assistance and technology transfer, most developed countries would also like to see offered. The risk is that if Washington is not seen to take on a serious emissions-reduction target (for example moving briskly to a peak in annual emissions) and to make generous financial and technological transfers, its reputation or soft power could be doubly damaged. This would make it harder for the United States to elicit strenuous efforts from other governments on issues that are salient to Washington, such as the 'war on terror' and counter-proliferation.

> *Climate change's aggregate impact could act as a drag on globalising processes*

How major countries react, respond or adapt to climate change holds implications for the globalisation process itself. Robust new habits and mechanisms for multilateral cooperation could help to reinforce global interaction. On the other hand, while climate change is not the main culprit, its aggregate impact is probably sufficient to act as a drag on globalising processes. Increased numbers of refugees, driven partly by climate, will probably lead to new controls on the movement of people. Shifting disease patterns will add to anxiety about public health and fuel prejudices about the dangers of foreigners. Circumpolar nations may appear to seek to arrogate to themselves new navigational and resource advantages in the Arctic (to the pique of those disadvantaged by geography).

The prevailing economic orthodoxy in the developed world on privatising utilities such as water may come under greater question, especially in vulnerable and traditional societies. And any resort to carbon tariffs by states with significant greenhouse-gas reduction commitments against those without would probably be followed by cycles of economic retaliation. States are likely to respect an international status quo under conditions of an expanding global economy, yet resort to narrow revisionist aims when expansion falters, as it has so drastically in 2008–09.

Assessing climate change and the way ahead

For security analysts as well as for scientists, climate change is an insidiously multifaceted problem. Climate 'winners', like Russia, may turn out to be political losers; witness the interplay of Russia with China. Worse, climate change is both devilishly uncertain and very long term. The political challenge of marshalling interest in a multi-decadal challenge in the teeth of the current and unfolding international economic crisis is daunting. That crisis makes it all the harder to demonstrate and communicate persuasively that a forward-looking pursuit of green technology and infrastructure creates jobs and could be a win–win strategy. Still, not moving now in response only allows eventual effects to be worse. Indeed, if climate scientists are gathered in a back room and asked what needs to be done, they respond 'everything, all the time'.

Yet the scale and scope of remedial actions needs to be commensurate with the problem – which the science has yet to convincingly measure. Years ago, at the very beginning of concern over climate change, a mentor of one of us, Nobel-Prize-winning economist (and strategist) Thomas Schelling, observed that he experienced more climate change commuting from Boston to Washington than the United States would experience in many decades. Both analytically and politically, one place to start is by disentangling the often confused debate about mitigation versus adaptation. So far, much of the discussion has focused on mitigation: how might the world slow, then turn around, the accumulation of greenhouse gases. Yet, even mitigation strategies well beyond ones that can be imagined now would still leave the world warming for decades. As a result, thinking about the security implications of global warming means thinking about how groups, nations and institutions adapt to what will in any case be the fact of climate change.

Hence, even if Schelling is right (and disagreeing with Schelling is always perilous) it is the cumulative, systemic consequences over time that matter. Climate change affects the biosphere which sustains all human endeavour. A single, simple policy line – branding a group 'terrorist', recognising a secessionist province as independent – is not enough. Rather, the climate dimension needs to be integral to all policy considerations from foreign aid, nation building and border controls, to food and energy security, technology transfer and trade policy, international law, and multilateral diplomacy. Not to recognise the climate angle behind a range of critical issues in security policy will put prospective policy actions at risk of failure.

Acknowledgements

The authors express their appreciation to Geoffrey Dabelko, Joshua Busby and General Richard Engel for their helpful comments on this article. Of course, any remaining errors are the fault of the authors alone.

Notes

1 The last two years seem to have witnessed a harmonic convergence of thoughtful analysts staking out climate change as a national-security issue. In April 2007 CNA Corporation released a high-visibility study on *National Security and the Threat of Climate Change.* November 2007 saw publication of both CSIS/CNAS's *The Age of Consequences* and the Council on Foreign Relations' *Climate Change and National Security.* Open sources have reported that the United States Intelligence Community has also plumbed this environment–security connection, recently conducting a large assessment of the national-security implications of climate change. 'National Security Analyst Appraises Risks of Climate Change', *University of Delaware Daily*, 16 May 2008; 'New Intelligence Assessment Sizes Up National Security Implications of Climate Change', *Inside Defense Newsstand*, 18 June 2008; House Permanent Select Committee on Intelligence/Select Committee on Energy Independence and Global Warming, Open Joint Hearing, 25 June 2008. These efforts, and others, were

under-girded by the release of the Intergovernmental Panel on Climate Change's authoritative three-volume Fourth Assessment Report *Climate Change 2007* (Cambridge: Cambridge University Press, 2007).

2 For one provocative analysis of political and social impacts, see Nils Gilman, Peter Schwartz and Doug Randall, *Impacts of Climate Change: A System Vulnerability Approach to Consider the Potential Impacts to 2050 of a Mid-Upper Greenhouse Gas Emissions Scenario* (San Francisco, CA: Global Business Network, March 2007), available at http://www.gbn.com/ArticleDisplayServlet.srv?aid=39932.

3 Intergovernmental Panel on Climate Change, *Climate Change 2007: Impacts, Adaptation and Vulnerability*, Fourth Assessment Report, Working Group II (Cambridge: Cambridge University Press, 2007), Summary for Policymakers, pp. 11–12.

4 Testimony, Dan Kimball, House Appropriations Committee, Washington DC, 26 April 2007.

5 IPCC, *Climate Change 2007: Impacts, Adaptation and Vulnerability*, p. 331.

6 As is already happening in the St John's River in Jacksonville, Florida, hometown of one of the authors.

7 *Assessment of Climate Change Impacts on Select U.S. Security Interests, Module 2: Country-Level Exposure to Potential Sea-Level Rise*, Report Prepared by Center for International Earth Science Information Network (CIESIN), Columbia University for the National Intelligence Council, 19 October 2007. Data available at http://sedac.ciesin.columbia.edu/gpw/lecz.jsp.

8 Thomas R. Karl et al., eds, *Weather and Climate Extremes in a Changing Climate. Regions of Focus: North America, Hawaii, Caribbean, and U.S. Pacific Islands*, U.S. Climate Change Science Program and Subcommittee on Global Change Research, Synthesis and Assessment Product 3.3, June 2008.

9 Not discussed here is the impact of warming on drying ground cover and lengthening fire seasons, a problem to which Californians and Australians can attest.

10 'U.S. 2008 Tornado Death Toll 58% Above Average', *Daily Green*, 5 May 2008.

11 For an excellent delineation of climate change as a security issue, see Joshua Busby, 'Who Cares about the Weather? Climate Change and National Security', *Security Studies*, vol. 17, no. 3, July 2008, pp. 468–504.

12 'U.S. Midwest Farmland Flooding Boosts Food Prices', Reuters, 18 June 2008.

13 CIESIN, *Assessment of Climate Change Impacts on Select U.S. Security Interests, Module 3: Water Scarcity*, 20 November 2007, www.ciesin.columbia.edu/documents/Climate_Security_CIESIN_July_2008_v1_0.ed70208.pdf.

14 See, for example, Aleksandr Khramchikhin, 'The Chinese Bicycle', *Novy Mir*, 15 March 2008.

15 Laurie Garrett, 'Food Failures and Futures', Council on Foreign Relations, 15 May 2008.

16 Idea conveyed by Michael Malley, Department of National Security Affairs, Naval Postgraduate School.

17 Fred Iklé and Lowell Wood, 'Climatic Engineering', *National Interest*, no. 93, January–February 2008, pp. 18–24.

The Rise and Fall of Resource Nationalism

Ian Bremmer and Robert Johnston

Resource nationalism has been a catalyst for the rapid rise of prices for oil and other commodities over the last five years. It encompasses efforts by resource-rich nations to shift political and economic control of their energy and mining sectors from foreign and private interests to domestic and state-controlled companies. High-profile cases such as the quasi-nationalisation of heavy-oil assets in Venezuela and the re-consolidation of the Russian oil sector under giant state-owned energy firms have created upheaval for foreign investors. Moreover, these cases have elevated the importance of energy security in policy discourse in the major energy-consuming states, while embedding in oil markets a deep sense of pessimism about prospects for future supply growth.

With sharply falling prices for oil and other commodities over the second half of 2008, the geostrategic and industrial implications of resource nationalism are rapidly changing. In geostrategic terms, several regimes that have pursued externally oriented resource-nationalistic policies – sometimes described as use of the 'energy weapon' – will have to revisit these policies. The most prominent examples are Russia and Venezuela. With the global economy slowing and commodity demand falling, a sustained period of weaker prices will shift the advantage back to international companies and

---

Ian Bremmer is President of Eurasia Group, the world's leading global political risk advisory and consulting firm. He is author of *The J Curve: A New Way to Understand Why Nations Rise and Fall* and, with coauthor and colleague Preston Keat, of *The Fat Tail: The Power of Political Knowledge for Strategic Investing* (2009). **Robert Johnston** is the Director of Eurasia Group's Global Energy & Natural Resources practice. He specialises in oil, gas, power generation, metals and agriculture research as well as client relations. He received his PhD in international relations from American University in Washington DC.

Survival | vol. 51 no. 2 | April–May 2009 | pp. 149–158 DOI 10.1080/00396330902860884

away from host governments, as international companies can now afford to be more selective about the fiscal terms and regulatory conditions they are willing to accept from host governments. Evidence of this is already clear for producers of base metals and natural gas, and higher-cost oil producers are beginning to feel the effects as well. The rapid shift of leverage from producer states to international companies will likely have destabilising effects on a number of regions, particularly sub-Saharan Africa, Central Asia and the Andes.

Beyond the headlines

Resource nationalism has been a mainstay of commodity-market headlines, but with little nuance. There are, in fact, at least four variants which differ in the factors motivating the policy and impact on industry and investment patterns.

The highest-profile, and most notorious, cases of resource nationalism in the current commodity-market cycle (2002 to the present) are Russia and Venezuela. Both exemplify revolutionary resource nationalism, which is linked to broader political and social upheaval, not merely directed at the natural-resource sector. In Russia, this encompasses the broader reconsolidation of state power under the Putin presidency beginning in 2000 and the larger rollback of privatisation in strategic sectors. In Venezuela, oil-resource nationalism was an important feature of the 'Bolivarian Revolution' in which political and economic power was transferred under the Chávez presidency from the technocratic business class (symbolised by the managment of state-run energy giant Petróleos de Venezuela (PDVSA) under former CEO Luis Giusti).

A second feature of revolutionary resource nationalism is its dangerous effect on international resource companies. Ownership of prized assets may be wrenched away through forced renegotiation of existing contracts, using perceived historical injustice or alleged environmental or contractual misdeeds by the companies as justification. These actions tend to be top-down, arbitrary and accompanied by little if any compensation or recourse.

Revolutionary resource nationalism is much less frequent than economic resource nationalism, which often takes place in relatively stable political environments, where turnover in elected governments or unelected power elites is not a necessary precondition. Economic resource nationalism tends to involve rebalancing, a focus on shifting a larger share of commodity revenues from international to domestic hands. Actual political control and ownership of the projects may be less significant than increasing the host government's fiscal take. A good example is Kazakhstan, where the government of President Nursultan Nazarbayev is widely perceived to have used environmental policy and project-development problems as a basis for negotiating a larger share in the super-giant Kashagan project for the state oil company KMG. While the renegotiations led to a larger stake for KMG and a greater fiscal take for the government, control of the Kashagan consortium remains in the hands of international companies. Similarly, in Algeria the Abdelaziz Bouteflika government successfully imposed a new windfall-profits tax on the upstream oil sector in 2005 without demanding control of projects run by Anadarko, Repsol and others. In Mongolia, the government has led a strong push to increase state ownership of the massive Oyu Tolgoi copper project to 34%, but has not insisted on majority control. Like many other frontier-market states – countries that are in the initial stages of new natural-resource exploration and industry development – Mongolia recognises that its rebalancing efforts in rewriting contracts and legislation governing natural resources cannot be so punitive that international companies exit the country. Without the deep pockets and technology of the mining multinationals, the Oyu Tolgoi riches would likely remain in the ground.

Mexican public opposition to allowing foreign ownership of hydrocarbons runs deep

A third mode of resource nationalism is legacy resource nationalism, as practiced in Kuwait and Mexico. Nationalisation of oil assets (Mexico in the 1930s, Kuwait in the 1960s) is central to national political and cultural identity in both countries. In Mexico, public opposition to allowing foreign ownership of hydrocarbons runs deep; even the tepid initial steps toward reform under the government of President Felipe Calderón met with massive public protest. In Kuwait, the royal family has been unable to overcome intractable opposition from the national parliament to international investment in the 'Project Kuwait' plans to develop the country's geologically complex but vast northern oil fields. Legacy resource nationalism may well be the most ingrained variant, with the most durable impact on industry and oil prices.

Finally, resource nationalism is not exclusive to frontier- and emerging-market countries. It is rampant in OECD countries such as Canada and Britain, and is emerging in the United States and Australia. In general, resource nationalism in the OECD countries (and Brazil) can be characterised as soft resource nationalism. OECD countries have the same motivations as those pursuing economic resource nationalism, but generally avoid tearing up existing contracts and using arbitrary tactics. Rather, these countries have generally imposed royalty increases or tax changes through established regulatory or legislative channels, rather than in arbitrary action. But there are exceptions, particularly in the Canadian cases, where 'forced renegotiation' without independent regulatory or legislative review has taken place. But because there are no state-owned national oil companies in these countries, resource nationalism is narrowly confined to fiscal measures, especially taxes and royalties, which benefit the state as a whole but not a government-owned competitor. This is not always the case; Canada and Australia are clear reminders that resource nationalism can be led by provincial and state, rather than national, governments. The 2007 royalty review in Alberta was an effort to rebalance oil-sands windfalls from the private sector to the province. Newfoundland pursued a similar tack with deepwater oil projects. Both cases involved effectively forcing renegotiations on existing contracts.

The other side of the coin

In its most virulently populist form, resource nationalism can pose political risks for governments that pursue it. It can deprive them of the foreign technology and expertise they need to expand, or even sustain, the output and revenue streams they need for long-term survival. So long as prices remain high, governments can extend international influence and sustain popularity at home. But if and when prices begin to fall and the cash cow begins to lose weight, resource-drunk politicians may face, or produce, serious local and regional instability.

Venezuela, for example, is thought to control some 270 billion barrels in conventional and non-conventional oil reserves, the deepest supply in the world. With prices hovering near or above $100 per barrel and PDVSA reaping most of the profits, President Hugo Chávez appeared to have all the cash he needed to spend his way toward greater popularity and to extend his influence abroad. Yet, his government and PDVSA have become international symbols of the economic decay wrought by the impact of populist politics on resource management.

In the mid 1990s, before Chávez's climb to power, PDVSA's leadership believed that joint development projects with foreign firms could increase production to 6.5 million barrels per day (b/d). In 1998, Venezuela produced about 2.9m b/d. But output has since fallen to about 2.35m, for two main reasons. First, during a 2003 power struggle with Chávez and his government, PDVSA's workers went on strike. The president responded by sacking some 18,000, including the vast majority of the company's best-trained and most experienced engineers. Five years later, the company has still not recovered from the loss of so much valuable human capital. Secondly, Chávez's government has pocketed much of PDVSA's profits, bleeding the company of the money it needs to maintain deteriorating infrastructure, buy new equipment and invest in bringing new crude supplies on line. In 2007, to buoy his domestic popularity, Chávez spent $14.1bn on social transfers, more than three times the amount devoted to oil exploration and the servicing of PDVSA's existing assets. Unaudited figures released by Venezuela's energy ministry suggested that the company's profits fell by about 32% in 2007 despite the surge in oil prices.

The rest of Venezuela's economy is already in rough shape. The most optimistic estimates put core inflation at 20%, and the real figure is probably closer to 30%. Foreign investment is severely limited by Chávez's habit of voiding contracts with international firms, creating shortages of a broad range of consumer goods. Venezuela is a net importer of virtually everything except oil and remains deeply dependent on its neighbours, including the United States, for goods and services vital to the country's economy.

Convinced that oil production will rise and that high prices are here to stay, Chávez has aggressively antagonised the United States, his best oil customer. He has awarded rights to future development deals in the country's oil-rich Orinoco belt to companies owned by friendly governments: CNPC (China), ONGC (India), Gazprom (Russia), Petrobras (Brazil) and NIOC (Iran). He has repeatedly threatened to divert oil exports now destined for the United States toward consumers in Asia.

But Venezuela needs access to US energy markets; crude-oil shipments to America represent more than half the country's total exports. Chávez cannot simply redirect that much oil toward China and India. Venezuela has no direct access to the Pacific Ocean. Its rusting tankers must pay transit fees to use the Panama Canal and take seven weeks to reach East Asia. More to the point, neither China nor India will have the capacity to refine that much of Venezuela's heavy crude oil any time soon.

What happens as oil prices fall? It will not take $40-per-barrel oil to drain Chávez's government of capital, leaving him at the mercy of a people who have come to expect cheap gasoline and generous federal spending on social projects. The consensus among market analysts is that sustained $60-per-barrel oil or lower (WTI) would create serious fiscal and currency headaches in Venezuela. And unless Chávez changes course, the danger point will rise. Meanwhile, PDVSA's inability to expand its output ensures that much of the oil from the world's deepest reserves will remain offline, even as demand for new supply rises across the developed world.

It will not take $40-per-barrel oil to drain Chávez's government of capital

Similar problems can be found in other energy-rich states. Following the chaotic privatisations of the 1990s, private companies owned a clear majority of Russia's energy reserves. Output growth was strong. Today, after concerted state efforts to reclaim the country's natural wealth, nearly half of Russia's oil and gas reserves are again under state control. Oil and gas revenues now account for more than 60% of Russia's GDP. Oil alone generates nearly 70% of state revenue. Russia's oil production reached a peak of 9.9m b/d in October 2007, but is expected to decline by as much as 4% in 2009. This decline would be the first year-on-year drop since 1998. State dependence on oil profits has not done much damage so far, but depleted Soviet-era fields in Western Siberia and a lack of infrastructure investment in new, previously undeveloped areas on the Arctic Shelf and in East Siberia suggest that the Russian fiscal picture will be under greater strain as production falls off.

Despite these worries and surging production costs, Moscow continues to impose punitive taxes on oil production, helping it finance a stabilisation fund and a sovereign wealth fund, but discouraging major oil company investments in new plant and equipment or exploration projects. And as Western firms like Shell, TNK-BP and Exxon find themselves at the mercy of political machinations in Moscow, Russia risks losing access to the foreign technology and expertise it will need to access the hard-to-reach petroleum deposits that could reverse the country's declining output.

The end of resource nationalism?

If most resource nationalism is economic rather than revolutionary, the long-term impact of resource nationalistic policies on commodity prices may be less severe than generally assumed. Economic resource nationalism tends to delay projects rather than force their cancellation. Moreover, most modes of resource nationalism are sensitive to commodity prices. The general rule is that when commodity prices are high, resource-rich nations have greater leverage, yet the moment of leverage can be fleeting. The resource nationalism of the OPEC countries in the 1970s triggered a massive shift in exploration and production to areas such as the North Sea and Alaska. The current wave of resource nationalism is empowered by the relative absence of similar oil prospects available at a comparable cost, but this dynamic is limited to oil. While peak-oil worries are driving growing industry willingness to accept tougher terms from host governments, the same cannot be said for copper, uranium, natural gas or gold.

This dynamic impacts resource-nationalistic governments in two ways. First, efforts to impose resource nationalism in sectors such as natural gas (Bolivia) or copper (Zambia, Democratic Republic of the Congo) will be undermined should the ongoing global financial crisis continue to put downward pressure on commodity prices. Natural-gas developers and mining companies will have greater resistance to resource nationalism because of the relative abundance of prospects in other markets. Mining companies may even elect to pre-emptively defer or cancel projects to wait for prices to recover. Producers could also elect to substitute aluminium for tin or coal for natural gas if resource security becomes an issue.

Secondly, even with peak-oil worries, the oil-rich states are not entirely immune to demand destruction or substitution. While alternative conventional resources are not as easy to find as they were in the 1970s, industry does have options in terms of unconventional oil (most notably from Canadian oil sands) and of alternative fuels ranging from biofuels to coal-to-liquids. While developing scale is a challenge for all alternative fuels, when confronted with resource nationalism, consumer governments have strong incentives to develop their own resources (for example the US outer continental shelf, Chinese coal) and to lower the energy intensity of their economies through greater efficiency standards for automobiles, power plants and buildings. These energy-security dynamics overlap with efforts to lower greenhouse-gas emissions.

Oil-rich states that have effectively squandered the recent windfalls – most notably Venezuela – may find it difficult to sustain resource-nationalistic policies even in the event of a moderate oil-price correction, where prices stabilise in the still historically high range of $70–80 a barrel. Venezuela has its 2008 government budget set at $35 a barrel, but is believed to be spending at a rate of $75 a barrel. Both Venezuela and Russia have failed to materially reinvest the recent windfall in new upstream projects, though Russia at least has been more fiscally responsible in building up a large foreign-exchange and fiscal surplus.

* * *

Frontier-market governments looking to conduct resource-nationalistic experiments on the back of abundant metals or natural-gas resources will likely see their hopes dashed. Within the oil sector, resource nationalism will be most persistent in states that have maintained strong leverage relative to the international oil companies through investments in the operating capacity of their own national oil companies and broader efforts to diversify their economies to limit the extent of exposure to lower oil prices. Saudi Arabia probably best fits this category. Along with Libya and Algeria, Saudi Arabia will also benefit from additional leverage gained from low production costs. This means that international oil companies will continue to pursue limited investment opportunities under tough fiscal terms.

In several frontier markets, the sharp reversal of commodity prices and dashed expectations for a natural-resource-led economic boom could add to geopolitical instability. In Bolivia, for example, the Morales government depends on mining and gas revenue to fund politically important electrification programmes. In the Democratic Republic of the Congo, a fall-off in expected mining investment could add an element of economic volatility to a country already beset by a severe humanitarian crisis in its Eastern regions. The copper-rich southern provinces could be less able to prevent similar problems from emerging closer to home. In Kyrgyzstan, a gas-exploration boom and high gold prices have helped sustain the 'Tulip Revolution' of 2005, although the country remains beset by corruption and remains a difficult operating environment for business. In other words, natural resources play an outsized role in the economies and politics of these frontier markets. If failed experiments in resource nationalism result in lost investment as global commodity prices fall and multinational energy and mining firms look elsewhere, the countries themselves could be in for a spike in political turmoil.

A better understanding of the complexities of resource nationalism suggests that its significance may be both more fleeting – or at least cyclical – and narrow than is generally believed. In the context of international politics, worries over security of demand for resource-rich nations may prove no less important than security of supply for the major energy- and commodity-consuming states. As commodity prices spiked between 2003 and mid 2008, countries such as Russia, Iran and Venezuela amassed substantial reserves of hard currency. They then used these reserves to spend lavishly on projects meant to bolster their political popularity. But as a range of factors depress prices for energy and other commodities, these governments face domestic economic and political problems for which they are not prepared. Rich-world states, which have grown to accept these countries' new strength, may again find themselves managing the fallout that comes with their weakness – and a slowdown in supply growth over the next several years.

'Underkill': Fighting Extremists amid Populations

David C. Gompert

The storming of Falluja, Iraq, by US Marines in April 2004 and the attack on Gaza by the Israel Defense Forces in January 2008 are defining battles of this young century. Enemy fighters hid in dense populations and challenged US or Israeli forces to attack. In both cases, a thousand or so innocent civilians were slain or wounded, with serious political effects. The threat of Sunni leaders to leave the Iraqi Governing Council was enough to induce Washington to halt the assault on Falluja.[1] Israel was widely denounced for the carnage in Gaza even though Hamas had blatantly provoked attack by launching rockets against Israeli towns, and then ducked behind the very Palestinian people who counted on it for security. In both cases, superb armies with precision weapons relied more or less entirely, for lack of better alternatives, on the use of deadly force against extremists who, dressed like everyone else, hid in tenements, mosques and hospitals.[2]

We have had a glimpse of 'war amongst the people', in Rupert Smith's arresting words, and it isn't pretty, visually or strategically.[3] Burrowing into the population and luring attack is becoming a favoured enemy strategy. Extremists are using populations both for cover and for painting intervening forces as aggressors, a two-for-one trick they learn from each other. This is not mere asymmetric warfare, but warfare turned on its head. The inferior force can survive to fight again only by melting into the population it pretends to defend, yet it can win by inducing the superior force to harm that

David C. Gompert is Senior Fellow at the RAND Corporation. He has been Senior Advisor for National Security and Defense in the CPA-Iraq, Vice President for RAND's National Security Research Division, a senior official at the US National Security Council and State Department, and a corporate executive in the information industry.

Survival | vol. 51 no. 2 | April–May 2009 | pp. 159–174 DOI 10.1080/00396330902860892

population. The extremists' real purpose in hiding among civilians is not to deter enemy attack but to ensure that enemy attack kills and maims civilians. The population is not just a medium for tactical defence but a means of strategic offense.

The rise of global media is indispensable in the conception and execution of this strategy. Hostile propagandists have a field day when US, Israeli or NATO soldiers kill or hurt innocent people.[4] The gunman in the school window is less interested in stopping approaching troops than in getting them to kill schoolchildren. The real target of the shooter in the minaret is the billion Muslims worldwide who may be outraged by footage of worshippers bloodied by infidels. Yet, to treat this as an information-operations challenge is to misinterpret and underestimate it. The West's disadvantage is not one of propaganda but one of strategy and, for all the firepower of its forces, one of capabilities. Lacking good alternatives to deadly force, US and allied forces are hamstrung in carrying out their missions and larger purposes in the face of this strategy. Progress in Iraq shows that US forces are getting better at counter-insurgency and other types of irregular operations. But they lack adequate options to act forcefully against insurgents in urban areas without risking death or serious harm to ordinary people.

In counter-insurgency, the population is not only the field of battle but also the prize. Success depends on earning the acceptance and, better yet, active cooperation of the people. Conversely, the security of the people is among the chief duties of intervening or occupying forces. This suggests the need for a compact between forces and population, not unlike that of successful law enforcement. Just because Falluja's jihadis, Gaza's rocketeers, and the extremists of battles to come invite deadly attack on contested populations does not mean the invitation should be accepted. Expressions of regret cannot repair the political damage of harming people whom soldiers are supposed to protect. The attitude that civilian casualties in such circumstances are unfortunate but unavoidable is logically, ethically and politically indefensible. Making the safety of people among whom forces operate paramount will not put their missions at risk but instead will increase the chance of success due to the cooperation of the people.

Missions without martyrs

There is no escaping the fact that harming innocent civilians abroad can gravely damage US and allied interests. This is the crux of the dilemma facing US and allied forces when pitted against combatants hidden among civilians, in situations that occur not by happenstance but by enemy strategy. Resolving the dilemma demands that forces be able to prevail over enemy fighters without harming people of similar appearance around them. Only with the right capability is it possible to meet a high standard of regard for innocent lives abroad without jeopardising the missions or safety of troops.

The challenge of carrying out dangerous missions amid populations is not confined to counter-insurgency. The swelling of the world's cities and their attractiveness to bad actors, from extremists to extortionists, make this a general problem. Peacekeepers are often interposed between warring parties in population centres. Humanitarian-relief efforts can place soldiers into contact with desperate and unruly crowds. Intervention to halt genocide can be confounded by the mingling of predators and their prey. Quelling public disorder and rounding up looters, abroad or at home, may face troops with the need to curb violence without using violence. The need to free hostages, isolate terrorists and board pirated ships with captured passengers is increasing.

Such missions are no longer of secondary importance to militaries designed to wage conventional war against conventional armies. Taken together, they are of equivalent importance to conventional combat, and far more likely.[5] The incidence and significance of operations amid populations suggest a need for regular military forces to be able regularly to gain control of situations, perform their tasks and protect themselves without necessarily using deadly violence.

The US military, for example, could remedy a major shortcoming in counter-insurgency and other important non-traditional missions if it equipped its units with effective non-lethal options and the skills to use them. Such options would give regular small units more flexibility, self-sufficiency and speed. This translates not only into reduced risk of making politically consequential mistakes but also into better odds of achieving the mission at hand. In the words of a former deputy commandant of the US Marine Corps, non-lethal capabilities can 'fill a vulnerabilities gap, and, in so doing, allow American forces to effectively address a wider variety of situations and better control the escalation of violence in many situations. *Non-lethal capabilities make our forces more, not less, formidable.*'[6]

Non-lethal options have long been essential in police work, where ensuring public safety with minimum violence is stock-in-trade. The blurring of the line between law enforcement and military missions unsettles both policemen and soldiers, but it cannot be denied. While it is rare for police to find themselves in combat, it is increasingly common for the military to be called upon to operate in conditions and missions that resemble police challenges. For one thing, military forces may have to provide law, order and public safety in situations abroad because of the lack of adequate police.[7] Thus, the relevance to military operations of police doctrine regarding use of force lies less in the low likelihood that police will engage in combat than in the virtual certainty that military forces must conduct missions in which police standards and practices may apply.

Non-lethal options have long been essential in police work

While police departments lament the lack of good non-lethal capabilities, the military establishment seems untroubled. Such capabilities have been regarded by the military as having limited utility at most, and then only in rare circumstances.[8] This absence of interest is evidenced by the \$50 million, less than 0.01% of US defence funding, spent each year on development of non-lethal weapons by the Joint Non-lethal Weapons Directorate of the US Department of Defense.[9] This is hard to square with the lessons of Falluja and Gaza.

The very term 'non-lethal' is inadequate. Given the nature of the missions and duties of US forces, being able to disable persons without killing them is the wrong standard. Even short of lethality, violence against populations whose trust and cooperation US forces need to earn, and which are the key to success, may ruin the mission and set back an entire campaign. Pain, shock or injury may turn a crowd into a mob, a mob into a confrontation, or a confrontation into a cause célèbre that can fuel insurgency. The ability to calibrate non-lethal force, from none to mild to moderate to intense, can be as important as avoiding death. The need is for a continuum of force in which forces are as effective at the non-violent end as they are at the most violent.

The continuum of force

Such a continuum must enable forces to affect the behaviour of but not harm non-combatants, while gaining advantage over enemy combatants who are indistinguishable in appearance from those non-combatants. For example, the ability to make innocent persons and enemy fighters respond in noticeably different ways would permit more focused and forceful, and if need be lethal, action against the former while minimising harm to the latter. Likewise, the ability to disorient but not injure individuals of unclear identity and intent could take the initiative from enemy fighters without jeopardising the well-being, good will and subsequent cooperation of the larger population in which they have embedded themselves.

The continuum of force should be based as far as possible on a more-or-less standard set of capabilities available to regular small military units involved in counter-insurgency, peacekeeping, humanitarian intervention and other irregular operations amid populations. The US military as a rule does not rely on specialised forces for such missions but instead uses the same sorts of 'general purpose' forces for all. Moreover, regular troops operating amid populations often do not know each morning what kinds of predicaments and persons they will face in the hours to follow. On any given day, a US unit in Baghdad might face hostile fire from a housing complex, a hostage situation, an angry crowd, a sectarian confrontation, rumoured terrorists in a marketplace, or a checkpoint challenge. Such circumstances can develop suddenly, whether by enemy design or spontaneously. The need for capabilities ranging from non-violent to lethal force is common, varied and unpredictable; and the need for small units to act swiftly argues against having to call in specialised capabilities from higher echelons or central locations.

This places a premium on versatile and portable capabilities that can be carried and used by small units (companies, platoons, squads) operating in populations and faced with uncertainty. Additionally, these capabilities should be scalable from non-harmful to extreme or even lethal effects to enhance the ease and speed of escalation and de-escalation as a situation unfolds.[10] Continuum-of-force capabilities should also be affordable enough that most small units could be equipped. Finally, missions and conditions that give rise to the need for a continuum of force are not of the distant future but now. Therefore, all else being equal, technologies for the continuum of force should be feasible (at hand or only a few years off) and not dependent on speculative science.

An effective continuum of force will require that troops have an ability to gain information and time and to exploit both in adaptive decision-making despite uncertainty and urgency; performance standards and skills to escalate to gain advantage while managing risk; and readily calibrated effects from non-violence to lethality. These prerequisites can be met thanks to advances in information networking and adaptive decision-making;[11] germane experience with non-lethal force in law enforcement;[12] and progress in a wide assortment of potentially relevant technologies.

Specific capabilities should be based on operating requirements. These can be identified by examining a large, diverse and indicative set of realistic scenarios encompassing counter-insurgency, peacekeeping, humanitarian relief, civil order and other missions and conditions that small military units might face. From analysis of 24 such scenarios, common themes emerge:

- There is a prevalence of small-unit engagements and a corresponding need for junior officers and non-commissioned officers to be able to decide in dangerous and urgent circumstances what measures to take.
- Information about the identity, motivations and intentions of persons engaged is usually incomplete, ambiguous, confusing or deceptive.
- Physiological and psychological effects of non-lethal systems on individuals and groups are hard to predict.
- Seizing the initiative from and exerting control over enemy fighters amid innocent people is essential.

- It is critical, yet difficult, to communicate with groups, especially large groups, of persons engaged by friendly forces.
- There is a need for mild, even non-violent, initial effects in order to gain time, information, initiative and control, including the differentiation or separation of combatants from non-combatants.
- Scalable, versatile and portable capabilities are needed.[13]

These findings suggest that the problem of acting forcefully against adversaries amid populations is as much one of gaining and using knowledge as it is one of causing desired effects. Extremists in places like Falluja and Gaza know we have no shortage of firepower, so they exploit our deficiencies in information. If the US Marines and Israel Defense Forces knew well enough who and how capable their enemies were, their knowledge of the populations behind whom those enemies crouched was much less good – thus the civilian deaths. It follows that we need an integrated solution – part information, part judgement and part physical capability – missing so far in the narrow current approach to non-lethal options. The search to date has been flawed if not doomed by the failure to see that the problem is as much of cognition as of physics.

The problem is as much of cognition as of physics

Some options with regard to physical capability appear to be efficacious under some conditions but not generally. For example, a small unit patrolling neighbourhoods without knowing whether, when and what threats might appear cannot regularly bring along a heavy truck with a necessarily large microwave transmitter. Anti-electronics capabilities are of value when enemy fighters are in vehicles or otherwise relying on electronics, but only then. Electroshock Tasers are useful only at short range against small numbers of individuals, are not scalable and can cause pain.[14] Tear gas and other chemical agents may alienate otherwise cooperative persons and raise legal problems.[15] Rubber bullets produce pain if not injury and are not scalable. While these options may help in certain circumstances, the need is for options of such general utility across missions and conditions that ordinary small units can be trained and equipped to carry and use them routinely.

Sound and light

Although no single technology satisfies this general need, the options of greatest promise involve sound and light. The tight focusing of these forms of energy is not a theoretical gleam in the eye (or buzz in the ear) but an increasingly practical option.[16] Both can be effective in hailing, inhibiting, disorienting, disrupting or degrading key sensory faculties of dangerous persons at distances up to hundreds of metres, without necessarily causing lasting harm to them or to innocent persons. Both sound and light are inherently and more or less continuously scalable. Their effects can range from mild to severe, affording opportunities to observe and adjust weapons effects, up or down. As intensity is increased, enemy combatants and non-combatants may react differently, isolating the former and scattering the latter, thus reducing the number of potential targets against which to direct even harsher measures. Sound and light can be used against large or small groups, or individuals. Adding a range of lasers – from low-energy to high-energy to extremely short pulse – can make the effects even more pronounced.[17]

Directed sound and light, including lasers, are sufficiently portable, on small vehicles, that platoons or squads can carry them on most missions and on daily patrols. They do not involve physical projectiles, violent contact or inhalation, any of which may be counterproductive if used against people whose only mistake was to be in the wrong place at the wrong time.

As part of an integrated approach, directed sound and light capabilities can be complemented by innovative but readily available communications techniques. Provided friendly authorities have privileged access to mobile-phone switches, a unit commander could request instantaneous calling of all cell-phones in a given neighbourhood or congregated group of people.[18] This would permit transmission of simple text or audio messages to alert, warn, reassure or instruct. Even if only a fraction of those present receive the message, the rest would be promptly told its contents. The utility of adding this feature to a directed-energy suite of capabilities is apparent in many scenarios. The Israelis used a rudimentary version of such a capability (along with leaflets) to alert residents of Gaza by mobile-phone text message that they should stand clear of target areas.

In addition to a mobile-phone warning system, the continuum of force could usefully take advantage of portable video technology. Recordings from vehicle-, weapon- or fixed-mounted cameras could aid in learning lessons; adapting systems and tactics; refuting unfounded rumours and propaganda; and collecting intelligence about, for instance, dangerous persons. Beyond that, live video could help in managing escalation or de-escalation during operations. As with mobile-phone applications, practical video technology is developing rapidly thanks to market demands beyond the needs of a continuum of force.

Assessment of options cannot be technical alone. Military operations amidst populations are fraught with political risks, which enemies and unfriendly media organisations are poised to exploit. The potential for adverse reactions among the people affected or the wider, even global, population is a function of both the severity and the strangeness of a given capability. The unfamiliar may give rise to panic, rumour, superstition or disinformation. However painful, rubber bullets will at least not be blamed for later tumours, impotence, infertility or mental disorder. Intense sound and light, while uncomfortable, are less likely to cause adverse psychological and political reactions than chemicals or shocks. At the same time, the use of lasers might be misunderstood by those illuminated or misconstrued by propagandists.[19]

In the same vein, cell-phone messaging to alert and inform citizens regarding non-lethal force may also raise psychological and political questions. While citizens may appreciate being warned, instructed or reassured, they may at the same time react adversely to the perception that foreign forces or their own government are able to send them messages at will and, it might be inferred, access their phones and conversations. One way to win public acceptance is to give individuals a choice of whether or not to subscribe to a public-warning option upon acquiring a mobile phone or service. While some would decline, those who subscribe ought not be suspicious but rather reassured when they receive alert messages. In time, more people would likely sign up. Likewise, many people might not appreciate being observed by video cameras; the key to acceptance lies in a convincing argument on the security benefits.

Without such communication, even careful use of non-lethal force can go awry. It is imperative to communicate early, persistently and accurately the rationale and facts of all aspects of a continuum of force to people who may be affected. The unifying theme must be that military forces accept their duty to safeguard the people of countries where they operate and, accordingly, are depriving killers of the benefit of hiding among the people. Contested populations should be helped to understand that those who claim to be their champions are really using them as shields and, worse, want them to be killed or hurt, and that opposing forces are using non-violent means to frustrate this cynical strategy. If heard, this message could help turn populations against extremists, as well as turn the tables on the extremists' new strategy.

Making it happen

Any impression that the continuum of force is more relevant to Buck Rogers than to today's soldiers is mistaken. The suite of capabilities requires no technological heroics. Quite apart from military needs, acoustic, electromagnetic, mobile-phone and video technologies are progressing apace thanks to commercial markets, revenues, and research and development. For the most part, what is needed is not scientific discovery but creative application. Still, some aspects of the continuum of force do require development:

- very-high-intensity sound that is precise, scalable, effective at hundreds of metres, and can cause discomfort, disorientation or incapacitation;[20]
- very-short-pulse lasers;[21]
- software that permits selective and instantaneous mobile-phone messaging to users in a particular area;
- deployable links for real-time video; and
- improved portability of all elements of the suite, with a view toward fielding some or all with dismounted troops, thus improving versatility.

With an eye toward portability and ease of use, capabilities should be engineered as a system with, for example, common power, displays, controls and physical packaging.

A more serious potential problem than the feasibility of the individual pieces of a suite of capabilities is whether the integration of the components, including important information and communications features, is feasible in the near-to-mid term, especially when the need for sophisticated operators and nuanced doctrine is taken into account. But it is well within the capability of the military and its system providers to meet the challenge of integration. In any case, such a suite does not depend on, and should not await, every component. It can and should grow and evolve.

A suite of continuum-of-force capabilities would in its fullest form comprise directed sound, directed light, lasers, mobile-phone communication and video observation. As a whole, this suite is remarkable in its non-kinetic character; for the most part, it affects the senses and perceptions of persons engaged rather than destroying or degrading their physical condition.

The continuum of force demands abilities to sense and grasp a fluid situation

Ensuring that the suite of capabilities can be incorporated into and used effectively by regular small military units is as important as developing and integrating the technology. The continuum of force demands abilities to sense and grasp a fluid situation; to judge how to respond when the nature and intentions of the persons engaged are unclear; to understand and anticipate behaviour; to communicate; to escalate and de-escalate wisely and to be sensitive to wider repercussions of actions. To use the continuum of force to best effect, methods of adaptive decision-making under pressure are also necessary, the better to exploit information, manage escalation, avoid miscalculation and shape the behaviour of the persons on the receiving end.

It would be better to rely on well-trained, experienced, specialised teams within small units than to prepare, encumber, involve and control every member of a unit. The former approach would let the unit commander concentrate on the critical tasks of sensing, reasoning and adapting during an operation. Placing high-powered sound, light and laser capabilities in a single vehicle fits this approach. Finally, a smaller team would allow most members of the unit to be concerned only with the use of deadly force, thus lowering the risk that non-lethal options might impede lethal ones.

For such an approach, militaries will need to invest in the requisite human resources and abilities. This will require the training and education of junior and non-commissioned officers in continuous sense-making and decision-making when faced with uncertainty, urgency and risk – physical and political – amid populations.[22] It will also mean selecting and developing non-commissioned officers with the temperament and aptitude for technical and behavioural aspects of the continuum.

A related matter is the nature and content of instructions to be issued to such teams within units and their commanders. A notable advantage of relying on a few well-trained and seasoned non-commissioned officers is that they will not require detailed or rigid instructions. Given the uncertainty and fluidity of situations demanding a continuum of force, clear but flexible guidelines like those on which police rely are preferable to infallible manuals and elaborate checklists.

As the US military fashions a continuum of force, it should pursue international collaboration, not only with close US allies but also with the UN's peacekeeping department and with a wide circle of like-minded countries that face similar needs. There are few if any security risks associated with such collaboration, and it is in the US interest to foster widely the fielding of capabilities that can be effective against enemy fighters without harming civilians. The United States cannot afford to hoard the know-how.

* * *

A continuum of force for regular troops operating amid populations is needed and possible. Scalable, versatile and portable technologies such as directed sound and light are in train or within reach. But they do not provide a complete solution: the capability to prevail against dangerous enemies without harming innocent people and jeopardising larger campaign goals depends crucially on skill, sensitivity and preparation. In turn, creating, mainstreaming and institutionalising this capability will require vision, initiative, commitment and persistence on the part of the military's civilian and uniformed leaders.

Imagine if the US Marines assaulting Falluja had had the ability to disorient, degrade, isolate or otherwise neutralise the extremists with little or no harm to the population around them. Imagine if the Israel Defense Forces had ways to discriminate and isolate Hamas fighters from ordinary residents of Gaza. Imagine if jihadis and insurgents could not use innocent people as shields or induce deadly violence against them, but instead had to fight or flee. Added to the recent significant improvement in counter-insurgency by the US military, the continuum of force could help defeat those who would sacrifice their own people even as we would try to spare them.

Acknowledgements

This article is based on a newly released study by the RAND Corporation: *Underkill: Scalable Capabilities for Military Operations amid Populations* (2009). Authors: David C. Gompert, Stuart E. Johnson, Martin C. Libicki, David R. Frelinger, John Gordon IV, Raymond Smith and Camille Sawak.

Notes

1 Falluja was eventually secured by US Marines in November 2004 after the resident population had largely left.

2 US military doctrine and training for urban warfare was influenced by the Israeli military, including training for US troops at mock villages in Israel's Negev desert. Scott Peterson, 'Tough US Tactics Quell Fallujah Unrest, but at What Cost?', *Christian Science Monitor*, 20 April 2004, p. 5.

3 Rupert Smith, *The Utility of Force: The Art of War in the Modern World* (New York: Alfred A. Knopf, 2007).

4 See, for example, 'Civilian Deaths Mount in Gaza War', al-Jazeera, 6 January 2009, for a slanted and scathing, but not fabricated, account of Palestinian casualties at the hands of the Israel Defense Forces.

5 US Department of Defense Directive 3000.05, *Military Support for Stability, Security, Transition, and Reconstruction Operations*, 28 November 2005.

6 E.R. Bedard, *Nonlethal Capabilities: Realizing the Opportunities*, Defense Horizons No. 9 (Washington DC: National Defense University, Center for Technology and National Security Policy, 2002) (emphasis added).

7 According to UN officials, the number of professional police available, with some warning and preparation, to deploy into difficult situations worldwide is only 17,000 on paper and 12,000 in reality – a tiny fraction of the

potential requirement for international security forces. Unless indigenous police are of sufficient quality in sufficient numbers (often not the case) most of the total security requirement in conflict and post-conflict situations must be met by military forces, be they UN, US, NATO or other.

8 For an explanation of current US Defense Department policy on and commitment to non-lethal weapons, see Air Land Sea Application Center, *NLW Multi-service Tactics, Techniques, and Procedures for the Tactical Employment of Nonlethal Weapons*, October 2007, available at http://www.fas.org/irp/doddir/army/fm3-22-40.pdf.

9 This assessment is widely shared. See, for example, Council on Foreign Relations, *Non-lethal Weapons and Capabilities: Report of an Independent Task Force* (New York: Council on Foreign Relations, 2004); National Research Council of the National Academies, Committee for an Assessment of Non-Lethal Weapons Science and Technology, *An Assessment of Non-lethal Weapons Science and Technology* (Washington DC: National Academies Press, 2003); Paul K. Shupe, 'Nonlethal Force and Rules of Engagement', *Military Police*, April 2003; Jeffrey L. Underhill, *Are the Department of Defense Non-lethal Weapon Capabilities Adequate for the 21st Century?*, US Army War College Strategy Research Project (Carlisle Barracks, PA: US Army War College, 2006).

10 The particular advantages of scalable-effects capabilities have previously been identified in military literature; see, for example, Timothy J. Lamb, 'Army Nonlethal Weapons/Scalable-effects Program: A Think Piece', *Military Police*, April 2003.

11 For a treatment of how to meet the need for adaptive reasoning and decision-making under conditions of urgency and abundant information, see David C. Gompert, Irving Lachow and Justin Perkins, *Battlewise: Seeking Time-Information Superiority in Networked Warfare* (Washington DC: Center for Technology and National Security Policy, National Defense University Press, 2006).

12 *City of New York Police Department Police Student's Guide: Use of Force* (New York: NYPD, 2005).

13 David C. Gompert, Stuart E. Johnson, Martin C. Libicki, David R. Frelinger, John Gordon IV, Raymond Smith and Camille Sawak, *Underkill: Scalable Capabilities for Military Operations amid Populations* (Santa Monica, CA: RAND, 2009).

14 A useful rule of thumb for range is what is known as the 'rock-throwing rule'. Non-lethal weapons that lack the range of a thrown or slung rock – 100 metres – are severely limited in utility.

15 There is disagreement about whether the use of such agents would violate the Chemical Weapons Convention, which says that riot-control agents may not be used as a 'method of warfare' but does not define this phrase. The United States has long held that tear gas should be available for certain defensive purposes, such as when civilians are being used as a screen in an attack. Even this interpretation could limit the utility of tear gas in military operations.

16 Long-range acoustic devices are already being used by police and other security forces to hail, warn or both potential threats. Intense light and mild lasers are also being introduced, for example to illuminate situations or targets. For both, advances are needed to attain sharp focus at extended range.

17 It should be pointed out that a laser of sufficient power could cause eye damage or even blindness, which could violate international law. The Fourth Protocol to the 1998 Inhumane Weapons Convention bans the use of laser weapons specifically designed to cause permanent blindness; see Massimo Annati and Ezio Bonsignore, 'Non-lethal Weapons: Possibilities, Programmes, Perspectives and Problems', *Military Technology*, no. 27, July 2003, p. 49. This is unlikely to be an issue with low-power lasers. Because their pulse is so short, femtosecond lasers are not necessarily injurious. Nevertheless, the potential to cause blindness must be a consideration in the development and employment of high-power lasers.

18 Martin C. Libicki, David C. Gompert, David R. Frelinger and Raymond Smith, *Byting Back: Regaining Information Superiority Against 21st Century Insurgents*, RAND Counterinsurgency Study, vol. 1 (Santa Monica, CA: RAND, 2008).

19 These findings were in part the result of getting the reactions of experts on Arab and Muslim populations to aspects of a continuum of force. Roundtable Discussion on Continuum of Force, RAND Corporation, Washington DC, 11 September 2008.

20 One reason directed sound is not adequate to satisfy the continuum requirement is that it is effective in significantly altering hostile behaviour only if intensified to levels that can also permanently damage hearing. National Research Council of the National Academies, *An Assessment of Non-lethal Weapons Science and Technology*.

21 Because a laser is not simply a bright beam of light but a focused beam of coherent single-wavelength energy, scalability of light from bright light to laser is problematic if not infeasible.

22 Training and education are important not only for operating units and individuals but at all levels. Bedard (*Non-lethal Capabilities*) stresses the importance of such training in service and staff schools not only to improve effectiveness but also to gain acceptance of non-lethal capabilities throughout military leadership. This view is echoed in the Council on Foreign Relations report *Non-lethal Weapons and Capabilities*: 'there is a need to integrate information and training regarding non-lethal weapons into the curricula of schools at all levels in each service; this in turn would increase the rate of integration into current force capabilities'.

Review Essay

Pragmatism and Principle

Douglas Hurd

The Responsibility to Protect: Ending Mass Atrocity Crimes Once and For All
Gareth Evans. Washington DC: Brookings Institution Press, 2008. £16.99/$24.95. 366 pp.

The international community operates as best it can out of institutions devised in the aftermath of the Second World War. These institutions in their time provided an ingenious and sophisticated post-war settlement. They worked out the necessary compromises between rules and power; they built on the experiences and mistakes of the previous settlements of Vienna and Versailles. But our institutions are now showing their age. Few of them, however well devised for 1945–50, are fit for the purposes of 2009. They stand like palaces on a hill, still impressive to the distant observer, still active with innumerable meetings, but no longer proof against the weather. From time to time, as now with the financial institutions of Bretton Woods, an effort at reform is attempted. But in a world of 192 self-conscious nation-states the procedures for reform are extraordinarily cumbersome; progress has been slow, in most cases negligible. In the central sector which deals with war and peace it has so far proved impossible to reform the central institution, the UN Security Council. It can be argued that the single important achievement in this sector in recent years is the agreement on the Responsibility to Protect.

Douglas Hurd was UK Foreign Secretary from 1990 to 1995. He is writing with Edward Young a book about the character and policies of 11 British Foreign Secretaries, to be published by Orion.

DOI 10.1080/00396330902860900

The phrase in itself is opaque, presumably because a blunter definition might be divisive; but the purpose was defined clearly enough in the Outcome Document of the UN World Summit in September 2005. The heads of state and governments declared that 'each individual state has the responsibility to protect its population from genocide, war crimes, ethnic cleansing and crimes against humanity'. Should national authorities manifestly fail to provide this protection and peaceful means prove inadequate, then the heads of states and government 'are prepared to take collective action, in a timely and decisive manner, through the Security Council, in accordance with the Charter, including Chapter VII, on a case by case basis and in co-operation with regional organisations as appropriate'.

This did indeed constitute a step-change which would have been inconceivable when I worked as a junior diplomat in the UK Mission to the UN in the late 1950s. At that time power had already shifted within the General Assembly into the hands of the newly independent nations, who were fearful of attempts by former colonial powers or the two superpowers to interfere in the way they ran their affairs. For them the sacred text was Article 2(7) of the Charter, which forbids interference by the UN in the domestic affairs of member states. They were prepared to argue that apartheid in South Africa, continued British rule in Cyprus or French rule in Algeria fell outside this clause and were international issues. But these governments would have vehemently rejected any idea that Article 2(7) could be pushed on one side to permit international intervention to protect their peoples from the consequences of their rule, however disastrous these consequences might be thought to be.

No one is better suited than Gareth Evans to describe this revolution of opinion and trace its consequences. He was a member of the Canadian-inspired International Commission on Intervention and State Sovereignty which launched the process in 2001. He was a member of UN Secretary-General Kofi Annan's high-level panel which carried the idea forward. He combines a thorough grasp of the legal and philosophical background with his practical experience as foreign minister of Australia for eight years. In that post he impressed his fellow foreign ministers with clear thinking and notably blunt speech. Nowadays he expresses himself more mildly but with equal clarity. As president of the International Crisis Group he is well placed to follow episode by episode the conception and birth of the World Summit declaration just quoted.

No one will be surprised that Evans emerges as a passionate supporter of the Responsibility to Protect. It is to him axiomatic that nothing like the massacres in Rwanda in 1994 or at Srebrenica in 1995 should ever be allowed to happen again. There is no equivocation in his determination to prevent such horrors, but a certain defensiveness about the prospects. The reasons for this are clear. The chief threat to the Responsibility to Protect comes not from those like the Chinese who quietly in their hearts oppose it, but from politicians who invoke it rhetorically in and out of season. It is notable that Evans does not include then British Prime Minister Tony Blair among those whom he salutes as one of the authors of Responsibility to Protect. In Britain Blair's speech on the subject in Chicago in 1999 at the time of the Kosovo crisis is regarded as pathfinding; to Evans it is 'not much more than a hodge podge of sound bites' (p. 34). He is irked by the shallow way in which Blair and US President George W. Bush used the rhetoric of humanitarian intervention to justify the attack on Iraq in 2003 once their original argument about weapons of mass destruction fell to pieces. The British and American governments ignored what for Evans is a crucial test for the use of force, namely 'the balance of consequences'. Whatever the political future of Iraq the consequences of the Anglo-American attack could not justify the death of 150,000 Iraqis, the four million refugees, and the other negative results of their decision. One of these negative consequences has been the discrediting of the concept of humanitarian intervention, which had gained favour as a result of failure to check the disasters of Srebrenica and Rwanda, and retained that favour as a result of the successful interventions in Kosovo and Sierra Leone. The dangers of failing to balance the consequences of intervention are now burned into the consciousness of all governments. No one will put troops into Darfur or Zimbabwe or indeed reinforcements into Afghanistan without undertaking this balancing exercise.

Evans does not deny this setback, but seeks to envelop it in the wider story. For him 'humanitarian intervention' is a misleading phrase because it has come to be interpreted as meaning simply the use of military force. He sees the use of military force as a last resort, and not the heart of the Responsibility to Protect. Indeed a useful by-product of this book is his painstaking description of the peaceful techniques and assets of the United Nations together with the occasions on which they have been and are today successfully used.

Of course work to prevent a man-made disaster and work to rebuild a society stricken by such disasters can achieve more than missiles, bombs and bullets. As an example of prevention Evans cites the peaceful transition of Indonesia from military to democratic rule. As an example of successful intervention to check a growing disaster he cites Kofi Annan's negotiation of a deal between the warring parties in Kenya after the recent election. But by including these examples he stretches the concept of Responsibility to Protect very wide. The Indonesian transformation is essentially an internal achievement, and Annan would have acted in Kenya with or without the agreement on Responsibility to Protect.

Moreover, prevention is often easier to imagine with hindsight than to practise at the time. For example, it is easy to forget that until shortly before its disintegration Yugoslavia behaved and was generally regarded as a successful state with a prominent position in what was then called the Third World. Yugoslav governments were most unlikely to accept that they needed the kind of political help and tutelage which with the benefit of hindsight Evans prescribes for them. The same is true of the government of Pakistan today. In advance of trouble governments remain sovereign, and few governments despair of their own ability to solve their country's problems.

Unlike most of its proponents, Evans frankly faces some of the innate difficulties of Responsibility to Protect. For example, he acknowledges the occasional clash between peace and justice. Politicians and archbishops tend to use these terms interchangeably in their prayers and speeches. The clash may be a matter of timing. Anyone who has followed the peaceful transitions in South Africa and in Northern Ireland must acknowledge that at times the interest of peace rightly prevailed over the pressing of criminal charges. It was right to try Slobodan Milosevic at The Hague, but only when he was politically useless, that is after he had signed at Dayton the treaty which ended the Bosnia War. Evans sets out fairly the relevant problems in Liberia, Uganda and now the Sudan. Is peace in Darfur or between the North and South Sudan more or less likely if the legal case against the Sudanese president is pursued? This is not an easy conundrum. Evans argues rightly that it should be a political decision to be settled by the Security Council under Article 16 of the statute which sets up the International Criminal Court. But we (and the chief prosecutor of the court) should refrain from demonising the Security Council as immoral if it were ever to exercise its political function to suspend a prosecution in the interests of peace. Justice should be done, but not if as a result the heavens fall.

Likewise Evans confronts the fundamental problem of authority. The UN Charter is clear; so was the summit document of 2005 already quoted. To be legal, military intervention under Responsibility to Protect has to be authorised by the Security Council. But we all know that because of the veto such action may sometimes not be taken even when the moral case for intervention is overwhelming. Evans, for once verging on casuistry, argues that intervention even if not *legal* can be *legitimate*. He cites five moral and evidential criteria, including of course the balance of consequences, by which legitimacy can be judged. He does not shirk the difficulty. While it is obviously best that action should be both legal and legitimate, as in his view was the Gulf War of 1991, he argues that 'military action that is technically illegal, but widely perceived to be legitimate (as with Kosovo in 1999) does far less damage than action which is generally perceived to be neither legal nor legitimate (Iraq in 2003)' (p. 139).

These tensions, the clash between peace and justice, the question of valid authority, are not new problems, freshly invented to thwart our modern attempts at creating a better world. In various forms they have been present for centuries; they were central in the mediaeval scholastic attempts to define a 'just war'. This history does not make them any easier to handle, but it should caution us against making expansive attempts to settle these problems permanently. Indeed, the question of justice in war can only be solved by a steady process of evolution, the definitions changing in response to the events on the ground.

Two conclusions seem inescapable. First, the principle of Responsibility to Protect is right. In this respect the moral conscience of the world is a reality, and has moved forward. The British foreign secretary, for example, is elected not just to protect British interests but to add a realistic British contribution to creating a more decent world. The proliferating and sometimes overweening array of texts on human rights rests on a similar foundation in all countries. But the principle when it requires the use of force cannot be universally applied. There will be repeated occasions when a man-made disaster of the type specified in the Responsibility to Protect is occurring but the international community finds that the balance of consequences is against intervention. No statement of principles will impel the rest of the world to insist that China grants freedom to the people of Tibet. The judgement of African governments, up to now determining the judgement of the rest of us, has been that military intervention cannot free the people of Zimbabwe from Mugabe despite the horrors of his rule.

At the very time when the cohort of rhetorical politicians were proclaiming that we had learned our lesson and there would never be another massacre such as that of Rwanda, brutal massacres were occurring in Darfur and the Democratic Republic of the Congo which the action of the UN had proved unable to prevent.

So there cannot be universal application of Responsibility to Protect. Yet the world's leaders continue to speak as if with a firmer application of political will (of which by definition they believe themselves capable though their predecessors were not) universality can be achieved. In taking this line they respond to a long-standing tradition. An important strand of Anglo-Saxon and indeed French political thinking, stretching from Canning to Lincoln and Gladstone, to Woodrow Wilson to George W. Bush and Blair, from Rousseau to the Universal Declaration of the Rights of Man, proclaims certain principles as universal. When these are not applied in particular cases those responsible are denounced as practicing double standards. This is an accusation which our leaders must learn to live with. They should make it clear that they will act where they can, and refrain where they cannot. If on the one hand they continue as one to proclaim as universal the principle of the Responsibility to Protect, and yet repeatedly fail, often for good reasons, to apply it in practice, then the principle will become discredited. Even when the criteria for intervention are met, and the balance of consequences can be judged as favourable, those concerned will draw back. Pragmatism is not a heroic policy, but it can be a safer protector of principle than enthusiastic pretence.

Review Essay

Limits of a New-Age Worldview

Adam Roberts

Terror and Consent: The Wars for the Twenty-first Century
Philip Bobbitt. London: Allen Lane, 2008. £25.00/$35.00.
672 pp.

We are living in a time of transition, indeed on the cusp of a new age, and these circumstances require us to have a radically changed view of strategy, of law and indeed of the state. This is the message of Philip Bobbitt's remarkable mixture of description, prescription and prophecy. More particularly, *Terror and Consent* is about change in the constitutional order of states, and about 'whether that change will result in the triumph of states of consent or states of terror'. This book has attracted some big-name support: the dust jacket includes notably warm commendations from Tony Blair, Henry Kissinger, General Rupert Smith and others. Does the book deliver what is promised and praised? Is it of the same standard as his earlier work, *The Shield of Achilles* (2002), in which he explored the links between the internal constitutional order of states and their role in the world? There are many grounds for criticism of the present work, and I will come to them later. First, however, it is necessary to outline the book's central propositions. Without doing too much violence to Bobbitt's wide-ranging survey, these can be reduced to eight.

Adam Roberts is President-elect of the British Academy and Senior Research Fellow at the Centre for International Studies in Oxford University's Department of Politics and International Relations. He is also an Emeritus Fellow of Balliol College, Oxford. He was the Montague Burton Professor of International Relations at Oxford University from 1986 to the end of 2007.

 DOI 10.1080/00396330902860926

1. The nation-state, which was the dominant constitutional order of the twentieth century, is being replaced by what Bobbitt calls the market state. The key difference is that whereas the nation-state 'based its legitimacy on a promise to improve the material welfare of its people', the market state 'promises to maximize the opportunity of its people, tending to privatize many state activities and making representative government more responsible to consumers'. The market state is seen as 'a minimal provider or redistributor'. It is likely to have an interest in enhancing the rule of law without which markets cannot flourish. However, if it is not careful it may 'enable the commodification of weapons of mass destruction'. Thus, just as nation-states were far from being generally benevolent, so the market state can assume many different forms, some of which could be corrosive of internal and international order.

2. It has been possible, ever since the emergence of modern states at the time of the Renaissance, to draw a sharp distinction between states of consent and states of terror. 'States of consent govern on the basis of authority freely derived from the unfettered consent of the governed, authority that must be regularly and frequently renewed and that can be withdrawn; states of terror govern by means of repression and are not bound by the freely given decision of the public.' Both can evolve into market states. Thus, although many states of terror have been nation-states, it is quite possible that some could be market states: 'al Qaeda is but a precursor of future market states of terror'.

3. The growth of terrorism, and the emerging availability of weapons of mass destruction through clandestine markets, are both a consequence of the change in the international constitutional order, and a serious challenge to it. Just as the anarchist terrorism of the late nineteenth and early twentieth centuries was the obverse to the imperial states of that time, so today's terrorism is partly a response to the globalised and interdependent world created by the growth of the market state. Although terrorism is notoriously difficult to define, it is seen here as 'the use of violence in order to advance a political agenda by preventing persons from doing what they would otherwise lawfully do'.

4. The 'war on terror' is not a misplaced metaphor. There is a global struggle to stop global terrorist movements and to foreclose their access to nuclear

weapons. It necessarily involves a complex amalgam of international intelligence and police work, and also military action in states unwilling or unable to control terrorist movements and their access to weapons.

5. If there is to be a coherent approach to international events generally, and to terrorism in particular, there will have to be an intellectual and political rapprochement between strategy and law. This must be based on rethinking fundamental tenets of each. Strategy needs to be revised to take into account the extreme difficulty of deterring non-state entities that have no homeland. 'The twentieth century triad of deterrence, containment, and arms control regimes must now give way to twenty-first century strategies of preclusion.' Law, both domestic and international, needs to be revised to enable more effective action to be taken against transnational non-state movements and the states that back or tolerate them. Indeed, only if there is a convincing legal framework will states of consent be able to forge an effective strategy, and effective coalitions, in the wars of this century.

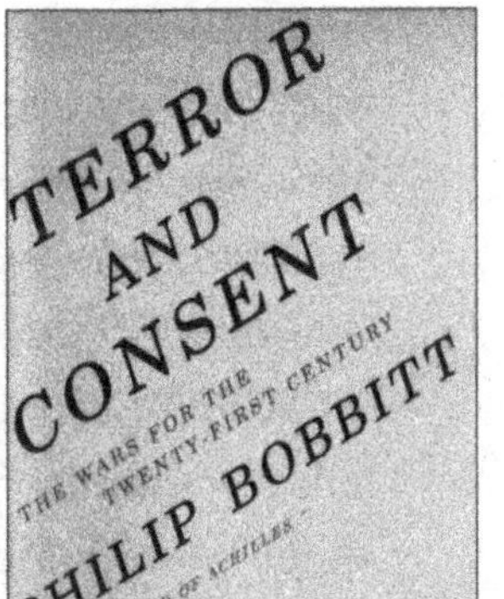

6. There is a case for preventive wars to enable states of consent to prevent certain states from acquiring weapons of mass destruction or supporting terrorist movements. However, the main effort to make such a case, the 'Bush doctrine' as enunciated in the White House's 2002 *National Security Strategy* document, is fatally flawed. Because it 'fails to provide neutral, general principles for action, it is not a doctrine at all'. A much more fully thought-out doctrine needs to be developed, on a more international basis. Such a development is seen as urgent, even overdue. Bobbitt suggests that the real case for the invasion of Iraq in 2003 was not to do with what weapons Iraq had at that time, but rather with the possibility of what it might acquire.

7. Sovereignty is necessarily changing from an absolute principle implying rejection of outside involvement to something more nuanced and qualified. The United States has moved towards a notion of transparent sovereignty which holds that 'because a regime's sovereignty arises from its compact with its people as well as with the society of states, sovereignty can

be penetrated when a state commits widespread acts of violence against its own people, or acquires weapons of mass destruction in violation of international agreements, or supports global terrorists'.

8. There is a need for a global alliance of democracies, based on a partnership between the United States and the European Union. The United States should aspire to the role of protector and conservator rather than hegemon, and states of consent should accept that role.

The case for these eight propositions, very crudely summarised here, is put with dexterity, and with much intriguing detail. The analysis of the woeful intelligence muddles in the United States and other states is masterly, and the critique of the handling of detainee issues is vigorous. Yet the book also has deep flaws. If it is brilliant and perceptive, it is also repetitive, over long and under checked. Worse, it presents a simplified description of, and prescription for, the world we face in the twenty-first century.

What Bobbitt offers is a 'new age-ist' view of international politics. He is in the tradition of a diverse group of figures – including Karl Marx, Norman Angell and George H.W. Bush – who have asserted in their time that a 'new age' was being born. All were vulnerable to the charge of painting with far too broad a brush to capture the complexities of the world, and of failing to relate their broader visionary sweeps to mundane facts that were at odds with them.

In *Terror and Consent*, the problem begins with the core proposition that the market state represents something fundamentally new, supplanting the nation-state from which it is born. The obvious objection to this is that, in previous centuries, states did not necessarily all have the character of nation-states as Bobbitt uses the term: hugely varied in their forms and purposes, some were multi-ethnic, and many had a confederal character that allowed only a very limited role for the centre. With the exception of certain extremely centralised communist regimes, all states, especially liberal democratic ones, have for centuries had an element of the market state. They have carved out a middle ground between what the state can do for its citizens and what other bodies, or indeed individuals, can do. The idea that governments are destined to have a more restricted role than hitherto suggests that the traffic is all one way, which it is not. Indeed, a possible collateral benefit of the recession into which we are entering is that we may hear a good deal less about the market state. The banking collapse post-dates the completion of this book: however, being such a clear reminder that markets can behave irrationally and that governments are needed to pick up the pieces and to regulate them better in future, it is bound to have political and administrative consequences that challenge at least some elements of the market-state idea.

The sharp distinction between states of consent and states of terror is also hugely problematical. It is crucial to Bobbitt's prescriptive vision – he argues that only states of consent should have an internationally agreed right to use anticipatory force – yet it is not worked out in detail. In particular, there is no systematic exploration of how actual states, with all their contradictions and complexities, do or do not fit into these two categories; nor of the problem of majoritarian tyranny over minorities; nor of how, even in many centralised and authoritarian states, there can be strong governmental opposition to terrorism. The way in which some authoritarian states have had liberal constitutional fig-leaves which in due course acquired real substance further calls into question Bobbitt's binary distinction.

The idea that states of consent could form the basis for action in a new international order has gained ground in the United States in recent years, and has found reflection in proposals for an international league of democracies. Bobbitt presents such ideas in a strikingly abstract manner, with little attention to the fundamental problem that in most democracies there is no significant support for them. The difficulty of deciding which countries count as democracies, the necessity to collaborate with many states that might not qualify as members, and the desire to make the best of a bad job with the institutions we have, all militate against acceptance of this idea; as, too, do profoundly different views about how the problems of terrorism are best addressed.

The rich discussion of terrorist movements that forms the heart of the book is weakened by occasional lapses in understanding of their positions and effects. Bobbitt states that the invasions of Afghanistan and Iraq came 'well before [Osama] bin Laden … showed any interest in Palestine'. This overlooks several of bin Laden's statements, including his interview broadcast on al-Jazeera television on 10 June 1999. Similarly, in arguing the perfectly valid point that suicide terrorism can be secular or at least non-Islamic in character, he cites as an example 'the Tamil Tigers fighting against the Hindu majority in Sri Lanka': the majority is Buddhist.

More serious is the consistent exaggeration of the effects of terrorist movements. It is important to his argument that 'terrorism is one of the principal forces destroying the legitimacy of the nation state and leading to the market state', but is it actually true? The evidence is not presented systematically. It can certainly be argued that what the Soviet Union labelled as terrorism in Afghanistan in the 1980s contributed not only to the Soviet withdrawal from Afghanistan, but also to the eventual collapse of the Soviet state. However, the Soviet Union was not exactly a nation-state. Indeed, in a process that is the inverse of Bobbitt's broad generalisation, the most important and largely unanticipated consequence of the Afghan struggle may have been the emergence of new nation-states out of the remnants of the old Soviet Union. Similarly, Bobbitt refers repeatedly to the Madrid bombings of March 2004, emphasising their effect in leading to a change of government and withdrawal of Spanish forces from Iraq, but he fails to note the crucial fact that it was the Spanish government's foolish response to the bombings, especially their instant attribution to the Basque group ETA, that influenced the electorate to kick the government out.

The most serious deficiency of this book concerns its most 'new age-ist' aspect: its argument that existing international institutions are completely unsuited to facing the challenges of today, including global terrorist movements, and need to be radically reformed or replaced. It is obvious that there is some force to this argument, but Bobbitt actually undermines it by failing to note the extent to which a process of adjustment has taken place. His comments on the United Nations must serve as an example of what is a more general problem in this book. He states that 'the *jus ad bellum* of the UN Charter simply does not contemplate a strategic context in which the anticipatory use of force is a necessity for a state's survival'. This is at best a half-truth. While the charter limitations on the right of states to use force are indeed stringent, he fails to note the care which those framing the charter took to keep open the freedom of the Security Council to act in a very wide variety of circumstances; and the roles assigned to regional organisations.

Of course no state will put all its eggs in the Security Council basket, but the UN framework is not as completely unsuited to current circumstances as this book suggests. Bobbitt argues, for example: 'The opaque sovereignty of the nation state that is enshrined in the institutions and rules of the society of nation states does not admit of any internal, domestic acts that empower the UN or any other body to strip a state of its sovereignty, thereby making it legally vulnerable to legitimate intervention'. Many acts carried out under UN auspices, including the US-led interventions in Somalia in 1992 and Haiti in 1994, suggest that there can indeed be UN-approved interventions as a result of largely internal crises. What the United Nations and United States have not done in these cases is what Bobbitt unwisely recommends: stripping states of their sovereignty – an approach which would be likely to inflame opinion both domestically and internationally.

There is a similar problem with the book's coverage of international law. Bobbitt claims that it is too closely tied to the interests of sovereign states, regardless of their internal structures and overall behaviour. He says that the 1948 Genocide Convention 'contained no provisions that might have qualified the sovereignty of the signatory states'. A glance at Articles 4, 6, 7 and 8 of the convention suggests that it had plenty of potential to qualify state sovereignty, and it has in practice been one basis for the establishment of the international tribunals in respect of the former Yugoslavia and Rwanda. Similarly, he argues that 'the entire system of the laws of war' is coming unravelled, but he is unspecific about what he would put in their place, and indeed how he would set about negotiating it. Likewise with his argument about the preventive use of force, it is impossible to imagine an international negotiation that would give carte blanche to such actions in advance. If the law is changed in this regard, it will be through a slow process of accretion.

Perhaps the greatest danger of 'new age' thinking is that it easily leads to an assumption that ideas, rules and understandings based on past experience can all be called into question, even ignored. Bobbitt sometimes avoids this trap – there are many rich historical vignettes in this book – but sometimes falls straight in. As a guide to our age, the book is interesting, illuminating, challenging, and frequently just plain wrong.

Book Reviews

United States

John L. Harper

The War Within: A Secret White House History 2006–2008
Bob Woodward. London and New York: Simon & Schuster, 2008. £18.99/$32.00. 487 pp.

Success has many fathers. So it was with the 'surge'. The fourth volume of Bob Woodward's series recounts the bureaucratic tug-of-war over how to salvage America's failing Iraq campaign in 2006. It is based on internal memos, off-the-record conversations and a long on-the-record interview with President George W. Bush and National Security Adviser Stephen J. Hadley in May 2008. Woodward admits that the book is 'much closer to the first draft of history than the last', but it is an interesting and revealing account.

Surge proponents included the hard-driving retired general (and David Petraeus patron) Jack Keane, Senator John McCain, Frederick Kagan of the American Enterprise Institute, and Iraq Study Group member Charles Robb. Supporters inside the administration included Hadley, his staff members J.D. Crouch, Meghan O'Sullivan and William J. Luti, as well as Bush himself. Proponents believed that a switch from US force protection to population protection would reduce the appalling level of violence in the capital and buy time for the Iraqi government to produce political results. Many also opposed a surge, extending the largely secret debate for months. Opponents believed that Iraq had become a black hole for US resources and that the Iraqis needed rapidly to take responsibility for themselves. They included Defense Secretary Donald Rumsfeld, Iraq commander George Casey, Central Command head John Abizaid, most of the Joint Chiefs of Staff, Secretary of State Condoleezza Rice and her advisers Philip Zelikow and David Satterfield, not to mention Iraqi Prime Minister Nuri al-Maliki, whose arm Bush had to twist to get him to request the additional five

 DOI 10.1080/00396330902860967

brigades. Vice President Dick Cheney's office was not initially pro-surge, preferring a policy of all-out support for the Shia. Abizaid's replacement, Admiral William J. Fallon, was a sceptic who, according to Woodward, made life difficult for Casey's replacement, Petraeus, before quitting over how to deal with Iran.

Woodward notes that Rice thought the decision to launch the surge had been made in 'textbook' fashion, 'even though she had opposed it and it had taken longer than half a year'. One wonders what textbook she was thinking of. Keane, the key player in the story, was a private citizen up to his neck in affairs of state. After the surge began, a back channel emerged from Petraeus to Keane to Cheney to Bush, by-passing the official chain of command through Fallon and Rumsfeld's replacement, Robert Gates. Woodward's story is a reminder (if any were needed) of the war-making power of a determined US president. Bush acted in defiance of much of his administration, the Iraq Study Group, the new Democratic majority in Congress and the American public, who had voted against an escalation in November 2006.

Surge proponents are probably right in thinking few will care about the method if the fall in violence (due partly to the surge) can be translated into a durable success. Will today's relative calm allow a stable Iraq to emerge? For Iraq's sake, even those who do not wish to see Bush's policy vindicated must hope this is the case. In the meantime, Rice's interview with Woodward raises doubts about the administration's grasp of basic history and strategy. Warning against an Iranian nuclear weapon, she observes, 'the Soviet Union became nuclear before it became powerful'. This would greatly surprise those who encountered the Red Army before September 1949. It also prompts a question: has anyone ever used the threat of a nuclear weapon to change the status quo in his favour? Rice also claims that the Iraq War has produced an anti-Iranian 'realignment' in the region and that 'a strong Iraq' will be Iran's 'worst nightmare'. It is hard to see how the anti-Iranian front, of which Saddam Hussein was a charter member, has been strengthened. An Iraq, strong or otherwise, under Shia influence is a relative gain for Tehran.

Between Virtue and Power: The Persistent Moral Dilemma of US Foreign Policy
John Kane. New Haven, CT: Yale University Press, 2008.
£27.50/$40.00. 403 pp.

This thought-provoking volume by Australian scholar John Kane examines the tensions and conflicts engendered by America's deeply embedded view of itself as peculiarly endowed with virtue, on one hand, and obliged to dirty its hands in the course of fulfilling its presumed historical mission to save the world, on the other. For Kane, a basic problem arises from the complexity of Americans' dearly held notion of their own virtue. Its content, he argues, includes the ideas of liberty and equality, simplicity and a missionary spirit. Its two essential, but basically incompatible, elements are innocence/incorruptibility, deriving from Christianity and calling for separation from the hurly-burly of world politics, and 'an active republican conception' emphasising the 'manly, martial qualities' needed for defence and conquest. The latter kind of virtue leads to the accumulation of power and generates 'nationalistic pride', calling into question America's innocence and selfless motives in the eyes of both Americans and the world.

Kane provides a lengthy account of how thinkers and statesmen (Presidents Woodrow Wilson and the two Roosevelts, for example) have tried to reconcile this contradiction in America's self-conception. A central argument is that thanks to the Second World War,

> America's leaders seemed to have achieved a synthesis that might be described as a recognition and acceptance of the need for *virtuous power.* The great lesson they had learned since 1919 was that power should not be regarded as antithetical to the reign of virtue but must be clearly understood as essential for its support.

With the Vietnam trauma, however, this fragile synthesis was shattered and, according to Kane, has yet to be reconstituted. If America's double-barrelled virtue demanded that the United States be both on the right side and the winning side, Vietnam was a devastating double blow. But Kane overlooks the fact that the 'Vietnam syndrome' had essentially disappeared by the mid 1990s, and that conservative Republicans and neo-conservatives have more often than not seen no contradiction between American virtue and the use of military power since Vietnam. Until recently, opponents of the war were curiously oblivious to the fact that influential supporters had drawn an entirely different set of lessons, namely that America was on the right side and the war could and should have been won.

The Limits of Power: The End of American Exceptionalism
Andrew J. Bacevich. New York: Metropolitan Books, 2008.
$24.00. 206 pp.

Drawing on the insights of Reinhold Niebuhr, William A. Williams and C. Wright Mills, Andrew Bacevich delivers a harsh sermon to his fellow Americans. His focus is a set of dysfunctional behaviour patterns and institutions that he believes impel the United States on a self-defeating course. The first is the tendency, especially since the 1960s, to identify 'freedom' with self-gratification and consumption. As the American appetite for freedom (so conceived) has grown, 'so too has our penchant for empire'. The connection is a 'causal one'. A turning point occurred between 1979 and 1983, when Americans rejected President Jimmy Carter's warning against the 'mistaken idea of freedom' (Carter's words) as selfishness and embraced Ronald Reagan, the 'modern prophet of profligacy'. Moreover, Reagan's Strategic Defense Initiative (SDI) prefigured the 'global war on terror' by introducing 'into mainstream politics the proposition that Americans could be truly safe only if the United States enjoyed something akin to permanent global military supremacy'. Abundance 'seemingly required access to large quantities of cheap oil', in turn requiring a firm grip on the Persian Gulf. 'It demanded oil wars.' Hence the Iraq War, a conflict that has eroded US power.

One problem with this is that, by Bacevich's own account, it was Carter's 1980 'doctrine' that laid the foundation for the US build-up in the Gulf. The recurrent notion that US security demands global military preponderance can be traced not to SDI but another fantasy-laden project, National Security Council Report 68, completed in 1950. Few would deny a link between America's thirst for oil and its Middle Eastern adventures. But the causal connection needs to be clearer. The rest of the book strongly suggests that even if America were to wean itself from Persian Gulf oil (representing 16% of oil imports in 2007, according to the International Energy Agency), its imperial behaviour would persist. Bacevich mercilessly dissects the workings of a self-perpetuating national-security bureaucracy that predisposes Washington to seek military solutions, and of a deep-seated 'ideology of national security' (incorporating the idea of a mission to spread freedom) that serves to legitimate executive action. So-called 'wisemen' (from James Forrestal and Paul Nitze to Dick Cheney and Paul Wolfowitz) have 'repeatedly misconstrued and exaggerated existing threats, with perverse effects'. It is hard to disagree.

Bacevich is particularly incisive in drawing the military lessons of recent experience. They are not that the US military should be retooled to fight 'small wars' on the periphery, that more authority should be given to professionals like Tommy Franks and David Petraeus, or (as some suggest) that conscription should be reinstated; rather, that 'the utility of armed force remains finite' and the United States needs a more modest, illusion-free foreign policy, one that does not try to make of the Middle East what it made of the Caribbean in the early twentieth century. Bacevich's alternative agenda, the defensive containment of radical Islam, the abolition of nuclear weapons, and the transition to a 'post-fossil fuel economy', does not seem particularly modest. But, as he points out, pursuing it would not put the United States on a collision course with the rest of humanity, and achieving it could hardly be more difficult than transforming the Greater Middle East.

Higher Realism: A New Policy for the United States
Seyom Brown. Boulder, CO: Paradigm Publishers, 2008. $24.95.
214 pp.

Timed to influence the new administration in Washington, this book by a distinguished international-relations scholar argues that the world is not, contrary to the assumptions of both Bill Clinton and George W. Bush, unipolar, permitting a *Pax Americana* based on US omnipotence and omniscience. Nor is it multipolar, allowing a concert of the great powers to emerge. The world system, for Brown, is 'polyarchic'. It features a plethora of non-state actors and networks, weakening alliances, and opportunistic, unpredictable behaviour by state actors subject to conflicting internal pressures. The foreign policy best suited to polyarchy, according to Brown, is neither conventional realism, with its strict focus on the national interest, nor neo-Wilsonianism, with its predilection for democratisation and military intervention, but 'higher realism'. Rejecting the notion that what is good for America is *ipso facto* good for everyone, this approach holds that US national interests are bound up with a set of collective 'world interests', and champions cultural and religious diversity.

US national-cum-world interests include avoiding nuclear war, reducing the role of force in international politics, arresting global warming and protecting vital ecosystems, preserving a well-functioning global economy, alleviating poverty and disease, and promoting democracy and human rights. Wherever possible the United States should work to transform the world 'society' into a world 'community', that is, one in which states are accountable for their conduct to the collectivity. Brown's is an attractive vision. He marshals polling data to show that on a number of points, higher realism enjoys wider support among ordinary Americans than one might suspect. Nonetheless, on at least one pair of issues the argument needs further elucidation to be persuasive. The first is that the United States, regardless of the position of others, should adopt a policy of no-use of nuclear, biological or chemical weapons and, in effect, unilaterally empty its arsenal of nuclear weapons. Brown, moreover, while wisely sceptical of the boilerplate 'democratic peace' argument for promoting democracy, doesn't really develop an alternative rationale. And on this point, at least, popular support is missing. From the days of Wilson, democracy promotion has been a project not of the broad American public but of the elites.

The Crisis of American Foreign Policy: Wilsonianism in the Twenty-first Century
G. John Ikenberry, Thomas J. Knock, Anne-Marie Slaughter and Tony Smith. Princeton, NJ: Princeton University Press, 2008. £17.95/$24.95. 168 pp.

This set of essays offers a spirited though inconclusive debate among liberal internationalists about the essence of Woodrow Wilson's message and its connection, if any, to the Bush administration's project of American predominance and democracy promotion. The historian Thomas Knock makes the case that Bush's foreign policy was light years removed, in letter and spirit, from what Wilson was about. True, Wilson intervened a number of times in Latin America, but he came to regard such action as counter-productive and saw democracy as a slow, organic process that could not be imposed from above. In any case, his 'claim to transcendent historical significance' rests not on the promotion of democracy but on the creation of a multilateral organisation whose members would act in concert and surrender a degree of sovereignty. In Wilson's words, 'only those who are ignorant of the world can believe that any nation, even so great a nation as the United States, can stand alone and play a single part in the history of mankind'. Another central plank in Wilson's platform was disarmament, a far cry from Bush's pledge to maintain US military might 'beyond challenge' by any power.

For political scientist Tony Smith, not multilateralism but 'the spread of democracy constitutes the first and most essential ingredient of liberal internationalism' because democracy is a precondition of peace and a system of collective security under American leadership. (On this point, at least, John Ikenberry seems to agree in his introductory survey.) As Wilson put it, 'a steadfast concert for peace can never be maintained except by a partnership of democratic nations'. Bush's foreign policy, in turn, was a kind of misbegotten joint venture of neoconservatives and liberal internationalists: the neocons provided its 'pillar of power', the notion of US military primacy, but the Wilsonians contributed its 'pillar of purpose', the idea of an America mission to foster democracy and free markets. Smith's particular quarrel is with 'neoliberals' (his term) who furnished intellectual fodder for a kind of 'progressive imperialism' after the fall of the Berlin Wall, and mounted the Iraq War bandwagon after 11 September 2001. Their seductive arguments included the democratic peace theory; the glib assumption that democracy promotion might now dispense with preconditions and 'sequencing'; and the redefinition of state sovereignty to accommodate a 'duty to intervene'. Smith makes a good case that the disagreements between the neocons and the liberals of the Democratic Party's Progressive Policy Institute (such as Rahm Emanuel, now White House chief of staff) over Iraq and the future world role of the United States have had more to do with means than ends.

Another of Smith's targets is the Wilson-inspired Princeton Project on National Security, which he dismisses as 'no more than a reformulation of the Bush Doctrine achieved through multilateralizing its terms'. Anne-Marie Slaughter, a co-author of the Projects's final report, rests her carefully argued reply to Smith on an interesting reading of Wilson's phrase, 'the world must be made safe for democracy'. According to Slaughter, this meant defending democracy where it existed, not intervening to spread it around the world. Moreover, multilateralism for Wilson was not a cover for US hegemony but 'a process of collective deliberation [that] produced better results for all concerned'. If these are the principles underlying the Princeton Project's proposed global 'Concert of Democracies', then such a body would indeed (as Slaughter says) have little to do with Bush's doctrine. At the same time, it is hard to imagine that the United States would join a concert of states that it did not intend to lead, and, when circumstances demanded, ignore.

Politics and International Relations

Gilles Andréani

Just Another Major Crisis? The United States and Europe Since 2000
Geir Lundestad, ed. Oxford: Oxford University Press, 2008.
£35.00/$60.00. 334 pp.

At a time when transatlantic expectations have been unusually high, thanks to Barack Obama's victory in the US presidential election, it may be useful, and sobering, to pause for a moment and ask whether these expectations are well founded. This volume, edited by Geir Lundestad, director of the Norwegian Nobel Institute and professor of international history at the University of Oslo, invites us to do just that. *Just Another Major Crisis? The United States and Europe Since 2000* stands in remarkable contrast to the usual literature on transatlantic relations. All too often, such studies emanate, if not always from true believers, at least from people who hardly ever question whether a close and cooperative relationship between the two sides of the Atlantic is either desirable or feasible. This usually results in tedious, repetitive recommendations that fail to reflect the increasingly complex and uncertain nature of the transatlantic relationship.

Bringing together a remarkable group of authors, including Charles Maier, Charles Kupchan, Michael Cox, John Ikenberry, Frédéric Bozo, Marcin Zaborowski, Helga Haftendorn, William Wallace, David Calleo, Rob Kroes, Steven Kull, Stanley Sloan and Gustrav Schmidt, *Just Another Major Crisis?* generally argues that the decline in relations between Europe and America since 2000 (some authors go further back, to the end of the Cold War), which culminated in the 2003 divide over Iraq War, is *not* 'just another crisis'. It is a sign of a seriously changed, and in many ways weakened, relationship: neither the security needs of Europe (Bozo), nor shared risks abroad (Haftendorn), unite the United States and Europe the way the Soviet threat did. The Iraq crisis has compromised the self-image of the United States, once widely endorsed in Europe as well, as the caretaker of the global liberal hegemony of the West. The necessary patterns of shared leadership that should have emerged after the Cold War have failed to materialise (Wallace). Culture itself has divided the people of one continent from the other (Kroes), and public opinion has not come together after the Iraq divide (Kull).

These essays, and the others not specifically mentioned in this review, point to a structural change in the relationship, and to a certain decline in transatlanticism as the dominant pattern in each side's foreign policy. The authors' viewpoints are diverse and nuanced, however, and their diagnoses and expectations for the transatlantic bond do not always coincide, which adds to the richness of the book. (That said, all the authors, in one way or another, would like the relationship to endure in a renewed form.) All in all, the least persuasive arguments emanate from those European contributors who believe a more united Europe has emerged as a consequence of the withering of the transatlantic relationship: for all the failings of US leadership under President George W. Bush, this has not helped – or so laments this European reviewer – the EU to assert global influence of its own, or offer an alternative source of leadership to that of the United States on the world stage.

The Return of History and the End of Dreams
Robert Kagan. London: Atlantic Books, 2008. £7.99/$12.95.
116 pp.

Once in a while, an American article or book (usually first an article, later turned into a book) will frame the debate on international affairs in a way that resonates globally and evokes a worldwide echo. Francis Fukuyama's *The End of History and the Last Man*, Samuel Huntington's *The Clash of Civilizations and the Remaking of World Order* and Robert Kagan's *Of Paradise and Power* (otherwise known as 'Americans are from Mars, Europeans from Venus') have achieved such eminence over the past 20 years. Pierre Hassner once commented on this phenomenon, making the somewhat sorrowful observation that 'if Americans have trouble shaping the world, they are second to none when it comes to interpreting it'.

Robert Kagan's most recent book, *The Return of History and the End of Dreams*, is a clear attempt to score another success, this time by taking aim at Fukuyama's *End of History*, to which the book's title and first quote explicitly refer: 'at the end of history, there are no serious ideological competitors left to liberal democracy'. Actually, this clear, concise and assertive volume could have been more accurately entitled 'The Return of Power Politics'. In the first part of this 100-page essay, Kagan describes the foreign policies of both established (United States) and emerging (Russia, China, Iran) powers as dominated by prestige, interests, the quest for hegemony and nationalism. That Kagan does not shy away from attributing these motives to the United States as well as to the non-democratic powers is illustrative of a broader trend: after the internationalist and liberal illusions of the immediate post-Cold War era, 'the world has become normal again'.

Against this background, the second half of the book describes the main political fault line of the future, one which, according to Kagan, will run between an association of authoritarian regimes (along with political Islam, admittedly a force of the past that cannot fulfill its aims) and a concert of democracies, led by the United States. This concert will provide legitimacy for action instead of the UN Security Council, a body hopelessly paralysed by divisions between autocratic and democratic countries.

It was clearly tempting, but imprudent, for Kagan to seek to make his point at the expense of Fukuyama's *End of History*, an intellectually far-reaching, elegant, creative and even visionary book, considering it was written in the late 1980s. All in all, Kagan does not dislodge Fukuyama's central tenet, that liberal democracy has no global ideological rival today. He convincingly describes political Islam as a force on the defensive that provides no effective traction, and his case that power politics is what matters today in international relations is perfectly compatible with a universe devoid of serious ideological divides, which is what *The End of History* was about. It is worth remembering that Europe in the classical age combined a uniquely homogeneous ideological and moral setting with the most ruthless power rivalry.

Also, if international relations are back to 'normal' power politics, where do the spontaneously harmonious relations among democracies and the desire for American hegemony described by Kagan come from? Geopolitics and the clash of interests should divide democracies just as they divide autocracies. If, on the other hand, there is a measure of genuine cooperation among states, especially among democracies, it is to be presumed that the states concerned have a view of world affairs and of their own interests which somehow transcends power politics. Like Bush's foreign policy, *The Return of History* tends to combine naivety and cynicism in an original, but unconvincing, way.

The Spirit of Democracy: The Struggle to Build Free Societies Throughout the World
Larry Diamond. New York: Times Books, 2008. $28.00. 448 pp.

Why does democracy take root, support itself and flourish in some places but not others? Do reversals in a number of countries such as Pakistan, Thailand and Russia over the last few years amount to a pattern of democratic recession, if not of renewed appeal and success of authoritarian regimes across the board? How can outside forces help foster democracy and counter these adverse tendencies? These are but a few of the questions addressed in *The Spirit of Democracy: The Struggle to Build Free Societies Throughout the World* by author Larry Diamond, a senior fellow at the Hoover Institution. Easy to read and well researched, *The Spirit of Democracy* offers an excellent synthesis view on some of the most vexing questions in the field of democracy studies.

Diamond first explores the democratic wave of the 1980s and 1990s, putting it into the context of a universal aspiration for democracy. In presenting his analysis, he tends to minimise the role of elites, as opposed to civil society, in bringing about democracy. He then turns to the recent 'democratic recession', insisting on the negative role of oil revenues, which he believes to be supportive of authoritarian control. He explores the underlying factors which contribute to the consolidation of democracy, emphasising external factors and in particular regional influences, which he sees as having played a major role in the consolidation of democratic achievements in Europe. This is followed by chapters devoted to Latin America, Eastern Europe, Asia, Africa and the Middle East, and to policy prescriptions addressing democracy promotion.

With his universalist mindset and his focus on the conditions of democracy, a perspective which belittles cultural factors and insists on the role of institutions and determined but careful political action, Diamond does not see a systemic trend in the recent reversal of democratic transitions. Nor does he believe in crusading from the outside for democracy, even less in achieving democracy by force; he concludes his stimulating book by recommending improvements in the functioning of US democracy at home as a necessary component of American efforts to credibly promote democracy abroad.

The Fate of Young Democracies
Ethan B. Kapstein and Nathan Converse. Cambridge:
Cambridge University Press. 2008. £16.99/$29.99. 188 pp.

More scholarly, and accordingly more narrow in scope, than Larry Diamond's *The Spirit of Democracy, The Fate of Young Democracies* explores in depth a question at the heart of democracy studies: why does democracy fail at the outset in certain cases? What constitutes the thin line between success and failure for newborn democracies? Using quantitative analytical methods, Ethan Kapstein (INSEAD and the Center for Global Development) and Nathan Converse (London School of Economics) have come up with original and thought-provoking answers to these questions, usefully questioning existing literature while resorting to new approaches of their own.

The authors first dissipate a number of prejudices: for example, while income inequality is often associated with authoritarian regimes, effective redistribution policies do not seem to be a factor in the initial consolidation of democracy. Likewise, parliamentary democracy is not more resilient than presidential regimes; the important thing in both cases is the existence of effective checks on authority. Time is also essential in allowing democratic culture – that is, the belief that democracy is the best way to peacefully reconcile differing views – to take root.

Using model regression, Kapstein and Converse next try to weigh the various factors which determine the outcome of democracies. Not surprisingly, they observe that democracies are most vulnerable in their infant years and that this vulnerability decreases over time. Ethnic fragmentation, closed economies and lower incomes are associated with higher rates of failure, but neither economic growth nor the reduction of inequality guarantees success per se. Institutional variables such as the existence of effective political checks play a decisive role, on average more decisive than economic factors.

Significant regional variables appear: in Europe and Latin America, democracy seems to have been more efficiently 'locked in' than in Asia and Africa, prompting one to wonder whether 'initial conditions' were more propitious to democracy in certain parts of the world. This is a question the authors discuss in some detail, continent by continent.

Kapstein and Converse conclude their excellent study by advocating democracy-promotion policies that take into account the vulnerability of young democracies in their first five years and provide adequate support at this crucial juncture. This can be best achieved with aid specifically dedicated to democracy promotion, despite its uncertain efficacy: general-purpose aid has proven to be poorly associated with the progress of democracy, and while *The Fate of Young*

Democracies does not dissipate the many doubts which surround democracy-promotion policies, it nevertheless makes commendable progress in narrowing them down and furthering our understanding of the delicate processes of democracy consolidation.

On Empire: America, War, and Global Supremacy
Eric Hobsbawm. New York: Pantheon Books, 2008. $19.95.
98 pp.

Short books, especially brilliant and incisive ones, set an example, and should prompt their reviewers to be brief themselves. *On Empire: America, War, and Global Supremacy,* by Eric Hobsbawm, is just such a book. In four essays, the famous British historian surveys the fate of empires and the future of war and hegemony in the post-Cold War era. A must-read, this small volume clarifies in a trenchant way issues often confused in public debate and academic works alike.

Empires no longer exist, and their demise is one of the great stories of the twentieth century. We should not regret their disappearance, nor retrospectively embellish their accomplishments for, as Hobsbawm points out, the twentieth century was one of the most murderous in history, witnessing a constant rise in the number of civilian versus military casualties, a record only offset by a significant decline in the number of inter-state wars since the 1960s. War in the next century will be different and depend on the stability of states rather than on rivalry among them. The disappearance of the great-power system has lifted a source of restraint on intervention in other states' affairs, and encouraged the fragmentation of states, which command less authority than they did before.

Altogether, we should expect less war, but a good measure of persistent armed violence. In this context, will some order be imposed by a return to a concert among the most powerful states? Or from a benevolent American empire? The distribution of power does not favour the first option, and the United States under Bush squandered its chance of sustaining a peaceful leadership role. Will the country now return to reason and exert global influence based on trade rather than on politico-military force? Will Washington be a source of order or disorder in the world? These questions, posed at the end of *On Empire,* may soon be answered in the real world; how they are resolved will do much to make this century either better or at least as bad as the previous one.

War, Conflict and the Military

H.R. McMaster

Eve of Destruction: The Coming Age of Preventive War
Thomas M. Nichols. Philadelphia, PA: University of Pennsylvania Press, 2008. £25.50/$39.95. 171 pp.

Why Not Preempt? Security, Law, Norms and Anticipatory Military Activities
Rachel Bzostek. Aldershot: Ashgate, 2008. $55.00/$89.95. 266 pp.

Striking First: Preemption and Prevention in International Conflict
Michael W. Doyle. Princeton, NJ: Princeton University Press, 2008. £14.95/$24.95. 200 pp.

Preemption: Military Action and Moral Justification
Henry Shue and David Rodin. Oxford: Oxford University Press, 2007. £45.00/$90.00. 276 pp.

As a new American administration defines its approach to national security, its leaders will attempt to define the conditions under which the United States will use military force to protect vital national interests. After the 11 September 2001 terrorist attacks, the George W. Bush administration shifted America's approach to national security from deterrence toward the pre-emptive use of force. As the 2002 National Security Strategy of the United States announced, 'we must be prepared to stop rogue states and their terrorist clients before they are able to threaten or use weapons of mass destruction against the United States and our allies and friends … To forestall or prevent such hostile acts by our adversaries, the United States will, if necessary, act pre-emptively.' The strategy of pre-emption, sometimes referred to as the 'Bush Doctrine', has generated a great deal of scholarly, as well as popular, controversy. Some have argued that the Bush Doctrine blurred the line between pre-emption, which requires conclusive evidence of an impending attack, and preventive war, which is more discretionary as it entails defeating threats before they coalesce. Recent books on the subject of pre-emption and prevention shed light on the advantages and disadvantages of these strategies from a broad range of perspectives and help place the contemporary debate in historical and ethical context. Taken together, their treatment of the subject illuminates the legal, moral and pragmatic dimensions of pre-emption and prevention.

In *Eve of Destruction*, Thomas M. Nichols, professor of strategy at the US Naval War College, argues that the international system is already moving toward a more permissive norm regarding prevention. Nichols argues that the shift toward prevention reflects the collapse of two norms: the presumption against preventive war and the inviolability of state sovereignty. He outlines two likely possibilities for the future, neither of which are sanguine: the use of 'ad hoc and unilateral violence' to attack perceived threats, or a failure to address more dangerous threats because powerful nations 'do not see a particular threat to their own people' (p. 117).

Nichols goes on to examine 'what might be done to maintain any possibility of international order in a new era of prevention' (p. 3). The alternatives he discusses include the possibility that great powers will grant each other the 'exceptional right to use violence as they will' in an effort to 'avert anarchy and to keep the carnage to a minimum' (p. 118). Nichols warns, however, that 'a system based on coercion rather than comity' is likely not only to breed resentment, but also to strengthen 'rogues and terrorists' through the damage done to 'ideas of the rule of law and the just use of force' (p. 118). Despite these clear disadvantages, the author sees even greater danger in what he describes as a 'vain attempt to preserve the current order' as 'old rules are still given a passing nod by the great powers even as they revise their defense doctrines and restructure their armed forces for preventive action' (p. 118). Ultimately, Nichols suggests a 'third alternative' involving the reform of international institutions, the United Nations in particular. Despite his doubts that the UN, as currently configured, would be able to act as a defender of the international order and his description of the organisation as 'one of the world's most dysfunctional bureaucracies', Nichols sees a US recommitment to the organisation and a demand 'that the international community be an actual community, imposed of likeminded and liberal states that will not tolerate thugs, madmen, and genocidal fanatics in their ranks' (p. 147) as the best way to avoid the 'advent of uncontrolled preventive war' (p. 144).

In *Why Not Preempt?*, Rachel Bzostek, assistant professor of political science at California State University, Bakersfield, examines whether states are bound by international law when contemplating 'anticipatory military activities', including actions taken in response to imminent threats or to counter more distant threats. Bzostek considers anticipatory military activities in the context of international law and just-war theory, and then uses case studies to distinguish between actions inspired by imminent threats and more distant threats. While there is no clear standard with respect to the legality or permissibility of anticipatory self-defence, Bzostek's analysis emphasises the centrality of the imminence of an attack, including knowledge of both the capability and the intention to attack, as justification for anticipatory action. Bzostek is more hopeful than Nichols. She concludes that the international community should 'not read too much' into the case of the US invasion of Iraq because 'legal and normative constraints' on anticipatory action remain and are likely to compel states to 'at least think twice' before using military force (p. 231).

Striking First contains two essays by Michael Doyle on the conditions under which preventive war is justified, and responses from Harold Hongju Koh, Richard Tuck and Jeff McMahan. Doyle, who was assistant secretary-general and special adviser to UN Secretary-General Kofi Annan, argues in his first essay that international law and the Bush Doctrine of prevention are both inadequate to meet contemporary challenges to national and international security. In his second essay, Doyle constructs 'jurisprudence, derived from cases, that the Security Council should draw upon when it deliberates the question of when to authorize preventive measures' or that, in exceptional circumstances, states might use to determine when they might use preventive force unilaterally (p. 44). The standards that Doyle argues should be applied to determine if preventive war is justified include the likelihood and lethality of the threat, and the legitimacy (proportionality, necessity, deliberateness) and legality of the response.

In his comment on Doyle's analysis, Koh, dean at Yale Law School, argues that 'problems of knowledge, proof, and prediction' make *ex ante* authorisation to take unilateral pre-emptive military action impractical and undesirable (p. 118). Koh contends that 'it is simply a category error to bestow prior legal authorization upon actions that are better addressed in the context of a post hoc defense' (p. 103). Richard Tuck, professor of government at Harvard University, objects to Doyle's argument, in part because politics, rather than 'impartial judicial decisions', should resolve issues involving the use of force. In his response, Doyle acknowledges that 'talking about standards for action in the absence of Security Council authorization can undermine the power of the established rules of law', but counters Koh's criticism with the observation that the 'states that ratified the UN Charter were not ratifying a suicide pact'. Doyle concludes that 'nineteenth-century rules' no longer fit and argues that political leaders should employ standards proposed by their citizens when contemplating the use of force (p. 159).

In *Preemption: Military Action and Moral Justification*, editors Henry Shue and David Rodin of Oxford University pull together interdisciplinary perspectives on the subject of pre-emptive attacks and preventive war. Contributors to this volume debate ethical, moral and practical dimensions of self-defence and examine the conditions under which preventive war might be justified. For example, David Luban, professor of law at Georgetown University, argues that preventive war can be regarded as defensive if enemies are conspiring to execute a murderous plan. In his essay, Walter Sinnott-Armstrong, professor of philosophy and legal studies at Dartmouth, contends that justification for anticipatory military action ought to depend primarily on a weighing of the relative consequences of action and inaction. In 'The Problem with Prevention', David Rodin disagrees. He argues that consequentialist and right-to-self-defence arguments are both inadequate to justify preventive war. He sets a high standard for the use of force, arguing that it can be justified only if 'those who we kill and maim have done something to make themselves liable to that treatment' (p. 170). In contrast to Rodin's conclusion that preventive wars cannot be morally justified, Shue contemplates what a justified preventive military attack might look like and outlines conditions for such an attack: it must be limited to the effective elimination of the danger, undertaken only when military action is urgent, based on solid intelligence, and grounded in reasons broadly acceptable internationally.

Essays by accomplished historians Hew Strachan of Oxford and Marc Trachtenberg of the University of California, Los Angeles, remind readers that the Bush policy of pre-emption is far from anomalous when considered in the context of American foreign and defence policy since the Second World War. Strachan observes that the US 'predisposition in favour of preventive war was obscured until the 1990s by the wider context of the Cold War, by America's endorsement of international law and multilateral institutions, themselves designed to curb preventive war, and by the use of special forces and covert operations which ensured that the United States' actions were largely overlooked' (p. 38). Trachtenberg stresses that it is important to view the question of preventive war in historical perspective because 'we can get some guidance by understanding that these problems are not entirely new, and that people had to face similar problems in the past' (p. 68).

Events of the past year, including the Israeli strike on the Syrian nuclear facility and the Russian invasion of Georgia, indicate that the subject of these books remain relevant and important to international security. A quick inventory of international-security issues – including Iran's nuclear programme and support for proxy forces, terrorist safe havens in Yemen, Pakistan and Somalia, and humanitarian crises in Africa – indicates that questions of pre-emptive and preventive war will remain very much on the international security agenda for the foreseeable future. Considered together, the analysis and arguments contained in these volumes are an excellent place to start for anyone charged with thinking through the difficult question of when and if pre-emptive or preventive force is necessary and justified.

Inside Defense: Understanding the U.S. Military in the 21st Century
Derek S. Reveron and Judith Hicks Stiehm, eds. Basingstoke: Palgrave Macmillan, 2008. £45.00/$89.95. 279 pp.

Concerned that citizens were ill informed about the role of the US military in defence policy and national-security decision-making, Derek S. Reveron and Judith Hicks Stiehm pulled together 21 essays on the subject from scholars, policy experts and military professionals. Although the quality of the essays in uneven, *Inside Defense* is a valuable book because it advances knowledge of military affairs critical to the development of sound strategy as well as the maintenance of a proper civil–military relationship in democratic societies. It seems clear that complex missions such as those in Iraq and Afghanistan will continue to demand that military efforts be directed toward achieving policy goals and integrated into comprehensive strategies that address fundamental causes of violence and instability. As Reveron and Hicks Stiehm observe, however, while the public is at least aware of military operations in armed conflicts, most are unaware of the military's role in 'less publicized activities' such as security cooperation and humanitarian assistance (p. xi). The editors and contributors shed light on these subjects as well as the military's role in diplomacy, the increasing role of private-security contractors, and the military's interaction with non-governmental organisations.

The editors cast their net widely, organising the essays into three sections: 'The Military and the International Setting', 'The Military and Government Institutions', and 'The Military and Civil Society'. Several essays examine how the military provides advice as part of the policymaking and national-security decision-making process. Others examine the relationships between the 'iron triangle' of the military, defence industry and Congress. Essays on the military and society cover such topics as the interactions between retired officers and the state; political partisanship and the military; the evolution of reserve and National Guard forces; and the role of women in the armed forces.

The volume might have benefitted from essays that placed contemporary military affairs in historical context. In their brief conclusion, Hicks Stiehm and Reveron argue that the military's role and the nature of civil–military relations are changing, asserting that the military is no longer 'solely charged with fighting and winning the country's wars' and that 'prior to the Vietnam era, the military was largely removed from politics' (p. 267). Although an examination of US military history might have revealed a greater degree of continuity with the past, the editors and the contributors succeed in providing a 'foundation for understanding the military' and suggesting 'questions that society must address' (p.

268). *Inside Defense* is suitable for use in graduate or undergraduate courses in US government and defence studies. It is also a practical book that might help orient those entering vocations that require interaction with the US military and defence bureaucracy.

America, Technology and Strategic Culture: A Clausewitzian Assessment
Brice F. Harris. Abingdon: Routledge, 2008. £75.00/$150.00. 220 pp.

In *America, Technology and Strategic Culture,* Brice Harris argues that America 'tends to substitute technology for strategy'. This tendency can be seen in the movement toward defence transformation and concepts such as network-centric warfare and effects-based operations (p. 2). These concepts neglect the non-technological dimensions of war, particularly the human dimension. While the orthodoxy of defence transformation and its associated concepts have been subject to increased criticism in Washington since Secretary of Defense Donald Rumsfeld's departure from the Pentagon against the backdrop of setbacks in Afghanistan and Iraq, Harris's book is valuable for two principal reasons. Firstly, the author explains the meaning and importance of strategic culture, a phrase often used but little understood. Secondly, he argues convincingly that America's fixation with technological solutions to the problem of war is not transitory, but based in a cultural predisposition to substitute technology for strategy.

The book is organised into two parts. The first examines the historical development of American strategic culture. Chapters on the 'theory and nature of war' and the 'art and science of strategy' could serve as useful primers on those subjects. The author then describes the evolution of America's defence-transformation initiative and its associated concepts. Harris concludes that, rather than representing a revolutionary break from the past, as its proponents often claimed, defence transformation was actually 'an artefact of American strategic culture' (p. 96).

In Part II, Harris applies nineteenth-century Prussian philosopher Carl von Clausewitz's theory of war to the concepts that underpinned defence transformation. In so doing he exposes the fundamental flaws in these concepts while demonstrating the enduring value of Clausewitzian analysis. He demonstrates convincingly that concepts such as effects-based operations and network-centric warfare are tactical rather than strategic constructs and are deficient as strategies in part because they do not describe 'how military force connects ends and means' (p. 151).

This is a well-conceived, well-researched, well-written book. Brice's argument that 'the network-centric/systems analytical approach to war is fundamentally inappropriate for meeting twenty-first century security challenges' is an important one: as he says, 'war is about politics, and politics is about people' (p. 153). This book deserves a wide readership among strategists, military officers and defence officials in countries beyond the United States because, although the wars in Afghanistan and Iraq have largely discredited the concepts associated with defence transformation in America, other militaries, including several in Europe, continue to pursue enthusiastically those concepts or concepts derived from the same flawed assumptions.

Africa
Jonathan Stevenson

Gulliver's Troubles: Nigeria's Foreign Policy after the Cold War
Adekeye Adebajo and Abdul Raufu Mustapha, eds. Scottsville, South Africa: University of KwaZulu-Natal Press, 2008. £30.95. 426 pp.

Nigeria, sub-Saharan Africa's most populous country and after South Africa its wealthiest, has also long been one of its most exasperating geopolitical stories. On one hand, as the region's ranking military power, it has been singularly and admirably willing to put its troops in harm's way for the sake of regional security and stability. On the other, despite its aspiration of establishing a 'Pax Nigeriana' in Africa, it has shown no real taste for acting as an exemplar of the kind of good governance that would enable African countries to sustain security and stability. The first essay in the wide-ranging and well-conceived *Gulliver's Troubles*, written by Adekeye Adebajo, ably characterises this schizoid quality as a wishful 'hegemony on a shoestring', whereby Nigeria has sought to exert its capacity to project hard power without nurturing the political legitimacy required to consolidate its influence (p. 14).

The remainder of the volume seeks to explain what constraints have dictated Nigeria's half-baked foreign policy and how they might be loosened. The sensible analytic model the editors have established is that of concentric circles – immediate neighbourhood, West Africa as embodied in the Economic Community of West African States (ECOWAS), continental challenges such as development and democratisation, and relationships with states and organisations outside Africa

– and the ensuing essays essentially follow this scheme. As a matter of form and editorial practice, quiet applause is due the editors for evidently insisting that each contributor conclude his or her chapter with a section that compresses and clarifies prior observations.

Substantively, the contributors deftly handle the expected domestic issues – the complications for political reform posed by the Muslim–Christian divide, the 'resource curse' of oil, and consequent internal political violence – and add a couple more novel and hopeful points, such as the relative competency of the Nigerian Foreign Service and its struggle against politicisation. Discussions of Nigeria's strategic competition with smaller Francophone countries and with France itself, as well as the deep and often fraught colonial roots of its relationship with the United Kingdom, are notably sophisticated and subtle. So, too, are Adebajo's probing chapter on Nigeria's interventions in the Liberia and Sierra Leone conflicts and Chris Landsberg's laudably textured and measured assessment of prospects for a 'concert of powers' between Nigeria and South Africa, notwithstanding their leadership roles in the formation of the African Union and the roll-out of the New Partnership for Africa's Development.

The part of the book on the global context features penetrating chapters on Nigeria's relationship with key multilateral organisations and its bilateral relations with the United Kingdom, United States, France and – inevitably – China. Concluding correctly that 'Nigeria's diplomacy is punching below its rightful weight' (p. 369), Abdul Mustapha distils a combination of committed constitutional and civic reform at home, more discriminating pragmatism in the region and wider strategic vision at the global level as the programmatic solutions. This fine book is a tour de force of scholarly teamwork, and should become a leading source on Nigeria's foreign policy.

The Trouble with Aid: Why Less Could Mean More for Africa

Jonathan Glennie. London: Zed Books, 2008. £12.99/$20.95. 184 pp.

One school of thought about the inefficacy of aid to Africa says that aid has been artlessly – and sometimes, as in the case of the international financial institutions' structural adjustment programmes, heartlessly – administered and siphoned off by kleptocratic officials. Another school holds that the developed world's largesse to Africa has engendered an insidious dependence on aid and with it disincentives to managing resources efficiently and achieving sustainable self-sufficiency. This line of thinking got some traction in the late 1990s with Michael Maren's forcefully argued *The Road to Hell: The Ravaging Effects of Foreign Aid and*

International Charity, but has never fully taken hold. In putting the case systematically and analytically in *The Trouble With Aid*, Jonathan Glennie, a perceptive veteran analyst of development-assistance policy, makes a good effort at reviving the less-is-more argument.

Glennie acknowledges that Western donor nations have generally responded to calls for increased aid to poverty-stricken Africa, but notes the discordant and conspicuous absence of urgency among members of African civil society for more outside aid. From such observations, he draws his basic thesis: 'dependency on aid from foreign donors has undermined the development of the basic institutions needed to govern and the vital link of accountability between state and citizen' (pp. 5–6). One important gloss on this idea is that putative donors tend to view providing money and emergency humanitarian assistance as the full extent of their moral obligation, which pre-empts consideration of more granular long-term policies that would move African communities towards sustainability. But Glennie does not believe either that the provision of aid should end or that the situation is hopeless. Instead, he dissects the ruling proposition that more aid means less poverty, applying what he calls 'aid realism', and exhorts donor governments to assess aid programmes not only on the basis of direct impacts – which they have myopically favoured – but also according to three additional criteria: policy impacts, institutional impacts, and macroeconomic impacts (p. 27).

As to policy impacts, he prudently declines to indulge in blanket condemnation of the IMF and World Bank's neo-liberal aid conditionality of the 1980s and 1990s, noting more discriminately that they 'were applied so rigorously and without regard for political context that they often generated negative outcomes' (p. 38). He also points out that aid influxes, to genuinely improve the lot of the people on the ground, must yield not only economic growth overall but also beneficial (or at least not inordinately detrimental) consequences for wages, prices, inflation and exchange rates, with trade-offs among these measures duly considered.

Perhaps the book's most profound point is that aid carries an inherent democratic deficit insofar as it increases the recipient government's autonomy vis-à-vis the domestic population and therefore decreases accountability, hinders the development of participatory government (in particular, through taxation and revenue distribution), and impedes the enhancement of institutional capacity. Thus, Glennie counsels donor governments to coordinate and harmonise their programmes and conditionalities; adopt more nuanced and sophisticated techniques for monitoring and measuring aid impacts; and exploit the greater efficiency and clarity thus gained to reduce aggregate aid and minimise the democratic deficit and institutional dysfunction it inevitably imposes on recipient governments. 'Rather than calling for more we should be sending our politicians back into their meeting rooms until they emerge with something that works' (p. 143). The objective, he notes provocatively, should be not to double aid by 2015 as currently advocated, but to halve it.

Diamonds, Dispossession and Democracy in Botswana
Kenneth Good. Oxford: James Currey, 2008. £14.99. 192 pp.

Botswana is often blithely characterised as sub-Saharan Africa's unique success story: a nearly middle-class country blessed with diamonds, a relatively small population and a stable government, its only blemish being one of the world's highest incidences (about 40% of the population) of HIV/AIDS. In his slashing if uneven polemic, Kenneth Good, an Australian political-science professor who taught at the University of Botswana until the government expelled him from the country, forcefully puts the lie to this sanitised portrayal. According to Good, Botswana is an illiberal democracy par excellence. While its leaders and Western admirers trumpet its rapid economic growth, pro-business policies and relatively low level of corruption, 'what actually exists under this deceptive image is an acute over-dependence on diamonds, the centralisation of power in a strong presidency and preponderant ruling party, and the weakness and dependency of parliamentary and judicial institutions and civil society' (p. 3).

The deconstruction that proceeds from this salvo is formidable. Good argues that Botswana has not truly escaped the resource curse – that the government's inordinate linkage of Botswana's economic fate to diamonds in general, and DeBeers in particular, has under-nourished other economic sectors, especially agriculture, left the country economically undiversified and highly vulnerable to negative developments in the world diamond market, and produced the kind of excessive military spending characteristic of mineral-rich countries to the detriment of education and health. It has also sharpened the division between the middle class and substantially rural 'destitutes', especially the pastoralist San ethnic group, who are stigmatised and consequently marginalised in terms of public policy. The basic political point of Good's analysis is that Botswanan democracy is largely illusory – the republic, he says, is really 'demo-feudal' (p. 69). The president enjoys comprehensive executive and political power and the presidency is handed down by one office-holder to the next, while parliamentary elections have never produced a change of government despite their procedural smoothness.

Rich in anecdotes and sardonic in tone, Good's book remains analytically compelling. His use of comparative examples, from both within and outside Africa, is particularly enlightening. The sketchy and hurried conclusion of the book is a disappointment, and his argument does, to be sure, sometimes take the form of an individual crusade. For instance, a 21-page appendix details the author's efforts to resist deportation. But since the Botswanan government's hostility stems from arguments Good advanced publicly before writing the book, his personal stake does not appear to unduly impair his intellectual integrity or objectivity. In the context of broader strife and dysfunction in Africa, Botswana still seems relatively well off. But Good demonstrates convincingly that it confronts many if not most of the obstacles to full and effective democratic governance that its neighbours face.

Understanding Somalia and Somaliland
Ioan Lewis. London: C. Hurst & Co., 2008. £16.99. 151 pp.

When Things Fell Apart: State Failure in Late-Century Africa
Robert H. Bates. Cambridge: Cambridge University Press, 2008. £40.00/$60.00. 206 pp.

The resurgence of Islamist extremism in Somalia and the brazenness of Somali pirates have made headlines of late. But underlying both phenomena is the insusceptibility of Somalis' arcane and complex clan system to effective central government, which Somalia as a whole has not had since the end of the Cold War. Thus, the succinct yet nuanced anthropological and historical treatment of the Somali people from Ioan Lewis – long the world's ranking expert on the subject – is a welcome source. Roughly the first two-thirds of the narrative text deals with Somalis' cultural and religious roots, fleshing out notions – glancingly familiar to many observers of African affairs – of patrimonial clanism and nomadic lifestyle, and their colonial history through independence, elaborating on the seemingly irresolvable tension between the decentralised clan system and Somalis' strong nationalism.

The last two chapters have the most direct relevance to Somalia's parlous current situation. Significantly, in Lewis's view, the rise of the Islamic Courts Union (ICU) has been 'the most positive recent development' (p. 85) in southern Somalia's fraught quest for political cohesion, and he downplays the al-Qaeda connections bruited by the United States and Ethiopia, which were responsible for overthrowing the ICU's de facto rule in late 2006 and installing the latest in a string of feckless transitional governments formed in exile. Equally importantly, he casts Somaliland's self-made political success and relative peacefulness as the logical model for the southern Somalis, thereby taking an implicit stand against the United Nations and other external actors who have insisted that a unitary solution is the only sustainable one. 'Pretending that Somaliland doesn't exist', notes Lewis, 'perpetuates [southern Somalis'] most profound political delusions' (p. 91). While he does not offer any explicit policy prescription, his deeply informed reflections on a promising way forward – which includes recognition of Puntland and the South Central Region as discrete federally autonomous entities – ought to register with policymakers.

Robert Bates, a Harvard political scientist, provides an interesting socio-political theory of state failure in late twentieth-century Africa. Although he does not specifically cover Somalia, his elegant analysis helps explain its woes. In an inventive Schelling-esque distillation of Africa's political dynamics, Bates posits an illustrative 'fable' involving a community consisting of a 'specialist in violence' – a metaphor for the state – and two groups of citizens capable of taking up arms. The factors determining the relative gains from the specialist's predation and, alternatively, taxation, along with the rates at which he discounts those gains, dictate whether he will behave like a venal thug or a responsible guardian and thus whether the community will be stable or degenerate into reactive sub-national violence. (pp. 16–20) This fable establishes useful parameters – of particular importance are public revenues – for a historical examination that, somewhat iconoclastically, focuses on the motives of governments rather than rebels. Bates concludes that when a state has collapsed, the people must be prepared to defend any wealth they seek to accumulate, so peace and prosperity are mutually exclusive in the short term. This insight, both daunting and clarifying, cries out for further exploration and current application.

China Returns to Africa: A Rising Power and a Continent Embrace
Chris Alden, Daniel Large and Ricardo Soares de Oliveira, eds.
London: C. Hurst & Co., 2008. £65.00/$75.00. 402 pp.

Crouching Tiger, Hidden Dragon? Africa and China
Kweku Ampiah and Sanusha Naidu, eds. Scottsville, South Africa: University of KwaZulu-Natal Press, 2008. £28.50. 357 pp.

China's rise as a world power and its economic and political interest in Africa have prompted two complementary edited volumes, both of them perceptive and useful, one providing largely major-power perspectives and the other predominantly African ones. Introducing the first book, the editors do not mince words: 'China's expanding relations with Africa are the most important dynamic in the foreign relations of the continent since the end of the Cold War' (p. 1). After furnishing valuable details on China's national economic interests and motivations in Africa, and examining its non-interference (or 'no ties') policy with respect to economic assistance, the book's focus widens to geopolitics, building a layered picture of China's designs in Africa. According to one contributor, Africa is a 'guinea-pig continent' (p. 139) for testing Chinese technological and industrial competitiveness through reliable, non-threatening allies and establishing China as the leader in South–South cooperation among developing countries, entrenching a multipolar world order and reinforcing the one-China policy via expanded international support.

On China's strategic rivalry with the United States, Bates Gill, J. Stephen Morrison and Chin-Hao Huang offer a balanced and considered chapter stressing Washington's limited understanding of Beijing's intentions and overwhelming distractions elsewhere, the risks that China itself faces in Africa, and the mutual tendency to concentrate narrowly on matters such as competition for access to oil and thus to apprehend the bilateral relationship in simplistic, zero-sum terms. As chapters discussing China's closeness with the Sudanese regime, its oil-based partnership with Angola and a growing strategic relationship with South Africa – a key 'anchor state' for US Africa policy – confirm, these factors compel the United States to develop 'new and longer-range thinking about US policies to engage China productively in Africa' (p. 169).

An insightful contribution on France's stake argues that Chinese prominence in Africa 'reinforces the credibility of a multipolar world' and, leaving room for pragmatic French involvement, helps keep alive the Gaullist vision of a 'great power Europe' implicitly led by France (p. 195). Unfortunately, there are no companion chapters on the calculations of the two other main European ex-colonial powers – the United Kingdom and Portugal. Such discussions certainly seem warranted, though their omission may derive from the editors' highly debatable suggestion that European involvement in Africa may be confined to a strategically minor 'residual presence' (p. 359).

At the same time, Alden and colleagues wisely note that 'China's role in Africa will be determined by African actors themselves' (p. 127), and Alden later forecasts not a Chinese imperialist 'scramble for Africa' but rather a more limited engagement in the wider context of Asian extroversion. Kweku Ampiah and Sanusha Naidu's volume provides qualified validation for these assertions in a series of thoroughgoing case studies on China's relations with nine African countries. While Adam Habib does see a geopolitical scramble between the United States and China tentatively taking shape, he and others also note that balancing on Europe and Japan's part and a gathering pan-African determination to pursue enlightened self-interest and enhanced strategic status through increasingly multilateral channels could well stave off such a contest. Together these volumes provide ample analysis for readers to draw their own informed conclusions.

Erratum: In the February–March 2009 issue of *Survival* (vol. 51, no. 1), the publisher of *Inside Egypt: The Land of the Pharaohs on the Brink of a Revolution* by John R. Bradley was incorrectly identified. The book is published by Palgrave Macmillan.

Brief Notices

United States

America and Its Critics: Virtues and Vices of the Democratic Hyperpower

Sergio Fabbrini. Cambridge: Polity, 2008. £15.99. 222 pp.

Asserting that the United States' status as the world's only 'hyperpower' exposes it to an unusual degree of criticism, Fabbrini aims to debunk the charges that American democracy is plebiscitary, devoid of voters, dominated by the rich and imperial in character.

The American Future: A History

Simon Schama. London: The Bodley Head, 2008. £20.00/$34.00. 392 pp.

In 2008, says Schama, the 'fate of America, and by extension the world, [hung] in the balance'. He looks at the deep historical roots of America's present crisis, arguing that the country has long had the ability to 'renew and rebuild … at times when it seemed overwhelmed by disaster'.

Barack Obama and the Future of American Politics

Paul Street. Boulder, CO: Paradigm Publishers, 2008. £14.99/$23.95. 280 pp.

The 'Obama phenomenon' is placed in historical context as Street attempts to discover to what extent Barack Obama truly represents 'change' within the American political system. While the new president could potentially bring about democratic transformation, in some ways he already adheres to 'long-prevailing power structures'.

The Myth of American Diplomacy: National Identity and U.S. Foreign Policy

Walter L. Hixson. New Haven, CT and London: Yale University Press, 2008. £27.50/$35.00. 377 pp.

Hixson believes that ever since the United States was founded, a 'mythical national identity', including the notion of American moral superiority, has led the country to wage war on a long list of external enemies. He critiques the US's 'pathologically violent foreign policy' and suggests ways America could help achieve a more just and peaceful world.

The Pornography of Power: How Defense Hawks Hijacked 9/11 and Weakened America

Robert Scheer. New York: Twelve Books, 2008. £17.99/$24.99. 250 pp.

Drawing on five decades of experience reporting on the 'military–industrial complex', Scheer attacks what he sees as wasteful, immoral, arrogant, dishonest and even 'insane' foreign and defence policies of the US government. He calls for nuclear disarmament and cuts in defence spending.

DOI 10.1080/00396330902860975

Daydream Believers: How a Few Grand Ideas Wrecked American Power
Fred Kaplan. Hoboken, NJ: John Wiley & Sons, 2008. £13.99/$25.95. 246 pp.

Kaplan seeks to explain what he sees as failures in recent US foreign policy, tracing them to the 'mistaken thinking' of President Bush and his aides. Among their false convictions, he says, was the belief that the world changed after 11 September 2001 and that new technologies had changed the nature of warfare.

Smart Power: Toward a Prudent Foreign Policy for America
Ted Galen Carpenter. Washington DC: Cato Institute, 2008. $24.95. 264 pp.

Carpenter calls for a more restrained US security strategy, which he believes would help the United States achieve 'strategic independence' and avoid 'becoming entangled in unnecessary wars'. He points out that the United States has engaged in at least 10 episodes of military force since the Cold War ended.

Souled Out: Reclaiming Faith & Politics After the Religious Right
E.J. Dionne, Jr. Princeton, NJ: Princeton University Press, 2008. £14.95/$24.95. 251 pp.

Dionne examines the role of religion in US politics, arguing that the era of the 'Religious Right' is now over. He attributes this not to a decline in evangelical Christianity in the United States, but to the desire of many believers to surpass the dogmatic, partisan and ideological politics of the past.

Turkmeniscam: How Washington Lobbyists Fought to Flack for a Stalinist Dictatorship
Ken Silverstein. New York: Random House, 2008. $24.00. 197 pp.

In this exposé of America's political lobbyist industry, Silverstein describes the results when he posed as a representative of a fictional firm with a large stake in the natural-gas fields of Turkmenistan. Several Washington firms were willing to work to improve the image of the totalitarian country.

Politics and International Relations

Globalisation and the Changing Role of the State: Issues and Impacts
Rumki Basu, ed. New Delhi: New Dawn Press Group, 2008. £19.99/$29.95. 240 pp.

This collection from India provides an overview of the phenomenon of globalisation. Divided into four parts, it looks at ways globalisation has influenced the nation-state and national sovereignty; political economy and ideology; human rights; and Indian politics and administration.

Political Ethics and the United Nations: Dag Hammarskjöld as Secretary-General
Manuel Fröhlich. Abingdon: Routledge, 2008. £80.00/$160.00. 272 pp.

Drawing on primary sources, including previously unpublished material, Fröhlich sketches the ethics and political innovations of Dag Hammarskjöld, the second secretary-general of the United Nations.

Rethinking Trafficking in Women: Politics out of Security
Claudia Aradau. Basingstoke: Palgrave Macmillan, 2008. £50.00. 225 pp.

Aradau situates her analysis of trafficking in women within a broader analysis of the relationship between security, subjectivity and politics. She argues that 'the reduction of politics to security limits struggles for equality and freedom'.

A Billion Lives: An Eyewitness Report from the Frontlines of Humanity
Jan Egeland. New York and London: Simon & Schuster, 2008. £18.99/$27.00. 253 pp.

Previously Undersecretary-General for Humanitarian Affairs and the United

Nations, Egeland has visited some of the world's worst disaster zones, including South Asia following the Indian Ocean tsunami and disputed territories in the Middle East. In this book he recounts his experiences confronting some of the world's biggest problems.

Who is a Normative Foreign Policy Actor? The European Union and its Global Partners

Nathalie Tocci, ed. Brussels: Centre for European Policy Studies, 2008. £17.00/$30.00. 329 pp.

The contributors explore claims by the European Union, Russia, China, India and the United States to have normative foreign-policy agendas. They ask how these actors define their foreign-policy priorities and how they will interact in a world characterised by the proliferation of global players.

World at Risk

Ulrich Beck. Trans. Ciaran Cronin. Cambridge: Polity, 2008. £15.99/$24.95. 269 pp.

According to Beck, the numerous risks faced by modern societies – terrorism, financial crises, climate change – and their use for political gain produce a need for security that can encroach on our liberty and view of equality, but also presents an opportunity to fundamentally change global politics.

War, Conflict and the Military

The American Way of War: Guided Missiles, Misguided Men, and a Republic in Peril

Eugene Jarecki. New York: Free Press, 2008. $26.00. 324 pp.

Jarecki seeks to expose what he sees as the corruption of the American political system by the economic, political and military systems that have been gradually evolving since the Second World War. 'The disastrous rise of misplaced power' predicted by President Eisenhower, he says, has come to pass.

Catastrophic Consequences: Civil Wars and American Interests

Steven R. David. Baltimore, MD: The Johns Hopkins University Press, 2008. £14.00/$25.00. 204 pp.

The greatest threat to the United States and its interests, says David, are civil war and 'other types of radical domestic upheaval' in countries of strategic importance, such as Saudi Arabia, Pakistan, China and Mexico. An emergency-response mechanism is urgently needed to address instability in these and other key states.

Dangerous Thresholds: Managing Escalation in the 21st Century

Forrest E. Morgan et al. Santa Monica, CA: RAND Corporation, 2008. $35.00. 274 pp.

According to the authors, 'escalation is a natural tendency in any form of human competition'. This volume analyses the escalatory threats faced by the United States in the military realm, and looks at how the government can 'dampen the mechanisms of deliberate, accidental, and inadvertent escalation' given current security conditions.

Ending Wars

Feargal Cochrane. Cambridge: Polity, 2008. £40.00/$49.95. 228 pp.

The underlying premise of this book is that war is 'a methodology rather than an ideology', meaning that when the context, issues or actors of armed conflicts change, violence can be controlled or even ended. Cochrane looks at how this can and has been done in a variety of conflicts.

First Strike: Preemptive War in Modern History

Matthew J. Flynn. Abingdon: Routledge, 2008. £18.99/$27.95. 261 pp.

Based on his analysis of numerous historical cases, Flynn argues that while pre-emptive warfare is a common and often well-regarded tactic, it usually proceeds from dubious moral logic and frequently fails to produce the desired outcome. Special attention is given to the Bush administration's interpretation of pre-emption in the case of Iraq.

The Forever War: Dispatches from the War on Terror
Dexter Filkins. London: The Bodley Head, 2008. £18.99/$25.00. 368 pp.

New York Times correspondent Dexter Filkins offers his first-person account of the 'war on terror', detailing his experiences in New York on 11 September 2001, in Afghanistan both before and after the fall of the Taliban, and in war-torn Iraq.

Global Threat: Target-Centered Assessment and Management
Robert Mandel. Westport, CT: Praeger Security International, 2008. £41.95/$75.00. 147 pp.

After analysing the nature of modern security threats, Mandel proposes what he calls a 'target-centered conceptual approach' to better recognise, assess, prioritise and manage them. He uses the cases of the Iraq War, the 2004 tsunami, the London Transport bombings and the US illegal-immigration debate to illustrate his approach.

Intelligence and National Security Policymaking on Iraq: British and American Perspectives
James P. Pfiffner and Mark Phythian. Manchester: Manchester University Press, 2008. £16.99/$27.50. 296 pp.

The contributors look at the way the decision to go to war in Iraq was made in the United States and the United Kingdom, asserting that both President George W. Bush and Prime Minister Tony Blair 'had to convince [their legislatures] and public that war was necessary, and both used intelligence in questionable ways to do so'.

How to Stage a Military Coup: From Planning to Execution (2nd ed.)
David Hebditch and Ken Connor. Barnsley: Frontline Books, 2008. £8.50. 224 pp.

Noting that the coup 'remains the single most common form of power change', the authors analyse numerous examples of government takeovers from around the world. They explore the conditions that give rise to coups and discuss the factors that determine their failure or success.

Military Transformation and Strategy: Revolutions in Military Affairs and Small States
Bernard Loo, ed. Abingdon: Routledge, 2008. £70.00/$140.00. 203 pp.

Asserting that most literature on the revolution in military affairs (RMA) 'tends to be American-centric', Loo and other contributors analyse the implications of military transformation for smaller states. Themes covered include transformations in strategy, war and operations, and the possible impediments to the RMA.

Politics of Civil Wars: Conflict, Intervention and Resolution
Amalendu Misra. Abingdon; Routledge, 2008. £21.99/$43.95. 183 pp.

Drawing on case studies from around the world, Misra analyses the causes, conduct, consequences and conclusions of civil wars. His study includes discussion of such topics as contested nationalism, violence, external intervention, post-conflict reconstructions, reconciliation and governance.

Power and Military Effectiveness: The Fallacy of Democratic Triumphalism
Michael C. Desch. Baltimore, MD: The Johns Hopkins University Press, 2008. £30.00/$45.00. 232 pp.

Challenging the belief that democratic governance renders states more likely to triumph in armed conflicts against non-democratic opponents, Desch argues that the challenges of warfare are the same for all states, regardless of their form of government, and that military effectiveness is almost entirely a function of material assets.

Renegotiation of the Just War Tradition and the Right to War in the Twenty-First Century
Cian O'Driscoll. Basingstoke: Palgrave Macmillan, 2008. £45.00/$79.95. 232 pp.

O'Driscoll looks at how notions of the 'just war' have been invoked and changed in the context of the 'war on terror', and compares current thinking on such issues as anticipatory war, humanitarian intervention and punitive war with 'classical ideas about when and how war might be justified'.

Shaping Strategy: The Civil–Military Politics of Strategic Assessment
Risa A. Brooks. Princeton, NJ: Princeton University Press, 2008. £15.95/$26.95. 352 pp.

Brooks examines several case studies, including the 1967 Arab–Israeli War and the Iraq War, to illustrate his view that the quality of pre-conflict strategic assessments depends on the character of a state's civil–military relations.

The Steps to War: An Empirical Study
Paul D. Senese and John A. Vasquez. Princeton, NJ: Princeton University Press, 2008. £15.95/$26.95. 314 pp.

By looking at the development of 'militarised interstate disputes' from 1816 to 2001, the authors attempt to identify the factors that increase the risk of two states going to war. They conclude that territorial disputes, alliances, rivalry and arms races precipitate conflicts by increasing threat perception and creating a security dilemma.

Africa

Africa Doesn't Matter: How the West Has Failed the Poorest Continent and What We Can Do About It
Giles Bolton. New York: Arcade Publishing, 2008. $15.99. 348 pp.

Bolton draws on his experience as a diplomat and aid worker in Africa to explain the continent's problems, focusing on poverty, aid, trade and globalisation. He suggests ways that interested Westerners might help Africa overcome the many challenges it faces.

The African Press, Civic Cynicism, and Democracy
Minabere Ibelema. Basingstoke: Palgrave Macmillan, 2008. £42.50/$79.95. 279 pp.

Ibelema argues that corruption and civic cynicism in Africa are a problem not just among ruling elites but also among the general population. He urges Africa's growing independent press to intensify its critique of harmful attitudes that stand in the way of the continent's democratic consolidation.

African Geopolitics
Philippe Hugon. Trans. Steven Rendall. Princeton, NJ: Markus Wiener Publishers, 2008. £47.95. 174 pp.

This volume provides an overview of Africa's encounters with foreign powers going back over 1,000 years, traces the continent's economic, socio-political and cultural development, and concludes with an analysis of the main challenges facing Africa today.

African Security Politics Redefined
Karin Dokken. Basingstoke: Palgrave Macmillan, 2008. £47.50/$84.95. 247 pp.

Africa, says Dokken, lost most of its strategic importance to the superpowers once the Cold War ended, and rarely figured in the political-security considerations of the West until the 11 September 2001 attacks. She discusses the new challenges that have emerged in Africa since then and the regional, continental and international responses to them.

Angola: The Weight of History

Patrick Chabal and Nuno Vidal, eds. London: C. Hurst & Co., 2008. £17.99. 246 pp.

Since Angola's civil war ended in 2002, expectations have been high that the country's booming oil sector will finally allow the country to enjoy sustained economic prosperity. The contributors to this volume evaluate these expectations in light of Angola's economic, political and social evolution since it achieved independence in 1975.

Bewitching Development: Witchcraft and the Reinvention of Development in Neoliberal Kenya

James Howard Smith. Chicago, IL: University of Chicago Press, 2008. £11.00/$21.00. 272 pp.

While some have criticised efforts to bring development to Africa as 'latter-day imperialism' rooted in colonial rule and neo-liberalism, Smith argues that this overlooks the importance of development to Africans themselves. He presents his study of the ways the people of Kenya's Taita Hills have interpreted development through the lens of their occult beliefs.

Kenya's Quest for Democracy: Taming Leviathan

Makau Mutua. Boulder, CO: Lynne Rienner Publishers, 2008. $65.00. 329 pp.

Mutua surveys efforts to build a sustainable democratic state in Kenya since it gained independence in 1964. He analyses the societal forces that have contributed to the country's political evolution and suggests that efforts to achieve constitutional reform provide 'a window for understanding the larger struggles confronting Kenyan society'.

The Failure of Democracy in the Republic of Congo

John F. Clark. Boulder, CO: Lynne Rienner Publishers, 2008. $59.95/£39.50. 308 pp.

Clark tests various hypotheses to explain why democracy collapsed in the Republic of Congo in 1997. He touches on the country's political culture and economic performance, the role of militias, the influence of French foreign policy, the design of Congo's institutions, and the current 'electoral authoritarian' regime.

Darfur's Sorrow: A History of Destruction and Genocide

M. W. Daly. Cambridge: Cambridge University Press, 2007. £14.99/$22.99. 388 pp.

Daly seeks to explain the Darfur crisis by examining its historical development, beginning with the origins of the Fur state in the seventeenth century. He attempts to show how years of imperial mismanagement left the region unprepared for independence.

Faith and Politics in Nigeria: Nigeria as a Pivotal State in the Muslim World

John N. Paden. Washington DC: United States Institute of Peace Press, 2008. $14.95. 140 pp.

Challenging the view that Nigeria's oil exports are its most important contribution to the world, Paden argues that the country's experience accommodating ethnolinguistic and religious diversity makes it a model for other states, and a potential bridging actor between the West and the Muslim world.

Identity, Diversity and Constitutionalism in Africa

Francis M. Deng. Washington DC: United States Institute of Peace Press, 2008. $19.95. 308 pp.

Deng argues that a new relationship must be established between governments and societies to address problems of democratic legitimacy and secessionism in Africa. He suggests that ideas of constitutionalism and self-determination hold the key to reconciling ethnic diversity and national identity.

The Wizard of the Nile: The Hunt for Africa's Most Wanted

Matthew Green. London: Portobello Books, 2008. £16.99. 352 pp.

Green journeys into war-torn Uganda to investigate the life and crimes of General Joseph Kony, the violent and elusive leader of the Lord's Resistance Army. Along the way, he meets refugees, teenage war veterans, international peacemakers and government officials who speak to the ruinous effects of Kony's rebellion.

Closing Argument

Moon Over Manhattan

Jeffrey Mazo

I

Every American president since the OPEC oil embargo and price shock of 1973 has proclaimed a goal of energy independence. Yet despite 35 years and $115 billion spent on research and development for alternatives, the United States imports more of its energy than ever before. The geopolitics of energy is at the centre of international concerns, and the spectre of climate change caused to a great extent by emissions from energy sources makes the search for low-carbon alternatives even more urgent.

In his speech at Denver's Mile High Stadium in August 2008 kicking off his general-election campaign, Barack Obama said that as US president he would 'set a clear goal': energy independence within ten years.[1] His language echoed President John F. Kennedy's 1961 call to land a man on the Moon within the decade, one of the defining symbols of the technocratic and 'big government' approach to policy. It was also a subtle reference – a 'dog-whistle', in the parlance of partisan politics – to a plan proposed by former Vice President Al Gore the previous month to commit to producing 100% of the nation's electricity from renewable and carbon-free sources within the same ten years.[2] Gore made the comparison with the *Apollo* space programme even more explicit; it was a central metaphor of his speech. The comparison was also made explicit in the Democratic Party Platform.[3]

Invoking *Apollo* as a metaphor for national technological efforts is not unusual. In the energy realm, a progressive think tank founded in 2001

Jeffrey Mazo is Managing Editor of *Survival*.

 DOI 10.1080/00396330902861015

devoted to catalysing a clean-energy revolution is even called the Apollo Alliance. Its 'New Apollo Program', launched in October 2008, calls for specific investments of $500bn over the next ten years to reduce emissions and imports and restore American technological and industrial pre-eminence.[4] Though this programme, Gore's plan and Obama's initiative differ in details they share common approaches, a common vision and a common metaphor.

But *Apollo*, however remarkable a technological achievement, was not born or nurtured in isolation. Although Kennedy's 1961 speech is now remembered almost exclusively as the launch-pad for the Moon landing, this was only one part of an address on 'Urgent National Needs' in the context of the Cold War struggle. In the equivalent of a State of the Union speech setting out his agenda, the new president called for increases in foreign military and economic aid and information programmes, military modernisation, civil-defence expansion and a nuclear test-ban treaty. Along with the goal of landing a man on the Moon, these were all framed as part of a 'freedom doctrine' aimed at confronting communism on the world stage.[5]

Apollo was thus first and foremost a soft-power effort par excellence, to put down a marker for American prestige, though it may also have been motivated by, and had the effect of, stimulating the economy and in particular industries critical to national defence. President Dwight Eisenhower had already recognised the symbolic potential of space, transferring in 1960 all non-military aspects of space research and development from the Pentagon's Advanced Research Projects Agency (ARPA) to the civilian National Aeronautics and Space Administration (NASA), both created two years earlier in response to the Soviet launch of *Sputnik*.

Kennedy stressed that the Moon project would require a dedicated and focused national effort and diversion of resources from other important areas where they were already thinly spread; a half-hearted effort would be worse than none at all. It was not without controversy: not until the end of 1963, just before Kennedy was assassinated, was the debate on funding *Apollo* settled. But Lyndon Johnson was even more committed to space than Kennedy. And the election of 1964 cemented the big-government revolution. Throughout the decade the *Apollo* programme was paralleled by the economic and social programmes that made up President Lyndon Johnson's 'Great Society'.[6]

Twenty years after Kennedy's Moon speech, in his first inaugural address, President Ronald Reagan marked a change in philosophy of government: 'in this present crisis, government is not the solution to our problem; government is the problem'.[7] The sorts of long-term aspirations and accomplishments Gore compared to the *Apollo* programme – the Marshall Plan in the 1940s, the interstate-highway programme in the 1950s – would be incompatible with this vision. Reagan scaled back the role of government in the social realm. Although spending continued to expand, shifting to the defence sector, the technocratic imperative seemed to have died. President Bill Clinton's statement in 1996 that 'the era of big government is over' marked the culmination of this trend.

As president, however, Reagan did propose two initiatives that superficially evoked the *Apollo* effort: the Strategic Defense Initiative ('Star Wars') and the National Aerospace Plane. Yet as he acknowledged in his Star Wars speech, the programme would take decades to come to fruition, well beyond the ten-year horizon of *Apollo*, and in the event the missile-defence systems being deployed now are a shadow of the original vision.[8] The language in his 1986 State of the Union Address proposing a hypersonic space plane echoed Kennedy's Moon speech, yet it was not accompanied by an equivalent commitment of resources.[9] The programme eventually fell prey to budget constraints and technical problems, though like Star Wars its more modest technological children live on.

The *Apollo* programme cost $96bn in modern dollars over its 14-year lifetime, peaking at $7bn, or 0.4% of America's gross domestic product and 1% of national government spending.[10] The Marshall Plan averaged as much as 1.1% of GDP and 7% of federal spending over four years, and the interstate-highway programme eventually cost $425bn over 35 years – in contrast to the $115bn spent on alternative energy R&D over a comparable period. The Strategic Defense Initiative and its offspring similarly cost $110bn over 25 years for a much smaller share of national investment.[11] Only $2–3bn was spent on the National Aerospace Plane, and much of that came out of the Star Wars budget.

Other presidents have invoked *Apollo* in proposing grand goals in space: on the 20th anniversary of the first Moon landing George H.W. Bush called for an initiative to build a space station (first proposed by Reagan), return to the Moon and ultimately land men on Mars. But he and Congress baulked at the estimated £500bn price tag, and only the space station went ahead. Even that was never built; under Bill Clinton, the project was scaled back and transformed into the International Space Station. George W. Bush, in turn, announced a Mars-landing programme in January 2004, with a return to the Moon planned for 2020, but only £1bn in additional funding was proposed.

II

Apollo is not the only example regularly invoked when large-scale government-led and -funded research and development programmes are proposed. The other is the *Manhattan Project* that produced the atomic bomb, at great expense and in great haste, during the Second World War. The two are often used interchangeably; the 2008 Democratic Party Platform, to take one example, says that in public meetings 'Americans called for a Manhattan or Apollo Project-level commitment to achieve energy independence'. Yet beyond the level of commitment involved, differences between *Apollo* and *Manhattan* offer important lessons for large-scale technical efforts to address national or international security challenges in the next decades. If the *Apollo* achievement was the epitome of a soft-power instrument, the Bomb was the same for hard power. *Apollo*, though a magnificent achievement, was ultimately a dead end, focused on a narrow and finite goal. Little of the technology that got us to the Moon survived in more recent space efforts such as the Space Shuttle. The *Manhattan Project*, in contrast, created not just the Bomb but, for good or ill, an entire industry.

But these different destinations are less important than the different paths taken by the two programmes. The *Apollo* engineers spent over a million man-hours investigating three competing paths and technologies to achieve a Moon landing before NASA committed to one of them, Lunar-orbit rendezvous, in October 1962, partly on the basis of estimated costs. To have done otherwise – to have pursued more than one option – would have been prohibitively expensive. For the *Manhattan Project*, on the other hand, time was of the essence; getting the atomic weapon before the enemy was an existential imperative. So General Leslie Groves, military director of the project, was given what amounted to a blank cheque. Every possible avenue was explored and financed, and construction of factories begun even before the technologies they would employ were perfected. In the end the *Manhattan* engineers achieved not one but two Bombs, the uranium gun-type (*Little Boy*) and the plutonium implosion-type (*Fat Man*). Two different methods of enriching and separating the fissionable isotope of uranium and two methods for producing plutonium were used on an industrial scale.[12] This approach, at its most basic trading money for time, is the main reason the United States could do in three years what took other states decades, even after the trail had been blazed. Money spent going down blind alleys is only wasted to the extent you discount the future. It is, fundamentally, a social and ethical question rather than an economic one. In any case the cost of the *Manhattan Project*, as a share of national wealth, was on the same order as that of *Apollo*.[13]

Wartime urgency allowed organisational as well as technical corners to be cut. Oversight within the executive branch was streamlined; Congressional oversight was side-stepped by selective disclosure and direct appeals to the patriotism of committee chairs. Large industrial contracts were entered into as handshake deals and executives committed corporations to huge financial risks, again on the basis of patriotic appeals. To the extent practical, hierarchical management structures were avoided and scientists and engineers allowed to operate in a collegial environment. This approach has continued to show its value in the success of government organisations such as ARPA (now DARPA; 'Defence' was added in 1972), which was critical to what eventually became the Internet, or Lockheed's Advanced Development Projects (the 'Skunk Works'), which produced the first operational US jet fighter, the U2 and SR-71 *Blackbird* spy planes and the F-117 Stealth Fighter.[14] In contrast, the commission that investigated the 1986 Space Shuttle *Challenger* disaster put the blame on a NASA organisational culture that had, since the end of *Apollo*, become inflexible and hierarchical.[15]

It is telling that both the DARPA and Skunk Works examples are from the defence sector. Defence is the area where the social futility of future discounting is starkest. The Marshall Plan and the interstate-highway programme, basically infrastructure projects, were both rightly framed in national-security terms, as was *Apollo*. When Al Gore called the embryonic Internet the 'information superhighway', he intended to highlight the shared element of large-scale government investment in infrastructure rather than any specific technological metaphor.

What makes *Apollo* and *Manhattan* appropriate metaphors, each in its own way, for large-scale R&D efforts in general, and energy transformation in particular, is the degree to which they each conform to an ideal. There should be a focused and inspiring national goal sustainable over several election cycles; commitment of resources an order of magnitude above the norm; a willingness to fail, and spend money on failure; and a 'lean and mean', flat, open and empowering organisational culture.

III

In an interview early in the 2008 presidential primaries, Obama compared himself to both Reagan and Kennedy in his ability to articulate a new vision and lead the country in a fundamentally different direction at a time things just didn't seem to be working. In contrast to Reagan's view of the role of government, though, he said he wanted to 'make government cool again'.[16] The global financial crisis that broke in the waning days of the presidential campaign, and has dominated the transition and first months of the Obama administration, brought this dynamic into sharp focus, raising issues such as the future of free-market capitalism and the roles of governments and international organisations. Obama's failure to gain bipartisan support for the $787bn Keynesian economic-stimulus bill in February reflects a fundamental ideological difference in approach.

In his inaugural address in January, he elaborated on his basic philosophy of government: 'the question we ask today is not whether our government is too big or too small, but whether it works'.[17] And in his address to a joint session of Congress on 24 February, like Kennedy's Moon speech essentially a State of the Union address, he said he had asked for the stimulus package 'not because I believe in bigger government – I don't'. But he rejected the view that

> our problems will simply take care of themselves; that says government has no role in laying the foundation for our common prosperity. For history tells a different story. History reminds us that at every moment of economic upheaval and transformation, this nation has responded with bold action and big ideas. In the midst of civil war, we laid railroad tracks from one coast to another that spurred commerce and industry. From the turmoil of the Industrial Revolution came a system of public high schools that prepared our citizens for a new age. In the wake of war and depression, the GI Bill sent a generation to college and created the largest middle class in history. And a twilight struggle for freedom led to a nation of highways, an American on the moon, and an explosion of technology that still shapes our world. In each case, government didn't supplant private enterprise; it catalyzed private enterprise.[18]

The immediate purpose of the stimulus bill is to respond to the clear and present danger of the current financial and economic crisis. In this respect, it does not really matter what the $787bn is spent on, as long as it flows into the economy. As Jonathan Chait put it, 'World War II was an effective stimulus that, economically speaking, consisted of 100 percent waste. If war hadn't broken out, we could have enjoyed the same economic benefit by building all those tanks and planes and dumping them into the ocean.'[19] Likewise *Apollo*'s contribution to economic growth would have been the same if the landings had failed, though it is unlikely it would still be invoked as a model to emulate.

But as Chait points out, Obama has framed the debate over the stimulus package as much on the merits of the spending proposals as on their stimulus effect. Most of the money is going to programmes advocated during the campaign. In particular, the massive government-led and -funded energy research and development programme Obama envisaged on the stump is reflected in the bill through over $71bn in direct spending and $20bn in tax incentives for clean energy, including improvements in efficiency. The bulk of this spending is on such infrastructure investment; perhaps 10% is for research and development into new technologies for low-carbon energy generation and clean coal.

Subsuming spending aimed at the ten-year target for energy independence and a low-carbon economy in the stimulus package may have had short-term political benefits in getting it approved, but risks diluting the clear, inspirational goal central to successful long-term big-government projects. Framing the debate over the merits of the spending, though, may help sustain the effort at levels of investment and for a long enough time. The levels of green spending in the stimulus bill are on the order of magnitude of the *Apollo* or *Manhattan* projects; if they can be sustained beyond the immediate economic crisis through inspired leadership they are a first step towards energy transformation. But the bureaucratic and organisational issues are just as important. The proportion, or amount, of money allocated to research and development would have to be increased substantially, but the ways in which it is allocated and monitored will also need to be carefully designed. It may be difficult, in an economic environment that resulted in part from a lack of regulation and oversight in financial markets, to strike the right balance between oversight and empowerment, but the Obama administration has pledged to do so.

The stimulus bill includes $400 million to establish the Advanced Research Projects Agency – Energy (ARPA-E), proposed in 2007 as part of the Department of Energy, on the explicit model of DARPA, as 'a lean and agile organization [that] will assemble cross-disciplinary research teams focused on addressing the nation's most urgent energy needs through high-risk research and the rapid development of transformational clean energy technologies'.[20] It will take some time to get the agency up and running – but Energy Secretary Stephen Chu has stressed the importance of moving quickly and everyone at the department is 'crashing' to work out the details.[21] NASA's first budget in 1958 was around the same amount in real terms, and grew exponentially even before Kennedy's Moon speech. From 1961 to 1964 it continued to double and redouble, from 6,000 personnel and a budget of less than $1bn to a peak of 34,000 employees and 411,000 contractors. The *Manhattan Project* followed a similar trajectory from a handful of uncoordinated researchers to over 130,000 workers between 1942 and 1945. So it is within the realm of the possible for ARPA-E to serve as the nucleus of a lean, mean but massive national effort for energy transformation.

Apollo, Manhattan and DARPA all had the US federal government as their only customer. But for energy transformation, development of technologies which can then be passed on to the private sector, and other nations, is critical. There is precedent for the idea, at least, of transferring national proprietary technology to other nations: Eisenhower's Atoms for Peace and Reagan's offer to share Star Wars with the Russians and other nations. And, in the context of negotiations towards a global regime to mitigate climate change, the soft-power implications of giving away new energy technologies may rival the prestige garnered by the Moon landings – not to mention the direct national benefits of helping other nations limit damage to the global commons.

When President Jimmy Carter addressed the nation in April 1977 on the energy proposals of his young administration, he called the effort to find alternatives to imported energy and fossil fuels 'the moral equivalent of war' – and was ridiculed for it.[22] But if there had been a real 'Manhattan Project for Energy' 30 years ago, the geopolitical landscape today might look very different. Among the many tests facing Barack Obama is whether he might actually put into effect what five predecessors have merely promised.

Notes

1 Barack Obama, Acceptance Speech at the Democratic Convention, Denver, Colorado, 28 August 2008, http://www.nytimes.com/2008/08/28/us/politics/28text-obama.html.

2 Al Gore, 'A Generational Challenge to Repower America', speech at the DAR Constitution Hall, Washington DC, 17 July 2008, http://www.washingtonpost.com/wp-dyn/content/article/2008/07/17/AR2008071701896.html.

3 *Renewing America's Promise*, the 2008 Democratic National Platform, 25 August 2008, http://www.democrats.org/a/party/platform.html.

4 See http://www.apolloalliance.org.

5 John F. Kennedy, 'Special Message to the Congress on Urgent National Needs', 25 May 1961, http://www.jfklibrary.org/Historical+Resources/Archives/Reference+Desk/Speeches/JFK/003POF03NationalNeeds05251961.htm;

6 For a detailed discussion of the roots and progress of the *Apollo* programme, see Walter A. McDougall, *...the Heavens and the Earth: A Political History of the Space Age* (New York: Basic Books, 1985).

7 Ronald Reagan, 'First Inaugural Address', 20 January 1981, http://www.reaganfoundation.org/reagan/speeches/first.asp.

8 Ronald Reagan, 'Address to the Nation on National Security', 23 March 1983, http://www.fas.org/spp/starwars/offdocs/rrspch.htm.

9 Ronald Reagan, 'State of the Union 1986', 4 February 1986, http://www.presidential-speeches.org/State-of-the-Union-1986-Ronald-Reagan.php.

10 Deborah D. Stine, *The Manhattan Project, the Apollo Program and Federal Energy Technology R&D Programs: A Comparative Analysis*, CRS Report for Congress RL34645 (Washington DC: Congressional Research Service, 24 September 2008), p. 7.

11 Steven A. Hildreth, *Ballistic Missile Defense: Historical Overview*, CRS Report for Congress RS22120 (Washington DC: Congressional Research Service, 9 July 2007).

12 For histories of the *Manhattan Project* see Stephane Groueff, *Manhattan Project: The Untold Story of the Making of the Atomic Bomb* (London: Collins, 1967); Richard Rhodes, *The Making of the Atomic Bomb* (New York: Simon & Schuster, 1986), chs 14–17.

13 Stine, *The Manhattan Project, the Apollo Program and Federal Energy Technology R&D Programs*, p. 7.

14 For discussion of the organisational factors key to DARPA's success, see W.B. Bonvillian, 'Power Play', *The American Interest*, vol. 2, November–December 2006. For a similar discussion of the Skunk Works, see Ben R. Rich and Leo Janos, *Skunk Works* (New York: Little, Brown and Co., 1994), ch. 16.

15 *Report of the Presidential Commission on the Space Shuttle Challenger Accident*, 6 June 1986, available at http://history.nasa.gov/sts51l.html.

16 'Afternoon with Barack Obama', *Reno Gazette-Journal*, http://www.rgj.com/apps/pbcs.dll/article?AID=/20080115/VIDEO/.

17 Barack Obama, 'Inaugural Address', 20 January 2009, http://www.whitehouse.gov/the_press_office/President_Barack_Obamas_Inaugural_Address/.

18 Barack Obama, 'Address to Joint Session of Congress', 24 February 2009, http://www.whitehouse.gov/the_press_office/Remarks-of-President-Barack-Obama-Address-to-Joint-Session-of-Congress/.

19 Jonathan Chait, 'TRB: Hurry Up and Waste', *New Republic*, 4 March 2009, http://www.tnr.com/politics/story.html?id=943f400a-335b-4173-90c3-3fa82fd12b8a.

20 HR 364, 10 January 2007, http://thomas.loc.gov/cgi-bin/bdquery/z?d110:HR00364. The agency was established in August 2007 by the America Competes Act (PL 110-69), but not funded in FY2008.

21 George Leopold, 'Stimulus: Energy Department Scrambles to Build New R&D Agency', *EE Times*, 23 February 2009, http://www.eetimes.com/news/semi/showArticle.jhtml?articleID=214502434.

22 President Jimmy Carter, 'Address to the Nation on Energy', 18 April 1977, http://millercenter.org/scripps/archive/speeches/detail/3398; William Safire, *Safire's Political Dictionary* (New York: Oxford University Press, 2008), p. 436.